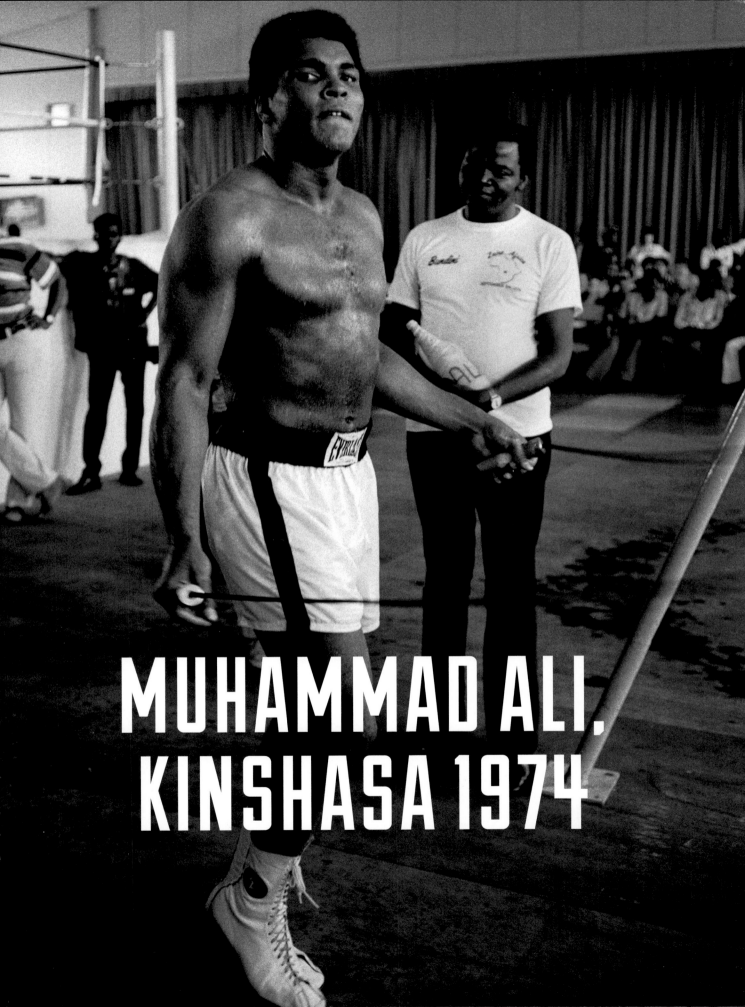

MUHAMMAD ALI, KINSHASA 1974

TRANSLATOR & LETTERER **JESSICA BURTON**

EDITOR **JAKE DEVINE**

TITAN COMICS

MANAGING EDITOR **MARTIN EDEN**
SENIOR CREATIVE EDITOR **DAVID LEACH**
ART DIRECTOR **OZ BROWNE**
ASSISTANT EDITOR **PHOEBE HEDGES**
SENIOR PRODUCTION CONTROLLER **JACKIE FLOOK**
PRODUCTION CONTROLLER **CATERINA FALQUI**
SALES & CIRCULATION MANAGER **STEVE TOTHILL**
MARKETING & ADVERTISING ASSISTANT **LAUREN NODING**
DIRECT MARKETING ASSISTANT **GEORGE WICKENDEN**
PUBLICIST **IMOGEN HARRIS**
MARKETING MANAGER **RICKY CLAYDON**
EDITORIAL DIRECTOR **DUNCAN BAIZLEY**
OPERATIONS DIRECTOR **LEIGH BAULCH**
EXECUTIVE DIRECTOR **VIVIAN CHEUNG**
PUBLISHER **NICK LANDAU**

Muhammad Ali, Kinshasa 1974

9781787736207

Published by Titan Comics
A division of Titan Publishing Group Ltd.144 Southwark St., London, SE1 0UP. Titan Comics is a registered trademark of Titan Publishing Group, Ltd.

A CIP catalogue record for this title is available from the British Library

10 9 8 7 6 5 4 3 2 1

First Published February 2021

Printed in China

Titan Comics

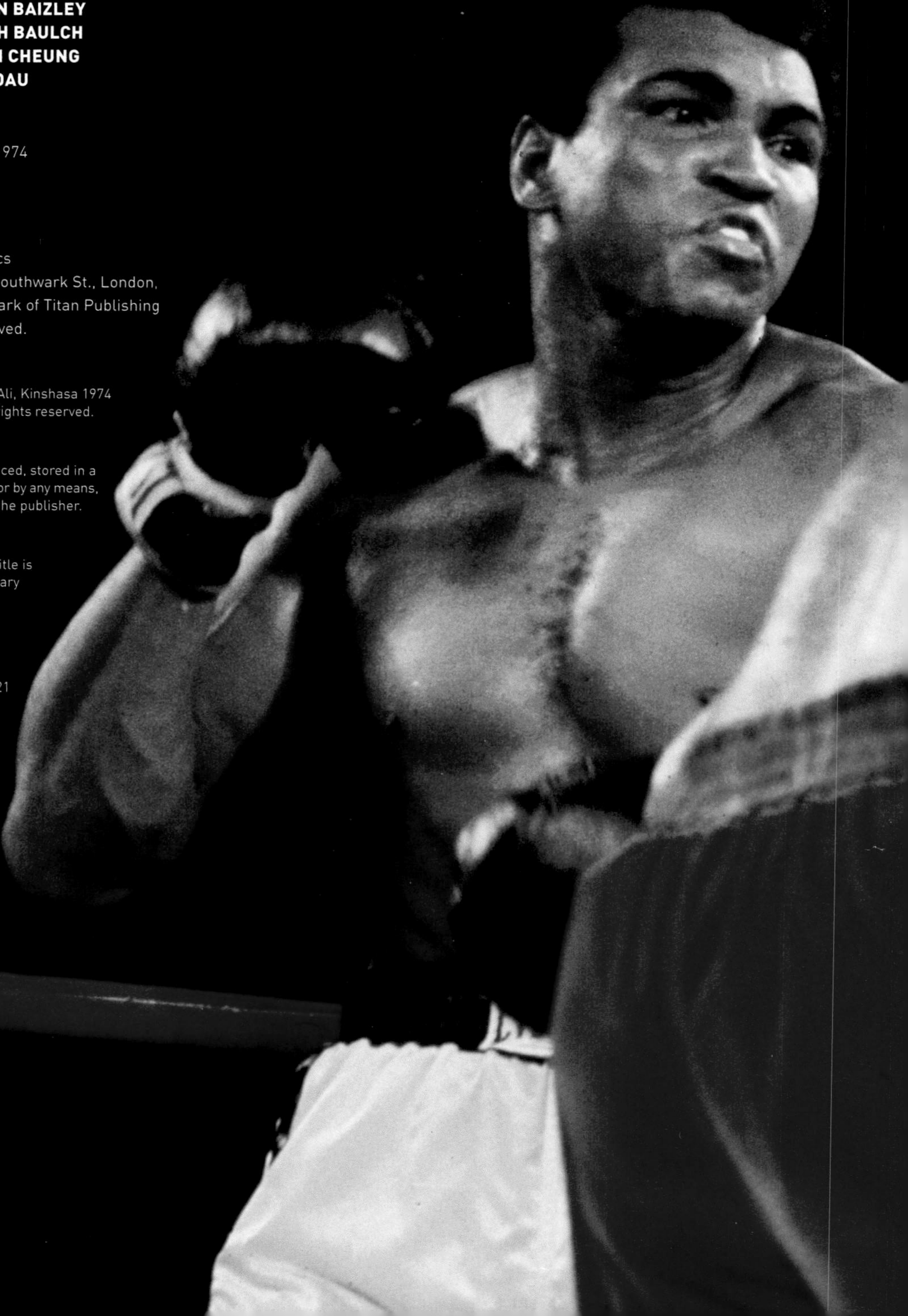

MAGNUM PHOTOS

MUHAMMAD ALI, KINSHASA 1974

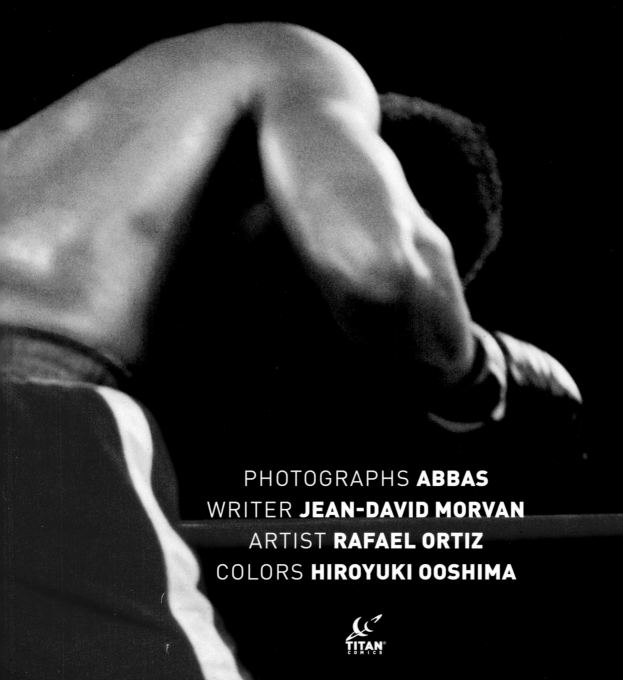

PHOTOGRAPHS **ABBAS**
WRITER **JEAN-DAVID MORVAN**
ARTIST **RAFAEL ORTIZ**
COLORS **HIROYUKI OOSHIMA**

TITAN COMICS

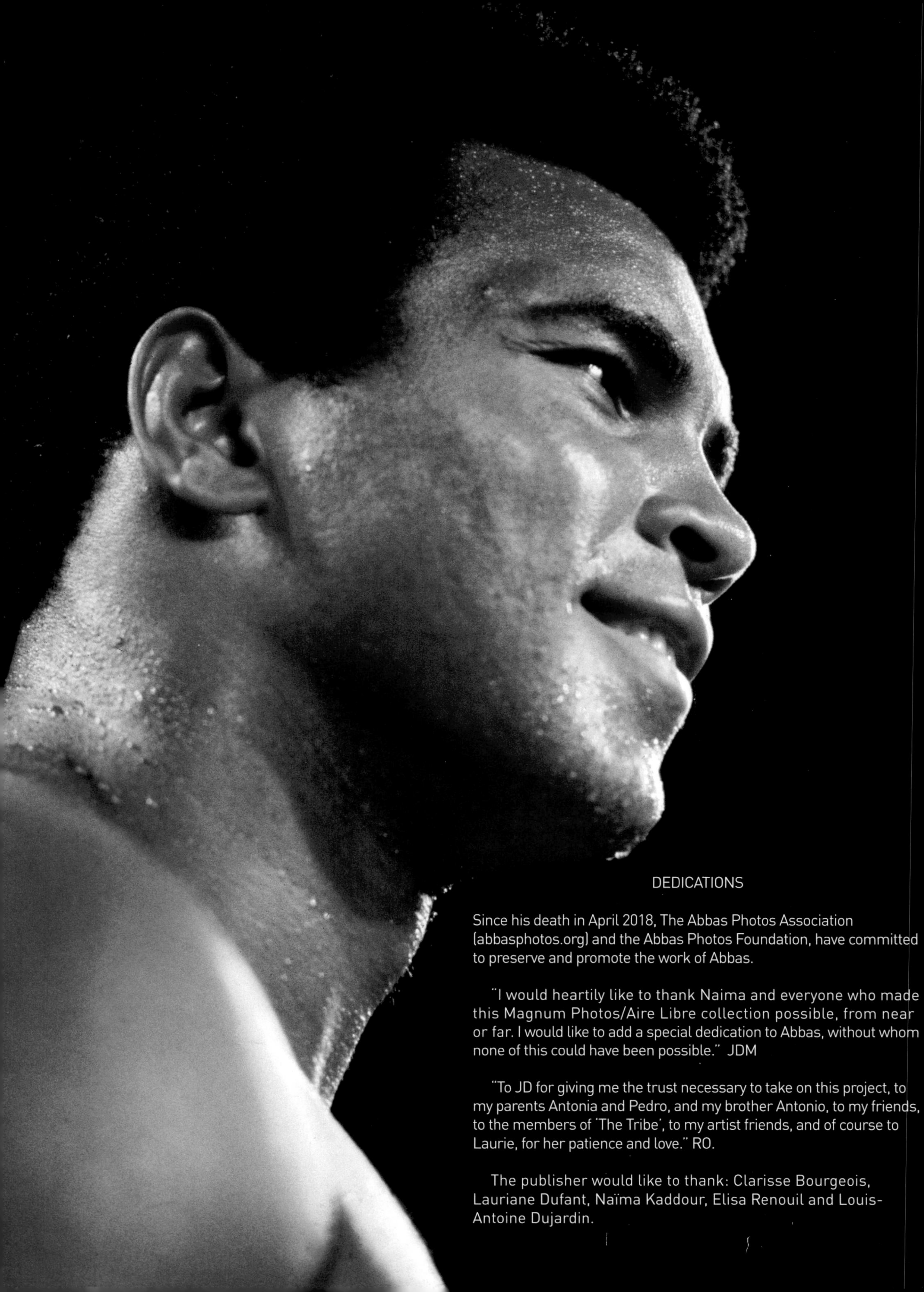

DEDICATIONS

Since his death in April 2018, The Abbas Photos Association (abbasphotos.org) and the Abbas Photos Foundation, have committed to preserve and promote the work of Abbas.

"I would heartily like to thank Naima and everyone who made this Magnum Photos/Aire Libre collection possible, from near or far. I would like to add a special dedication to Abbas, without whom none of this could have been possible." JDM

"To JD for giving me the trust necessary to take on this project, to my parents Antonia and Pedro, and my brother Antonio, to my friends, to the members of 'The Tribe', to my artist friends, and of course to Laurie, for her patience and love." RO.

The publisher would like to thank: Clarisse Bourgeois, Lauriane Dufant, Naïma Kaddour, Elisa Renouil and Louis-Antoine Dujardin.

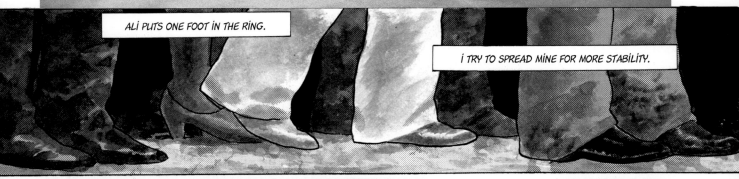

ALI PUTS ONE FOOT IN THE RING.

I TRY TO SPREAD MINE FOR MORE STABILITY.

ALMOST SWALLOWED BY THE CROWD, I HAVE ONLY INCHES WORTH OF SPACE AVAILABLE TO TAKE MY SHOTS.

HE HAS ONLY 15 ROUNDS TO ACHIEVE THE GREATEST FEAT OF ALL TIME.

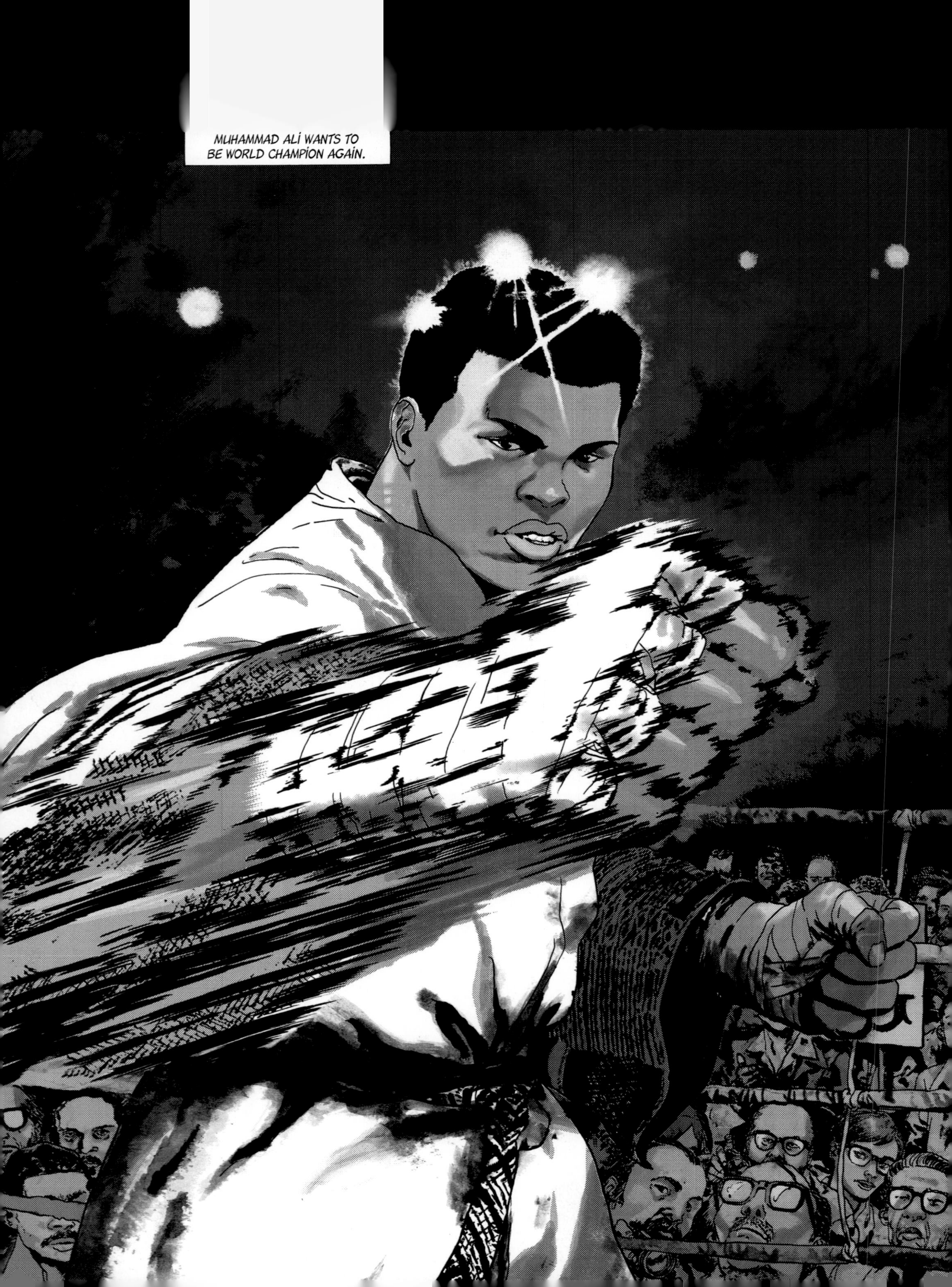
MUHAMMAD ALİ WANTS TO BE WORLD CHAMPİON AGAİN.

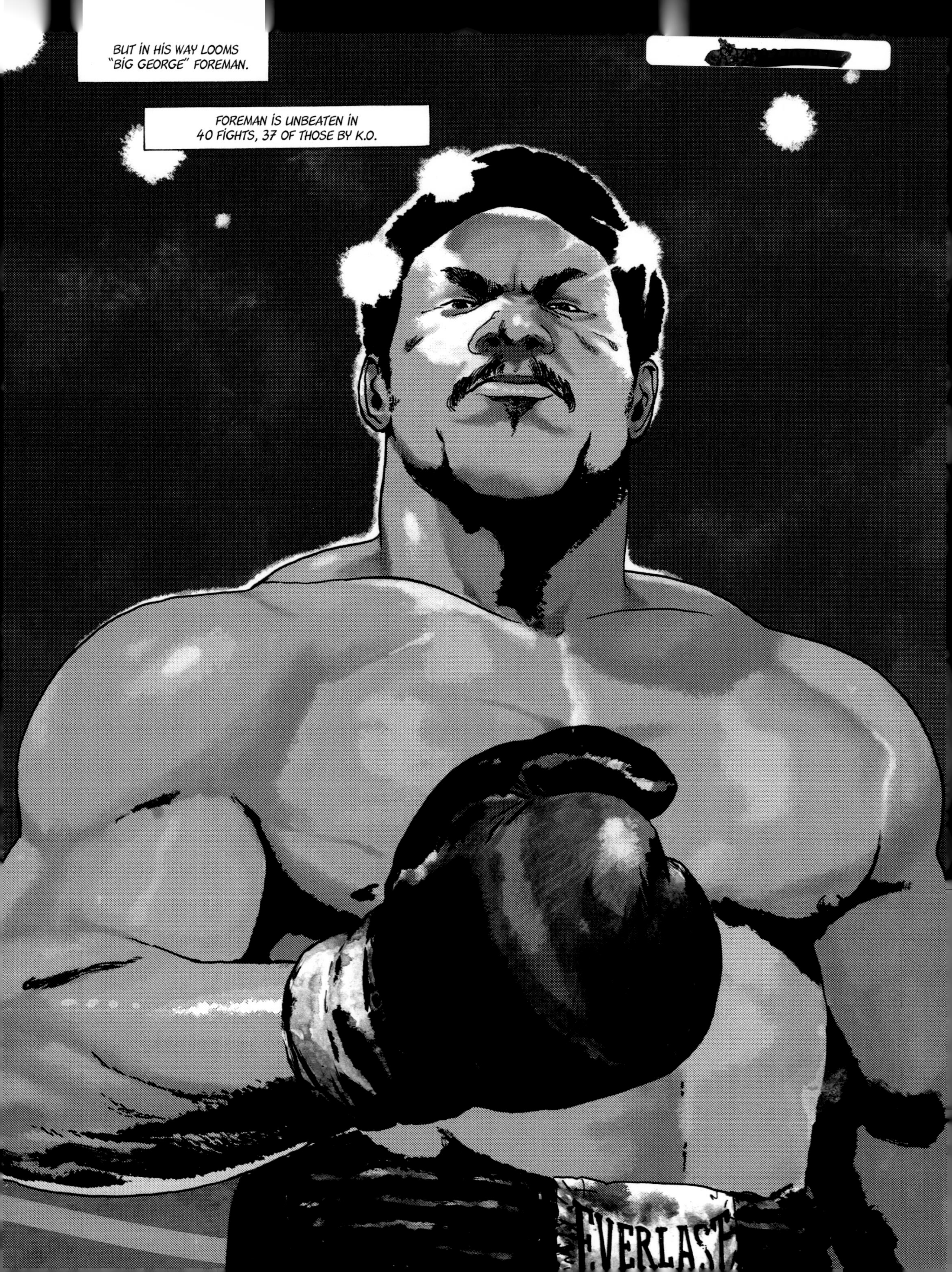
BUT IN HIS WAY LOOMS "BIG GEORGE" FOREMAN.
[redacted]
FOREMAN IS UNBEATEN IN 40 FIGHTS, 37 OF THOSE BY K.O.
EVERLAST

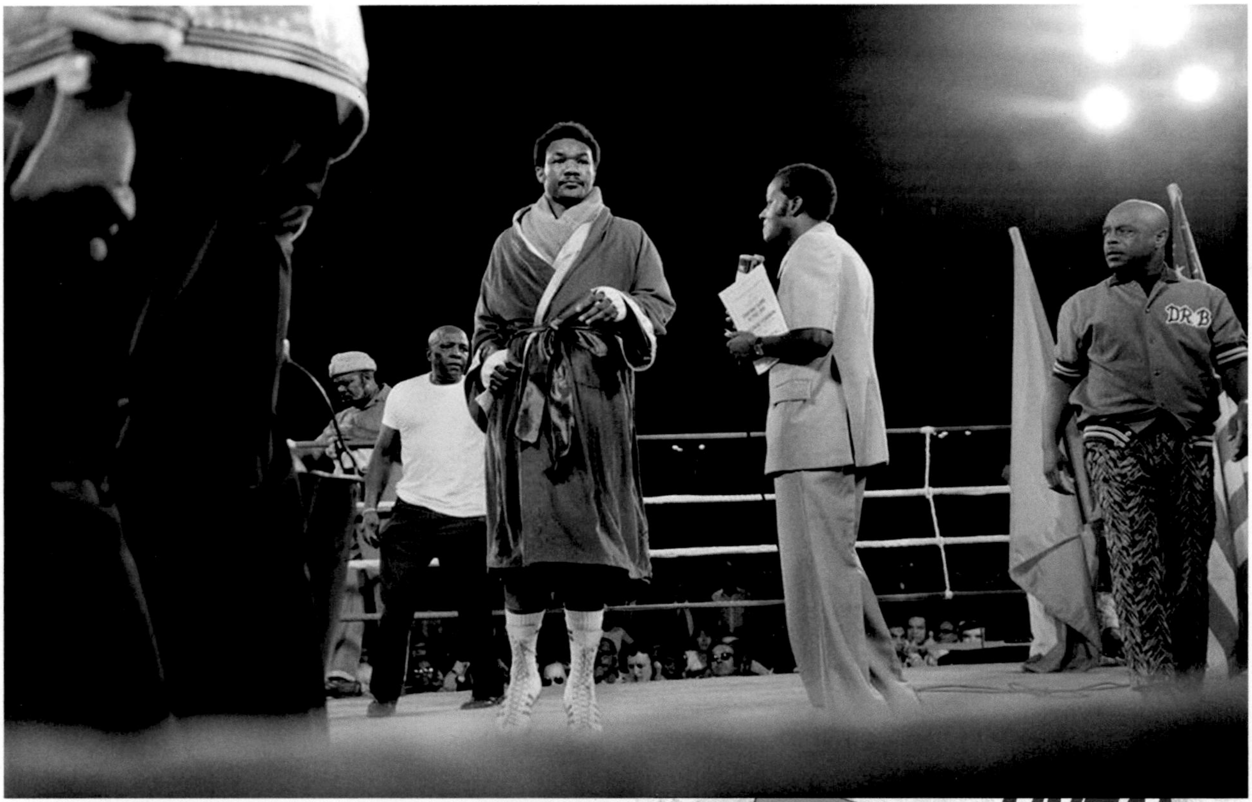

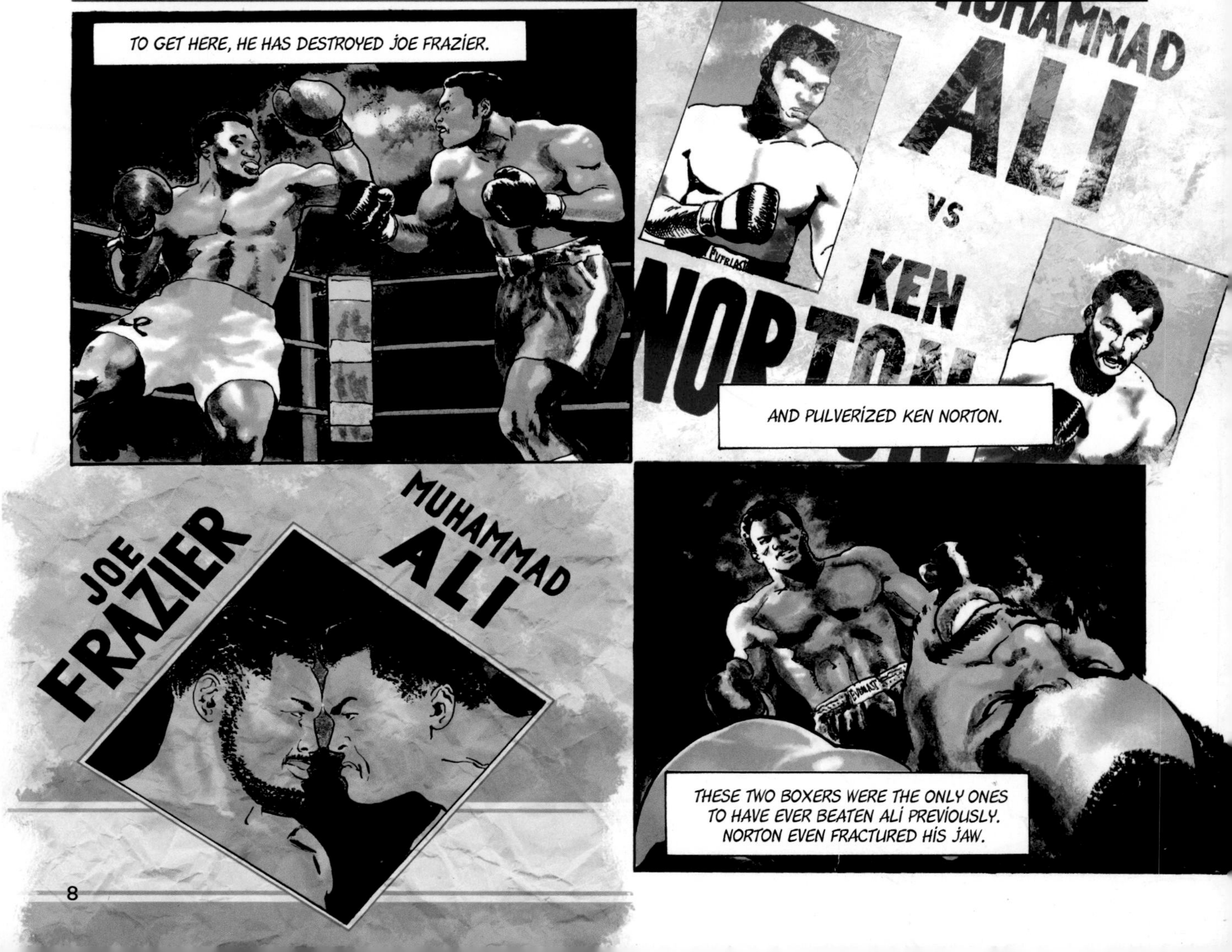
TO GET HERE, HE HAS DESTROYED JOE FRAZIER.
MUHAMMAD
ALI
VS
KEN
NORTON
AND PULVERIZED KEN NORTON.
JOE
FRAZIER
MUHAMMAD
ALI
THESE TWO BOXERS WERE THE ONLY ONES TO HAVE EVER BEATEN ALI PREVIOUSLY. NORTON EVEN FRACTURED HIS JAW.

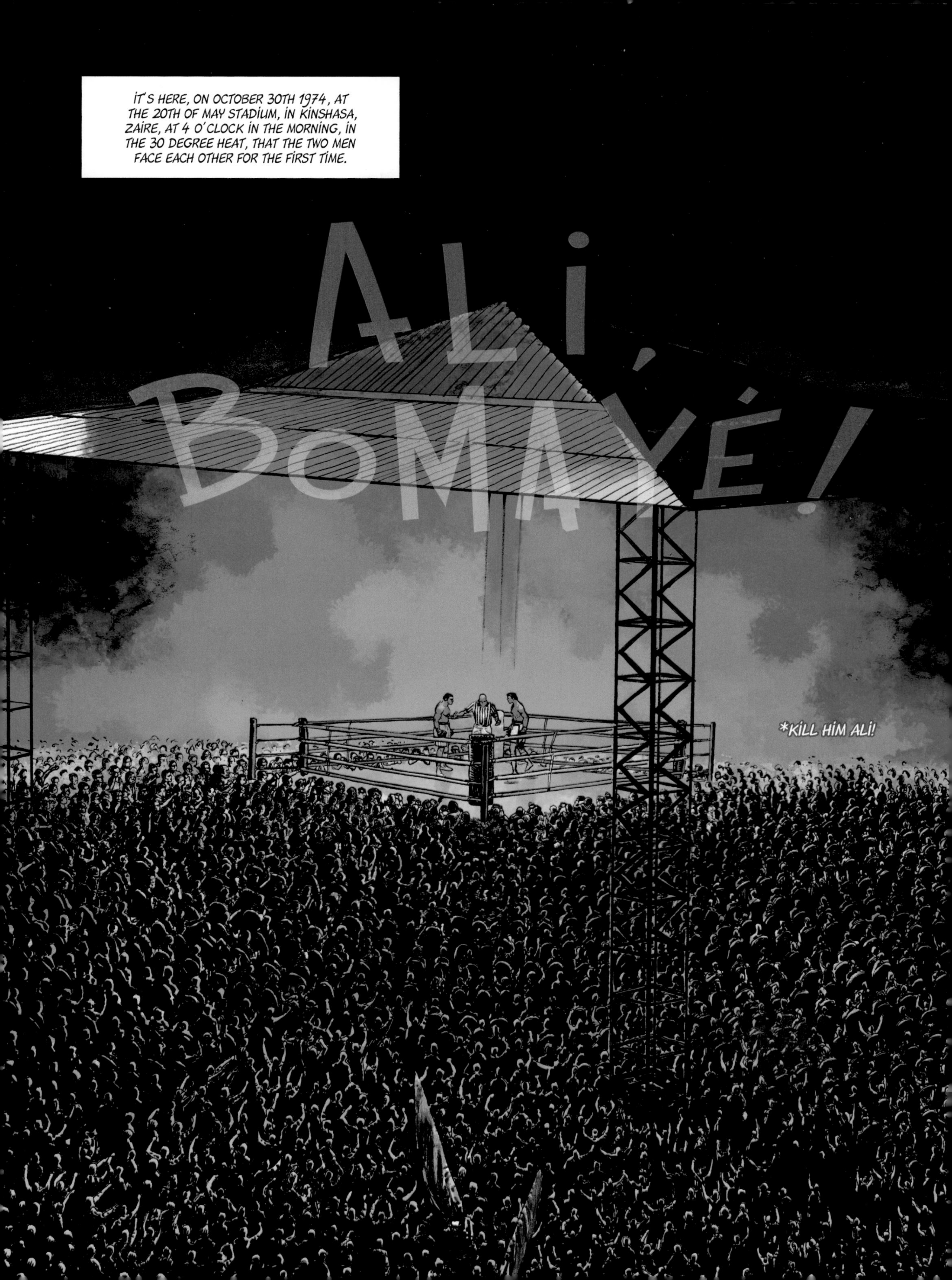
IT'S HERE, ON OCTOBER 30TH 1974, AT THE 20TH OF MAY STADIUM, IN KINSHASA, ZAIRE, AT 4 O'CLOCK IN THE MORNING, IN THE 30 DEGREE HEAT, THAT THE TWO MEN FACE EACH OTHER FOR THE FIRST TIME.
ALI, BOMAYÉ!
*KILL HIM ALI!

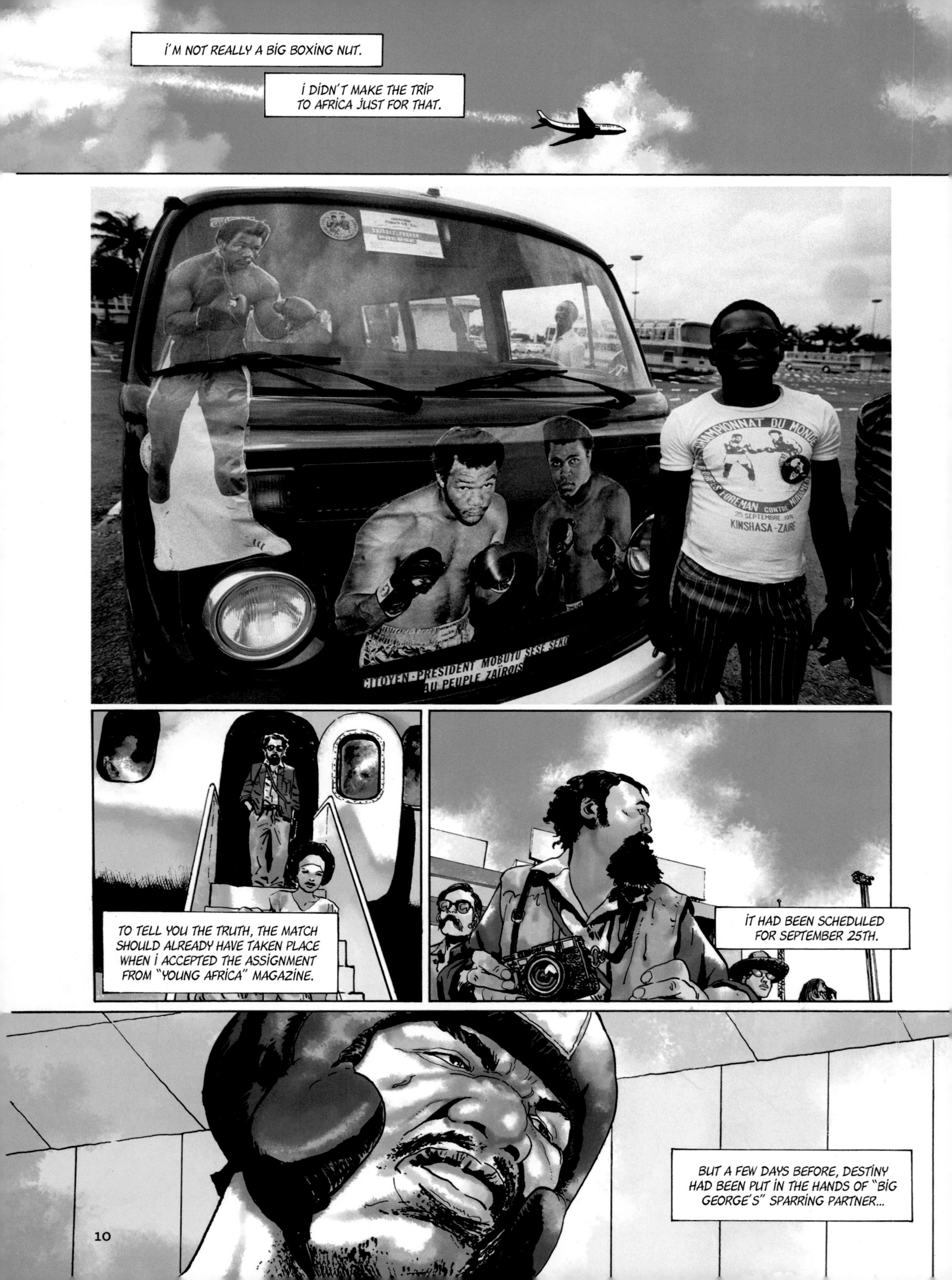
I'M NOT REALLY A BIG BOXING NUT.
I DIDN'T MAKE THE TRIP TO AFRICA JUST FOR THAT.
25 SEPTEMBRE 1974
KINSHASA-ZAIRE
CITOYEN-PRESIDENT MOBUTU SESE SEKO
AU PEUPLE ZAÏROIS
TO TELL YOU THE TRUTH, THE MATCH SHOULD ALREADY HAVE TAKEN PLACE WHEN I ACCEPTED THE ASSIGNMENT FROM "YOUNG AFRICA" MAGAZINE.
IT HAD BEEN SCHEDULED FOR SEPTEMBER 25TH.
BUT A FEW DAYS BEFORE, DESTINY HAD BEEN PUT IN THE HANDS OF "BIG GEORGE'S" SPARRING PARTNER...

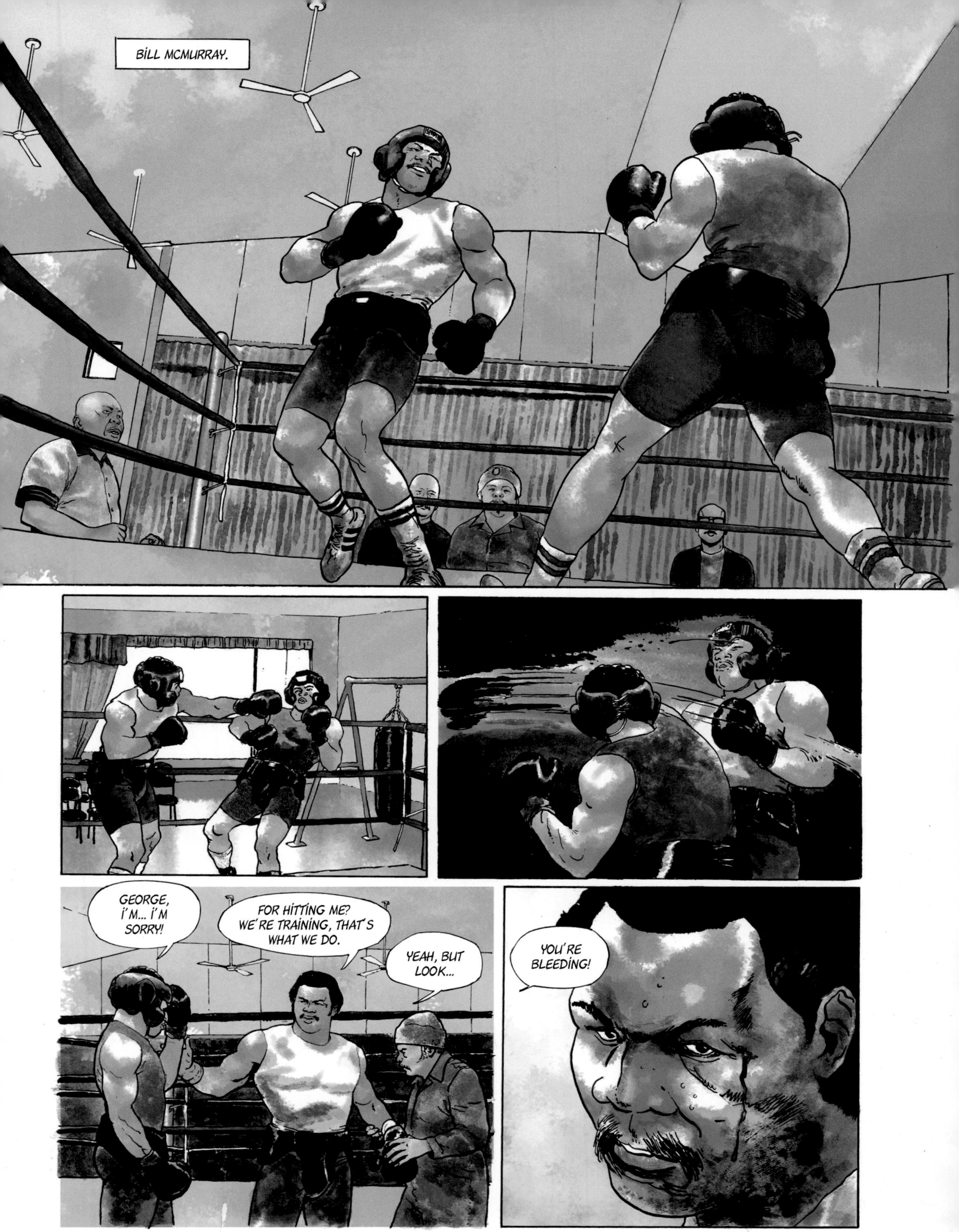
BILL MCMURRAY.
GEORGE, I'M... I'M SORRY!
FOR HITTING ME? WE'RE TRAINING, THAT'S WHAT WE DO.
YEAH, BUT LOOK...
YOU'RE BLEEDING!

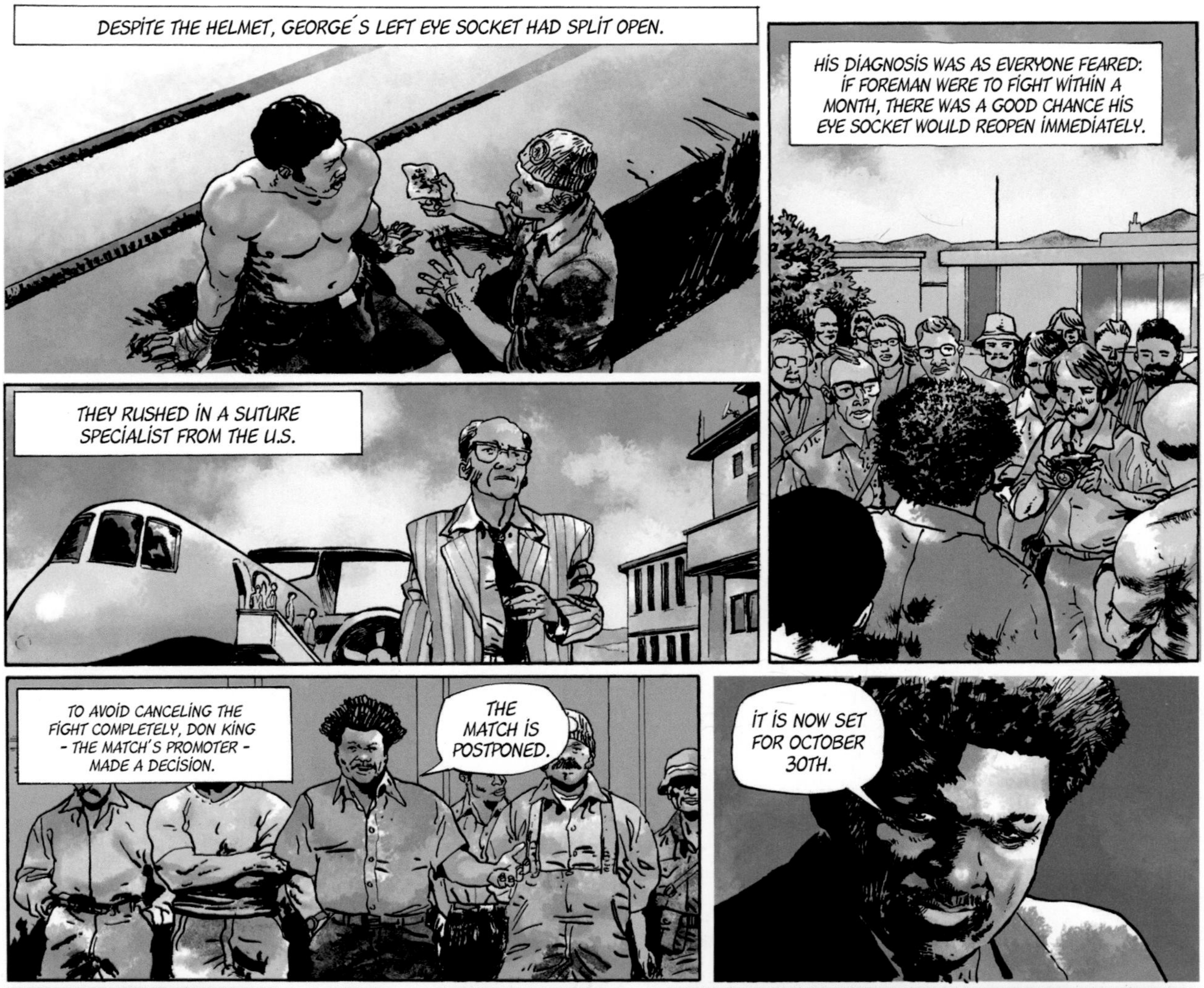
DESPITE THE HELMET, GEORGE´S LEFT EYE SOCKET HAD SPLIT OPEN.
THEY RUSHED IN A SUTURE SPECIALIST FROM THE U.S.
HIS DIAGNOSIS WAS AS EVERYONE FEARED: IF FOREMAN WERE TO FIGHT WITHIN A MONTH, THERE WAS A GOOD CHANCE HIS EYE SOCKET WOULD REOPEN IMMEDIATELY.
TO AVOID CANCELING THE FIGHT COMPLETELY, DON KING - THE MATCH'S PROMOTER - MADE A DECISION.
THE MATCH IS POSTPONED.
IT IS NOW SET FOR OCTOBER 30TH.

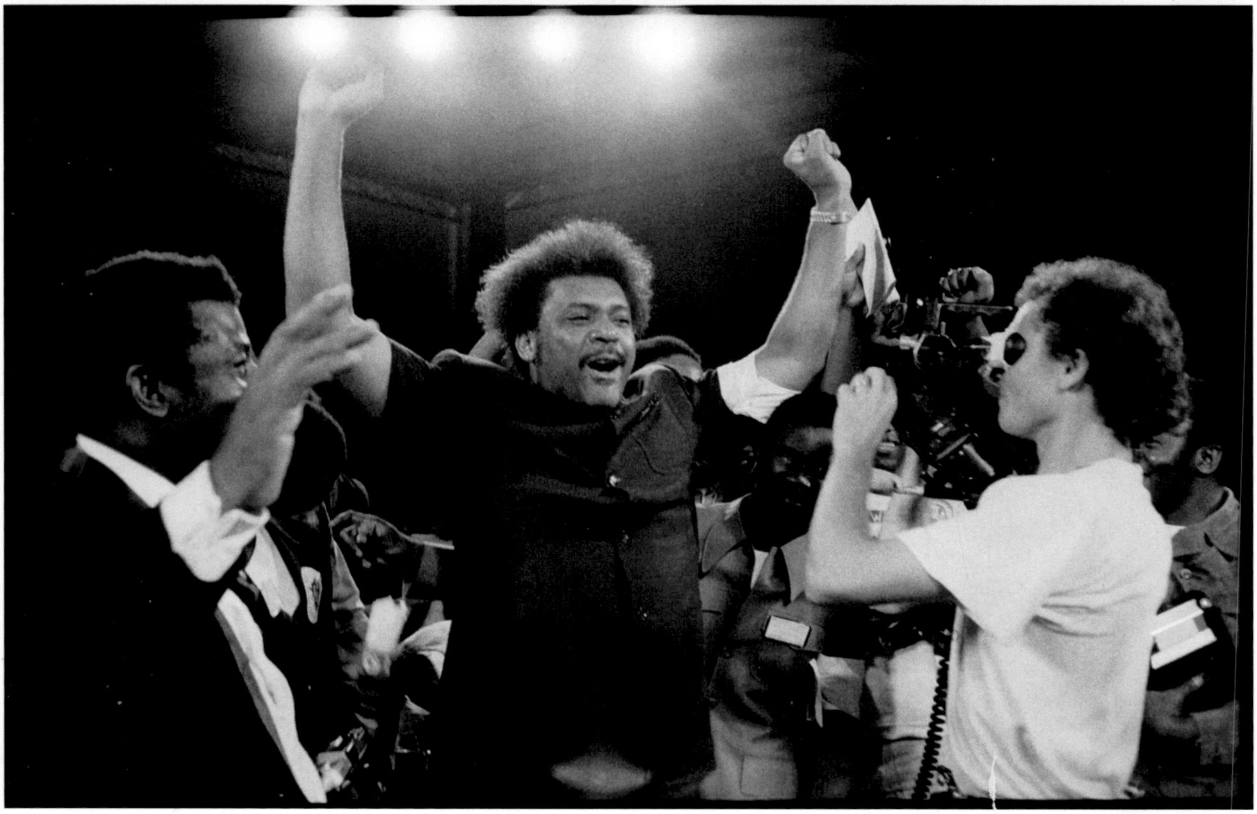

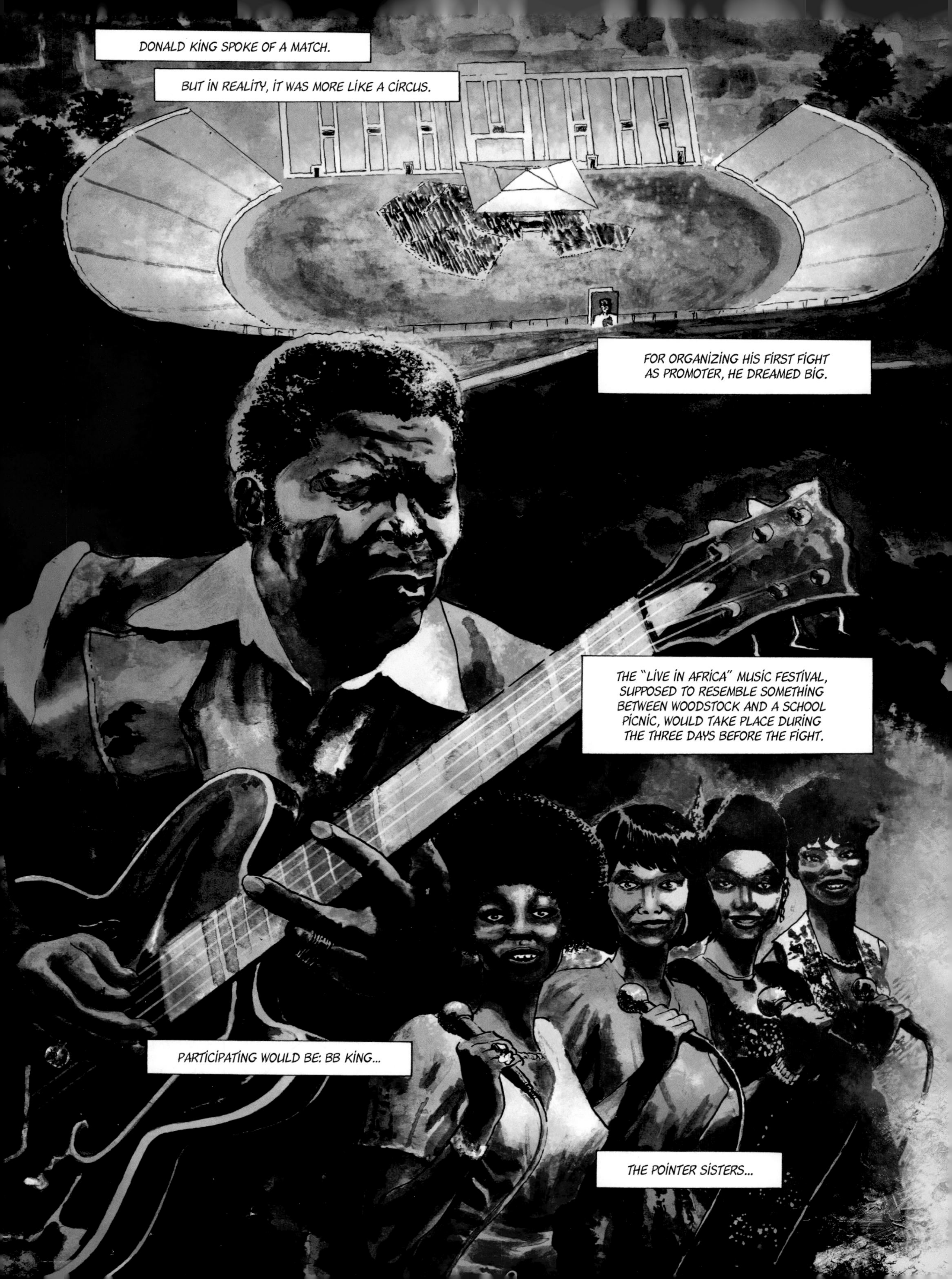
DONALD KING SPOKE OF A MATCH.
BUT IN REALITY, IT WAS MORE LIKE A CIRCUS.
FOR ORGANIZING HIS FIRST FIGHT AS PROMOTER, HE DREAMED BIG.
THE "LIVE IN AFRICA" MUSIC FESTIVAL, SUPPOSED TO RESEMBLE SOMETHING BETWEEN WOODSTOCK AND A SCHOOL PICNIC, WOULD TAKE PLACE DURING THE THREE DAYS BEFORE THE FIGHT.
PARTICIPATING WOULD BE: BB KING...
THE POINTER SISTERS...

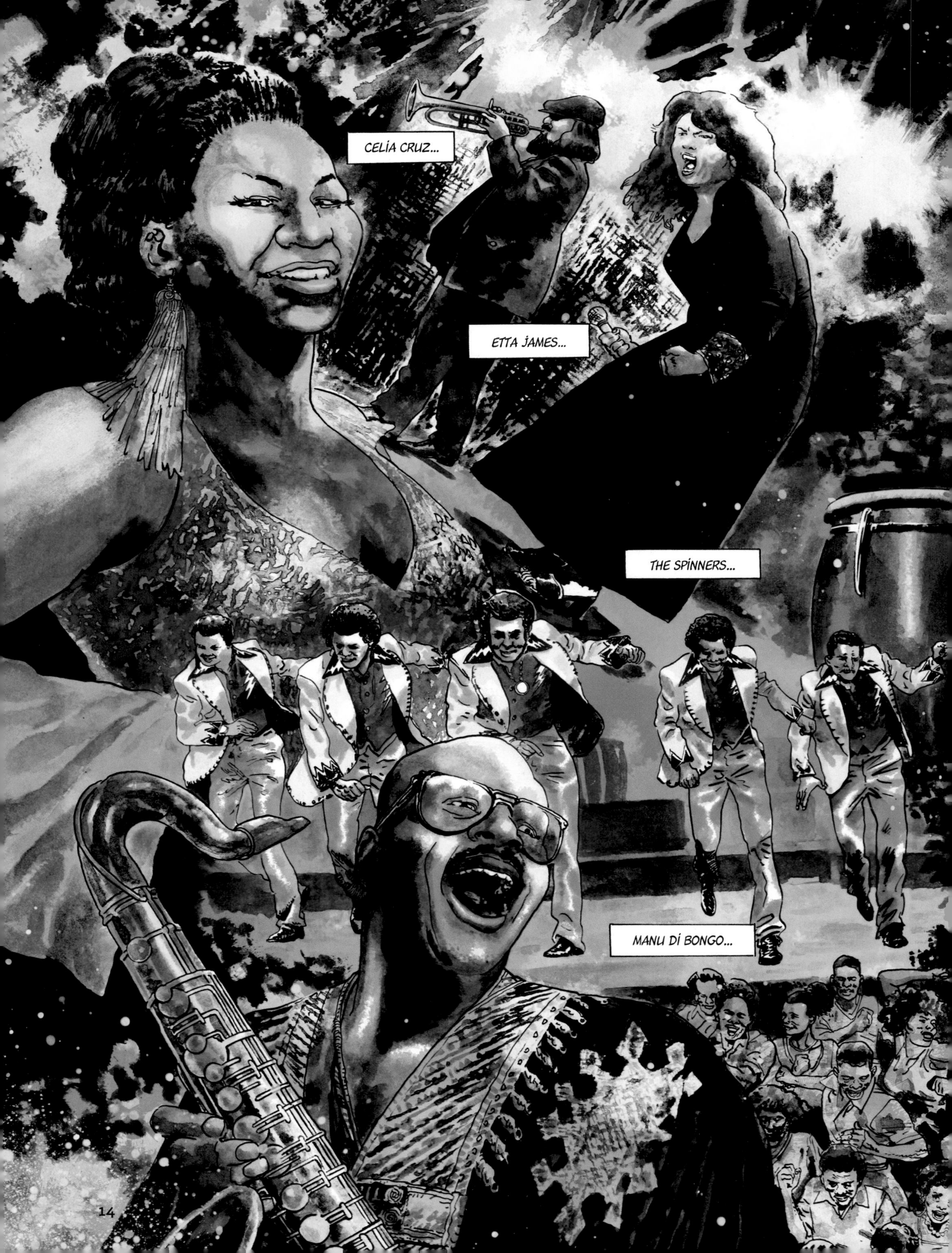
CELIA CRUZ...
ETTA JAMES...
THE SPINNERS...
MANU DI BONGO...

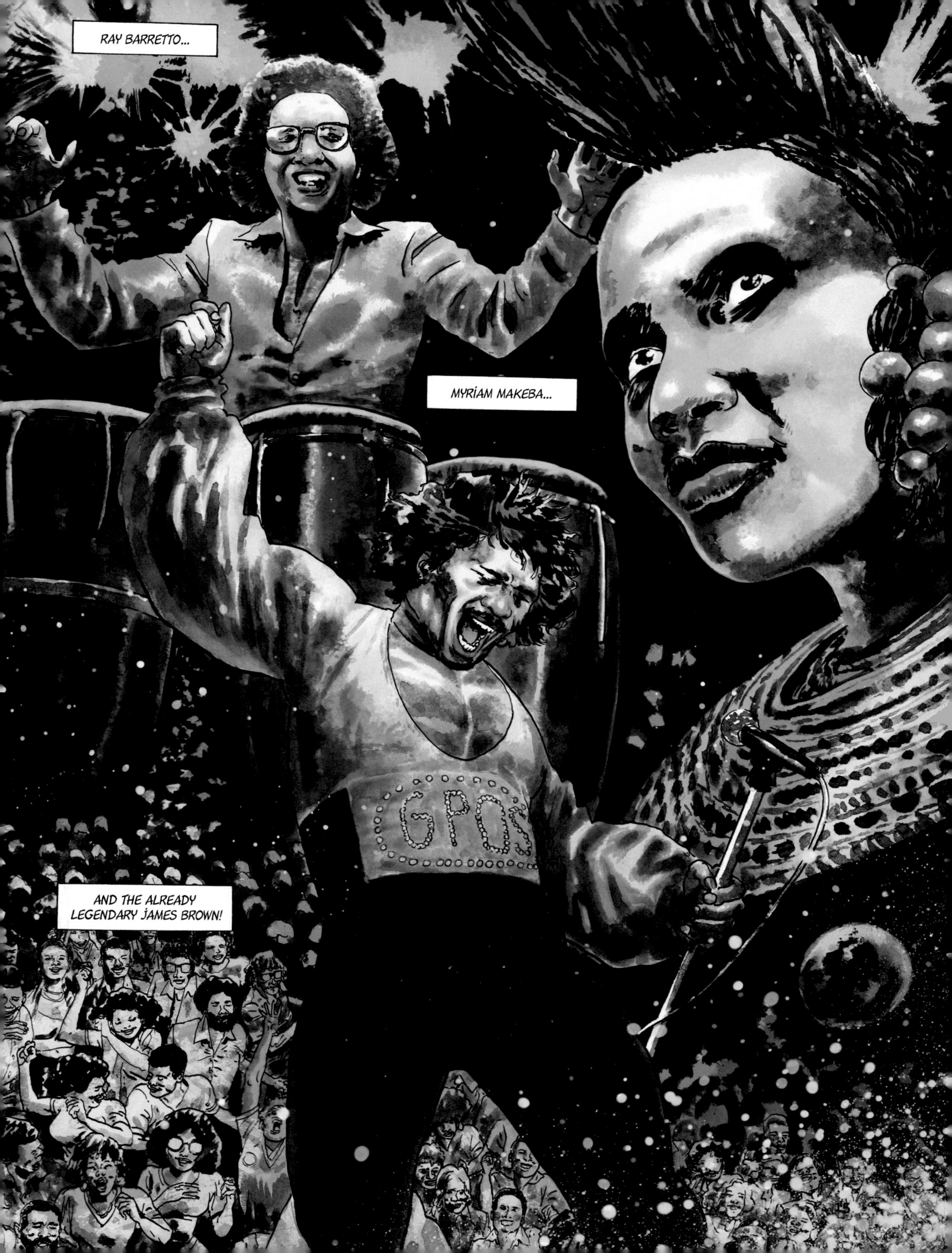
RAY BARRETTO...
MYRÍAM MAKEBA...
GROS
AND THE ALREADY LEGENDARY JAMES BROWN!

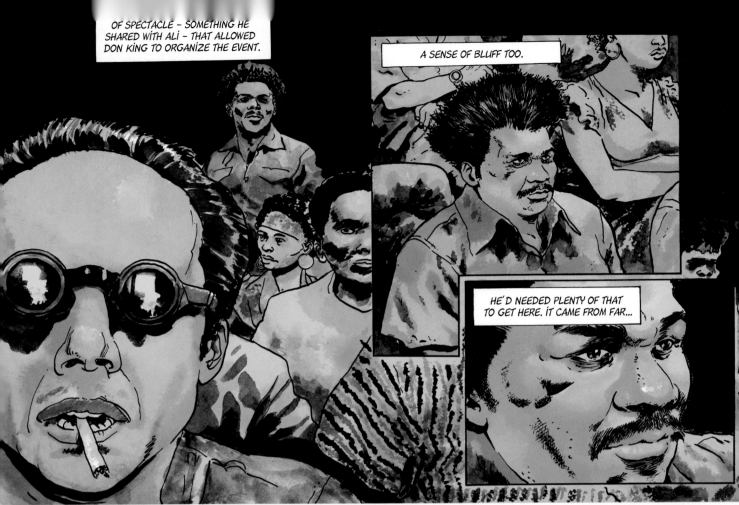

OF SPECTACLE – SOMETHING HE SHARED WITH ALİ – THAT ALLOWED DON KİNG TO ORGANIZE THE EVENT.

A SENSE OF BLUFF TOO.

HE'D NEEDED PLENTY OF THAT TO GET HERE. IT CAME FROM FAR...

...FROM CLEVELAND, OHİO, WHERE HE WAS BORN ON AUGUST 20TH 1931.

AT AGE 18, HE ENROLLED İN COLLEGE.

HİS HOBBY: GAMBLİNG.

THE WORLD OF MORE-OR-LESS İLLEGAL BETTING FLİRTED İRREDEEMABLY WITH CRİME, FRAUD AND LACK OF MORALS.

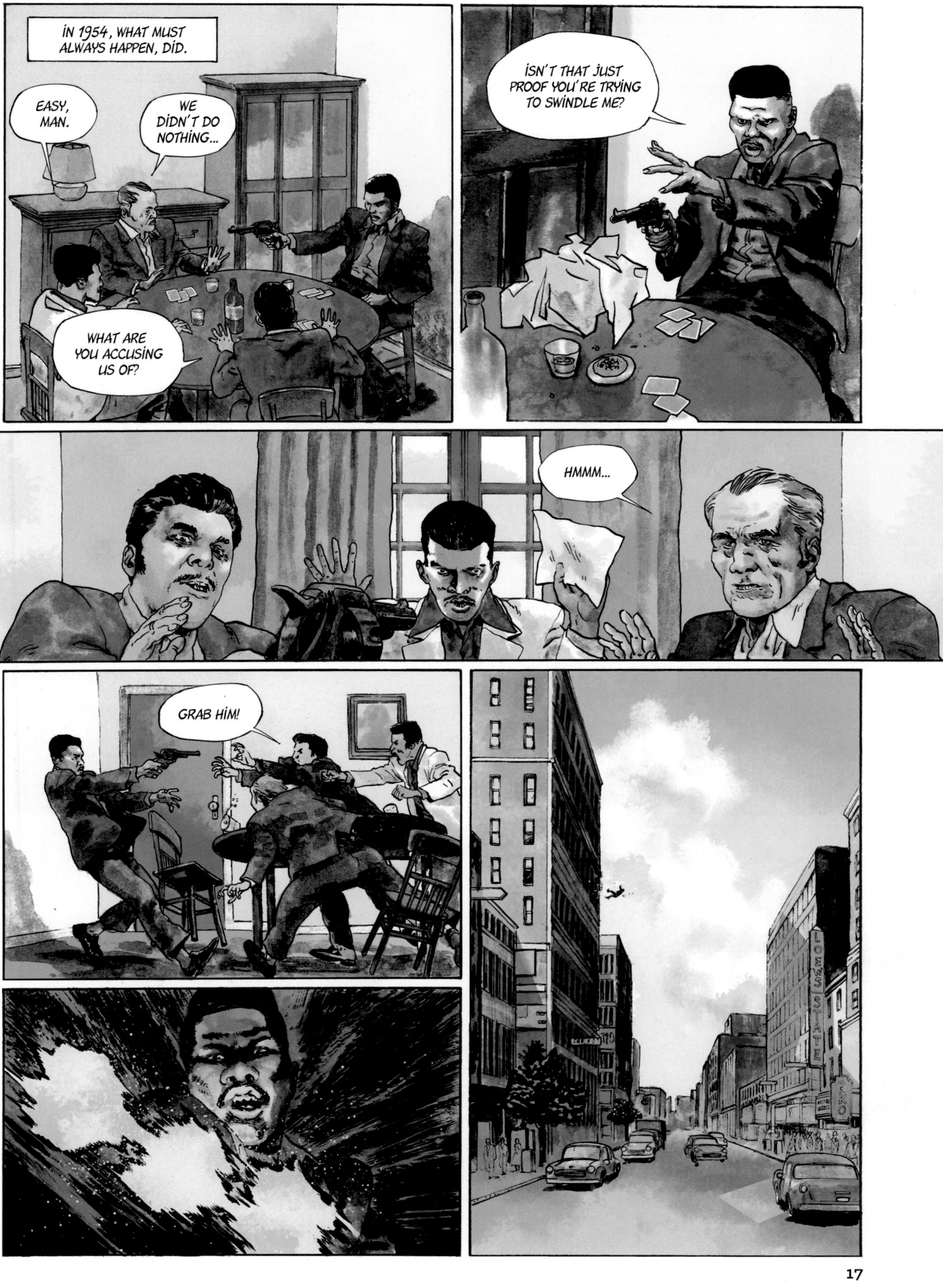
IN 1954, WHAT MUST ALWAYS HAPPEN, DID.
EASY, MAN.
WE DIDN'T DO NOTHING...
WHAT ARE YOU ACCUSING US OF?
ISN'T THAT JUST PROOF YOU'RE TRYING TO SWINDLE ME?
HMMM...
GRAB HIM!
LOEWS STATE
RKO

ONE OF THE CROOKS WAS KILLED BY THE SHOT. BUT DONALD DID NOT STAY IN PRISON, HIS CLAIM OF SELF-DEFENSE STOOD IN COURT.

98718

WHAT DOESN'T PUNISH YOU MAKES YOU FEEL STRONGER.

AND ONE DARK DAY IN 1966...

I WON'T PAY YOU BACK, GOT IT?

YOUR INTEREST IS INSANE...

YOU CAN GO SHOVE IT...

BOOHOOHOOC BOOH B BOHOOO BOHC

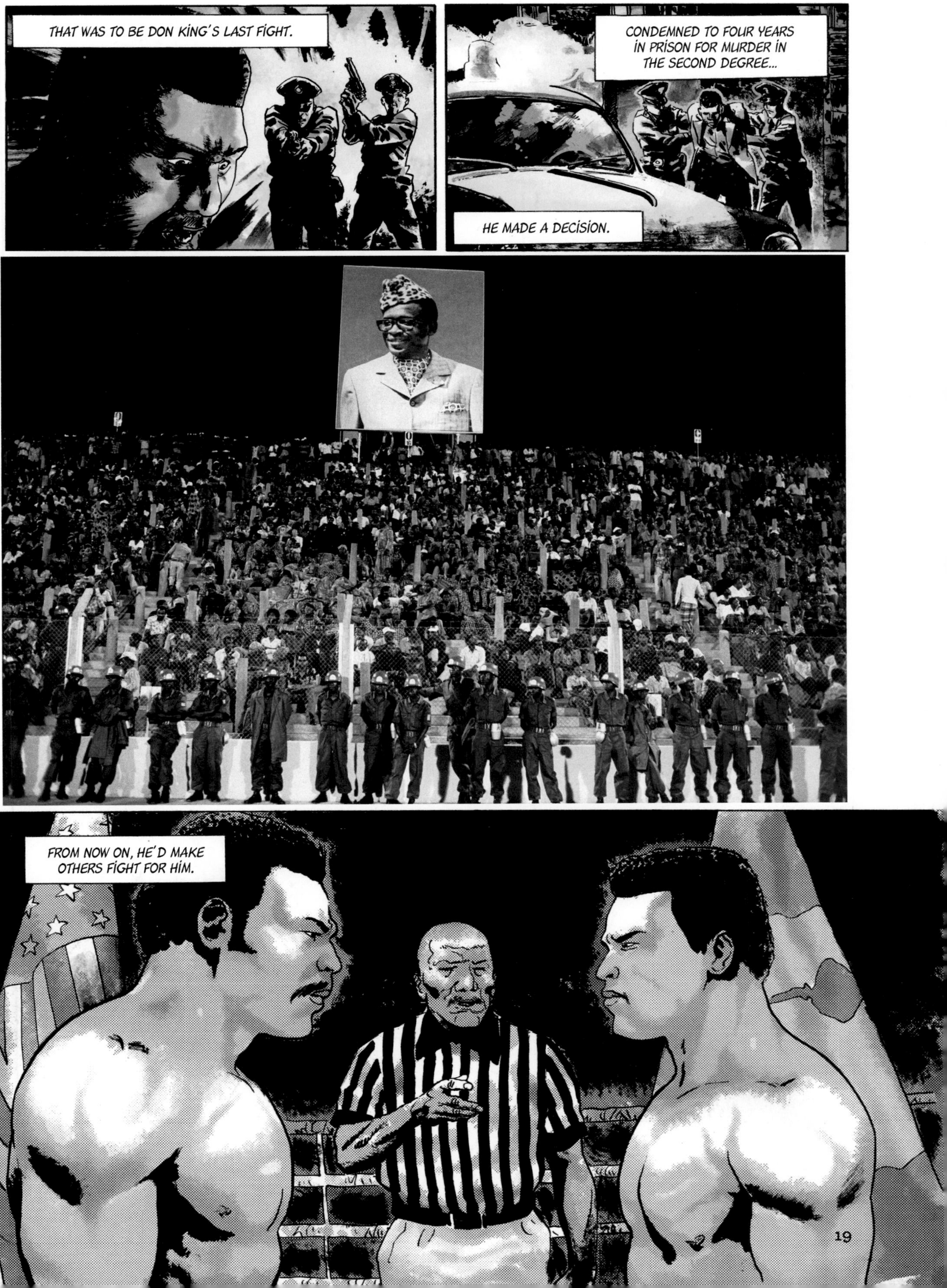
THAT WAS TO BE DON KING'S LAST FIGHT.
CONDEMNED TO FOUR YEARS IN PRISON FOR MURDER IN THE SECOND DEGREE...
HE MADE A DECISION.
FROM NOW ON, HE'D MAKE OTHERS FIGHT FOR HIM.

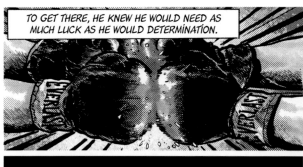

TO GET THERE, HE KNEW HE WOULD NEED AS MUCH LUCK AS HE WOULD DETERMINATION.

UPON HIS RELEASE FROM PRISON, HE NEEDED MONEY QUICKLY. AND WHAT OTHER SPORT BUT BOXING COULD MAKE HIM SO MUCH?

THE STAR OF THE TIME WAS ALREADY MUHAMMAD ALI.

IN JOINING THE NATION OF ISLAM THE YEAR BEFORE, ALI HAD RENOUNCED HIS BIRTH NAME OF CASSIUS CLAY.

THANKS TO LLOYD PRICE, A MUTUAL SINGER FRIEND, KING SET OUT TO APPROACH THE GOAT.*

(*GREATEST OF ALL TIME)

AND CONVINCED HIM TO PARTICIPATE IN A CHARITY GALA FOR A CLEVELAND HOSPITAL.

WITH THIS FIRST EVENT A SUCCESS, KING BEGAN TO MAKE A NAME FOR HIMSELF AMONG CONTACTS IN THE PUBLICITY WORLD.

IN 1973, HE PUT ALI INTO THE RING FOR AN EXHIBITION. ANOTHER FAVOR FOR A HOSPITAL ON THE EDGE OF COLLAPSE.

THIS HOSPITAL WOULD CLOSE ITS DOORS SHORTLY AFTERWARDS, HAVING NEVER SEEN A CENT OF THE THOUSANDS OF DOLLARS RAISED.

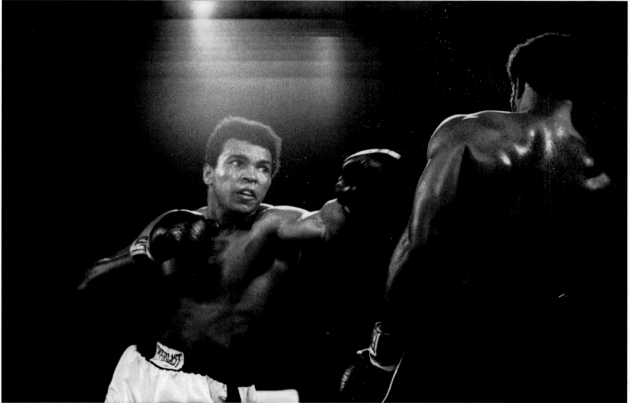

NOT ONLY DID KING GET RICH, BUT EVEN BETTER, HE NOW HAD A DIRECT LINK TO ALI WHO WAS FIGHTING TO WIN BACK THE TITLE HE HAD LOST IN 1970.

GEORGE FOREMAN, THE CURRENT UNBEATEN CHAMPION, NEEDED A SPECTACULAR FIGHT TO SOLIDIFY HIS REPUTATION.

DON KING HAD A VISION!

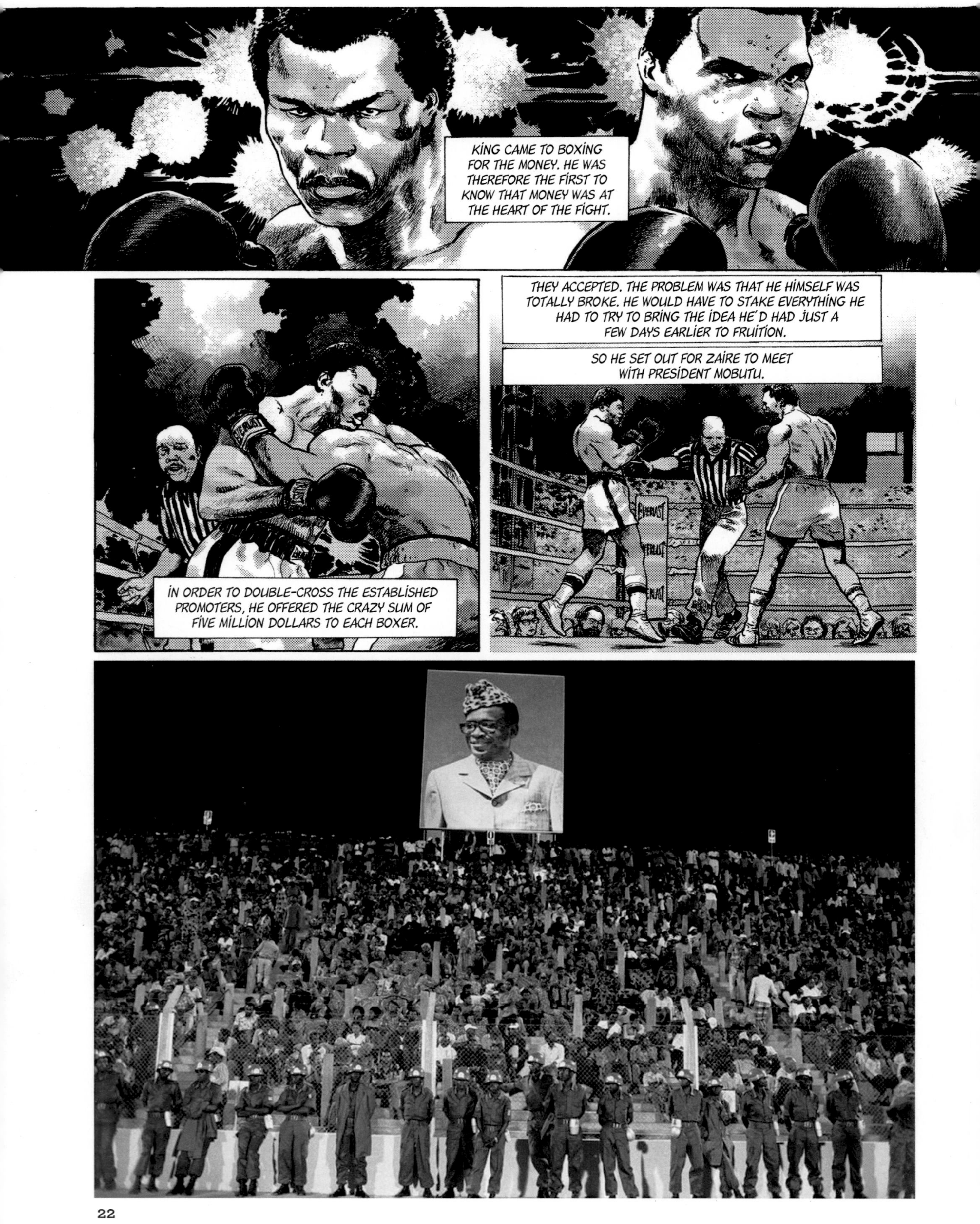
KING CAME TO BOXING FOR THE MONEY. HE WAS THEREFORE THE FIRST TO KNOW THAT MONEY WAS AT THE HEART OF THE FIGHT.
IN ORDER TO DOUBLE-CROSS THE ESTABLISHED PROMOTERS, HE OFFERED THE CRAZY SUM OF FIVE MILLION DOLLARS TO EACH BOXER.
THEY ACCEPTED. THE PROBLEM WAS THAT HE HIMSELF WAS TOTALLY BROKE. HE WOULD HAVE TO STAKE EVERYTHING HE HAD TO TRY TO BRING THE IDEA HE'D HAD JUST A FEW DAYS EARLIER TO FRUITION.
SO HE SET OUT FOR ZAIRE TO MEET WITH PRESIDENT MOBUTU.

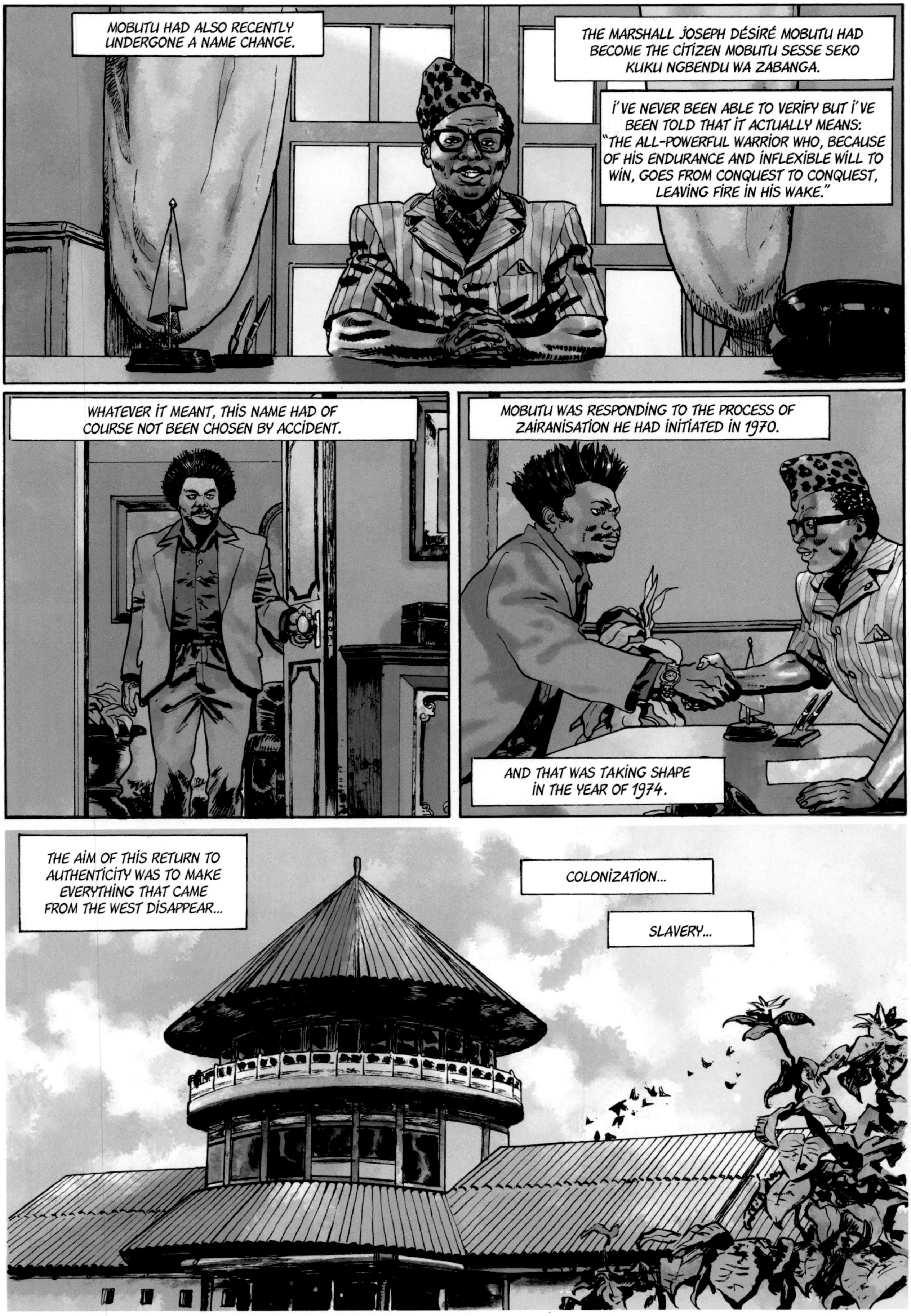
MOBUTU HAD ALSO RECENTLY UNDERGONE A NAME CHANGE.
THE MARSHALL JOSEPH DÉSIRÉ MOBUTU HAD BECOME THE CITIZEN MOBUTU SESSE SEKO KUKU NGBENDU WA ZABANGA.
I'VE NEVER BEEN ABLE TO VERIFY BUT I'VE BEEN TOLD THAT IT ACTUALLY MEANS: "THE ALL-POWERFUL WARRIOR WHO, BECAUSE OF HIS ENDURANCE AND INFLEXIBLE WILL TO WIN, GOES FROM CONQUEST TO CONQUEST, LEAVING FIRE IN HIS WAKE."
WHATEVER IT MEANT, THIS NAME HAD OF COURSE NOT BEEN CHOSEN BY ACCIDENT.
MOBUTU WAS RESPONDING TO THE PROCESS OF ZAIRANISATION HE HAD INITIATED IN 1970.
AND THAT WAS TAKING SHAPE IN THE YEAR OF 1974.
THE AIM OF THIS RETURN TO AUTHENTICITY WAS TO MAKE EVERYTHING THAT CAME FROM THE WEST DISAPPEAR...
COLONIZATION...
SLAVERY...

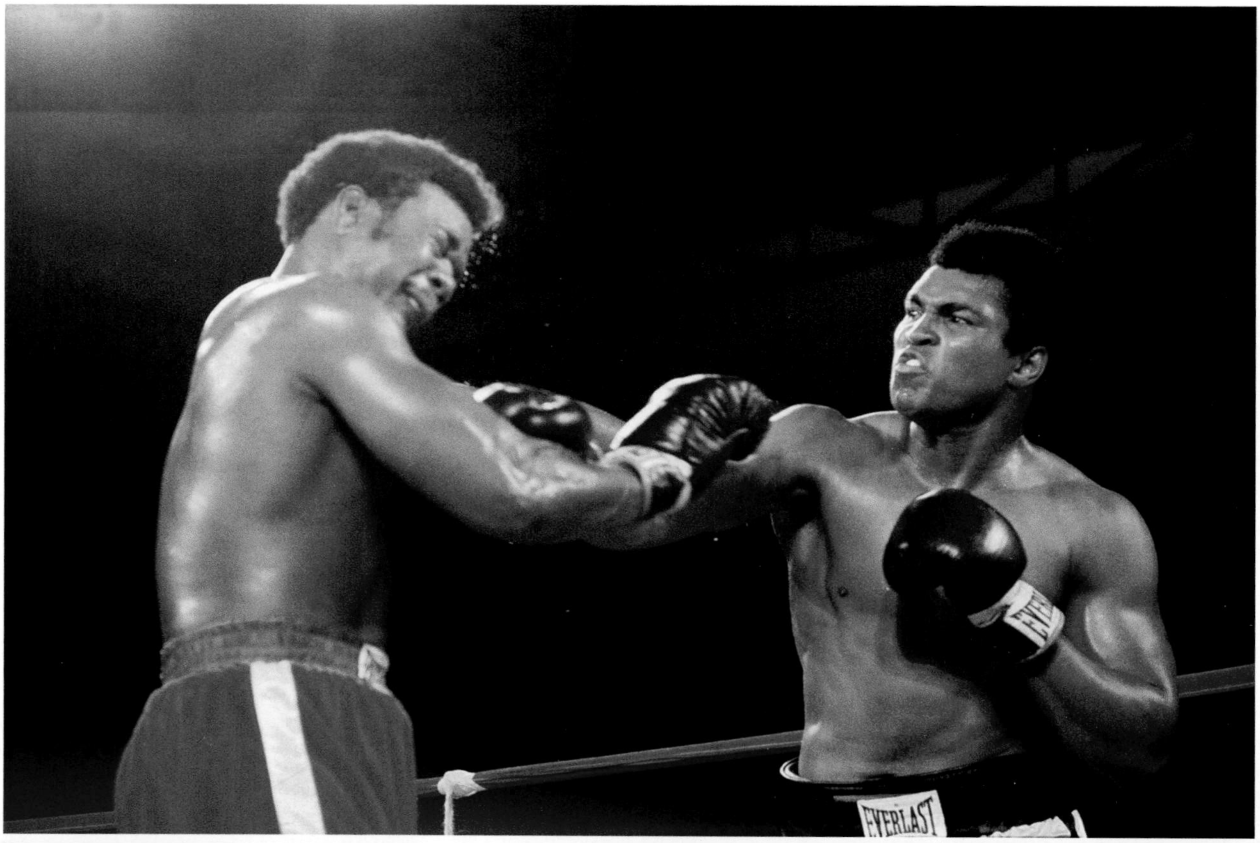
EVERLAST

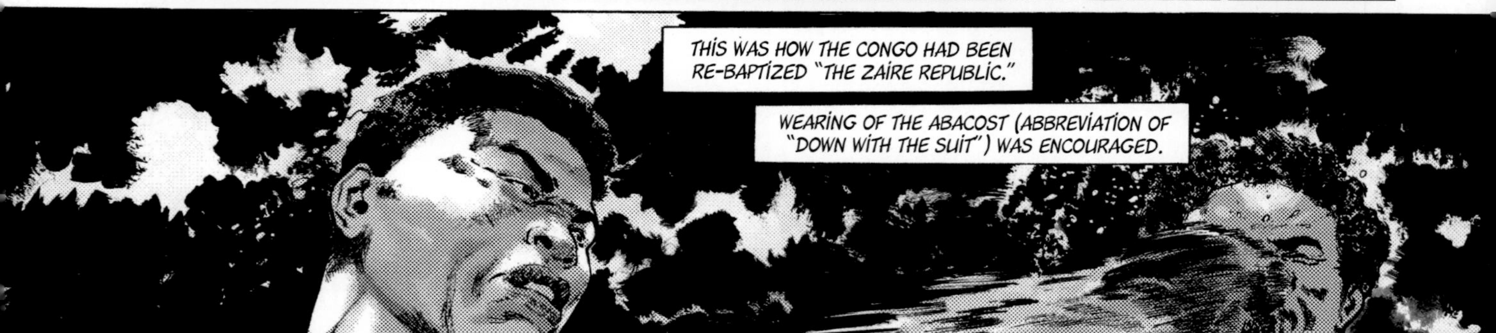
THIS WAS HOW THE CONGO HAD BEEN RE-BAPTIZED "THE ZAIRE REPUBLIC."
WEARING OF THE ABACOST (ABBREVIATION OF "DOWN WITH THE SUIT") WAS ENCOURAGED.

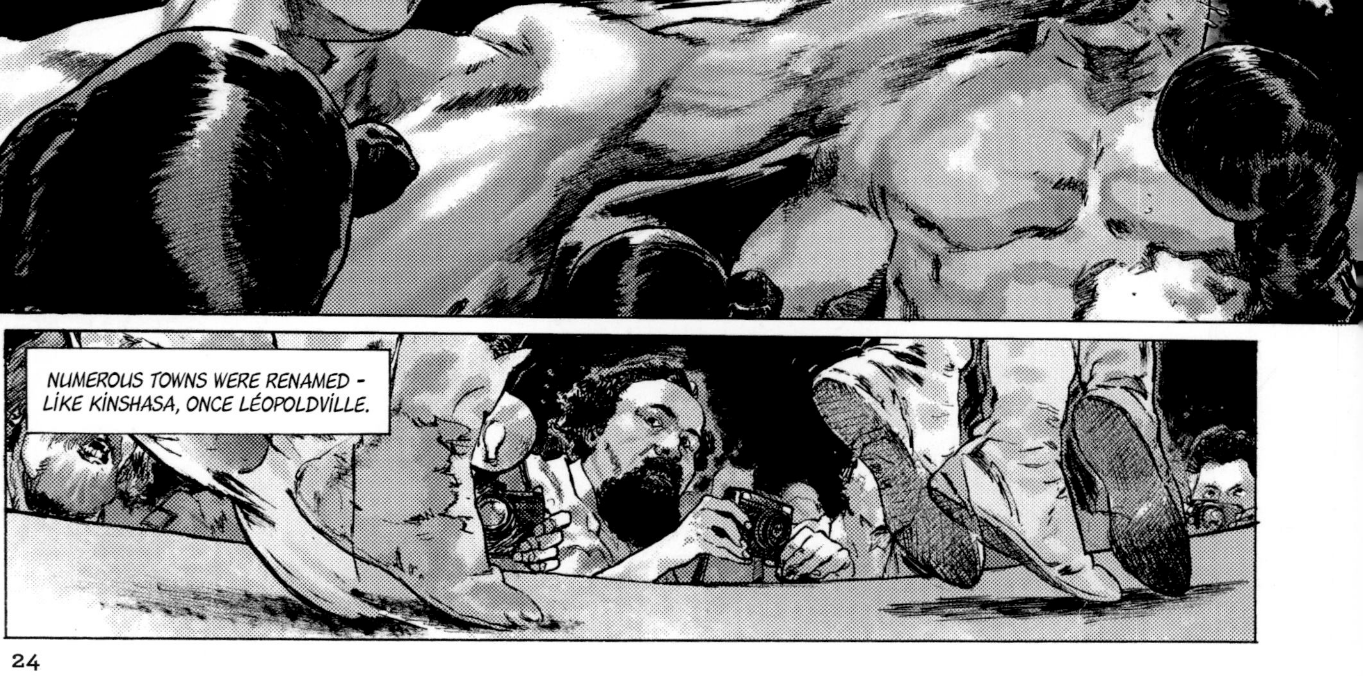
NUMEROUS TOWNS WERE RENAMED - LIKE KINSHASA, ONCE LÉOPOLDVILLE.

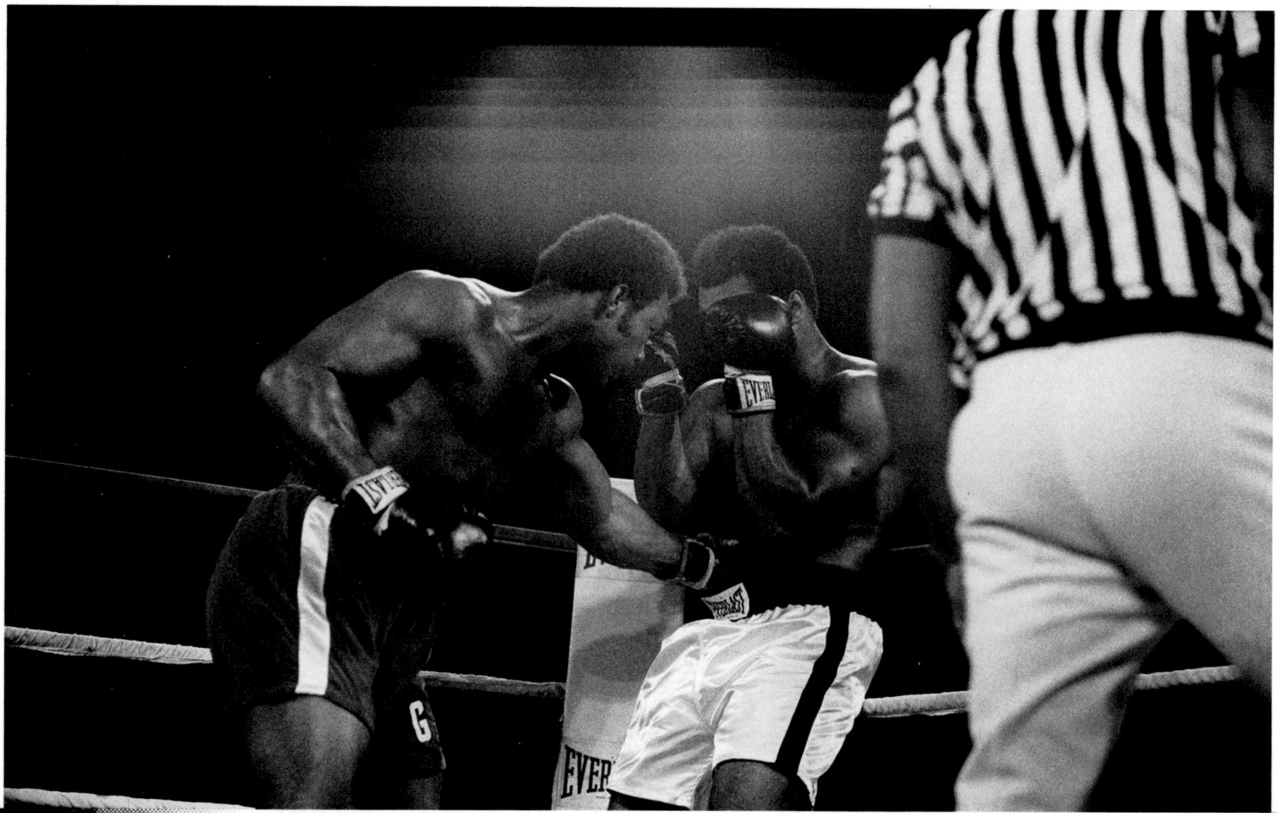
EVERLAST
G.F.

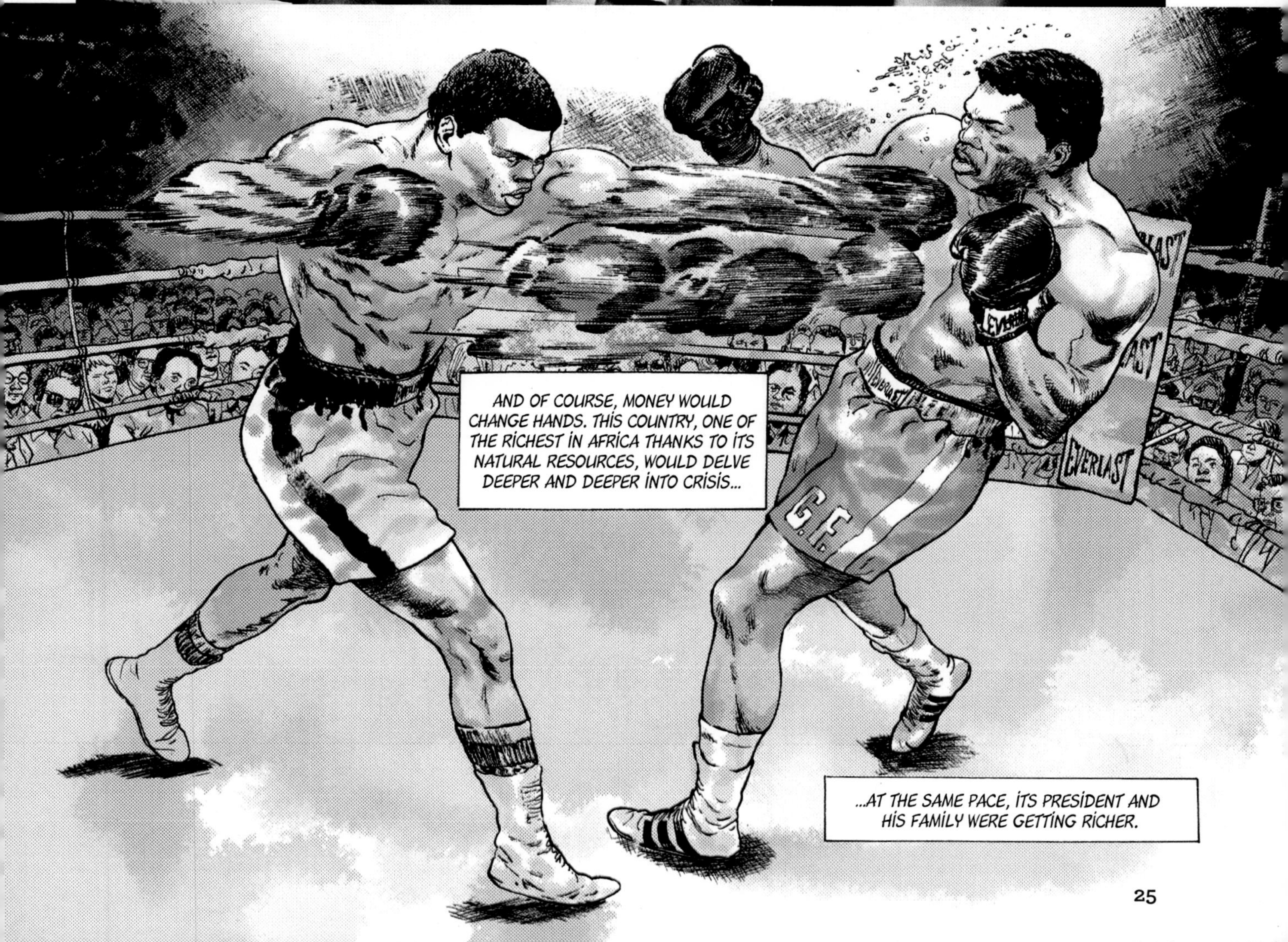
AND OF COURSE, MONEY WOULD CHANGE HANDS. THIS COUNTRY, ONE OF THE RICHEST IN AFRICA THANKS TO ITS NATURAL RESOURCES, WOULD DELVE DEEPER AND DEEPER INTO CRISIS...
...AT THE SAME PACE, ITS PRESIDENT AND HIS FAMILY WERE GETTING RICHER.
EVERLAST
G.F.

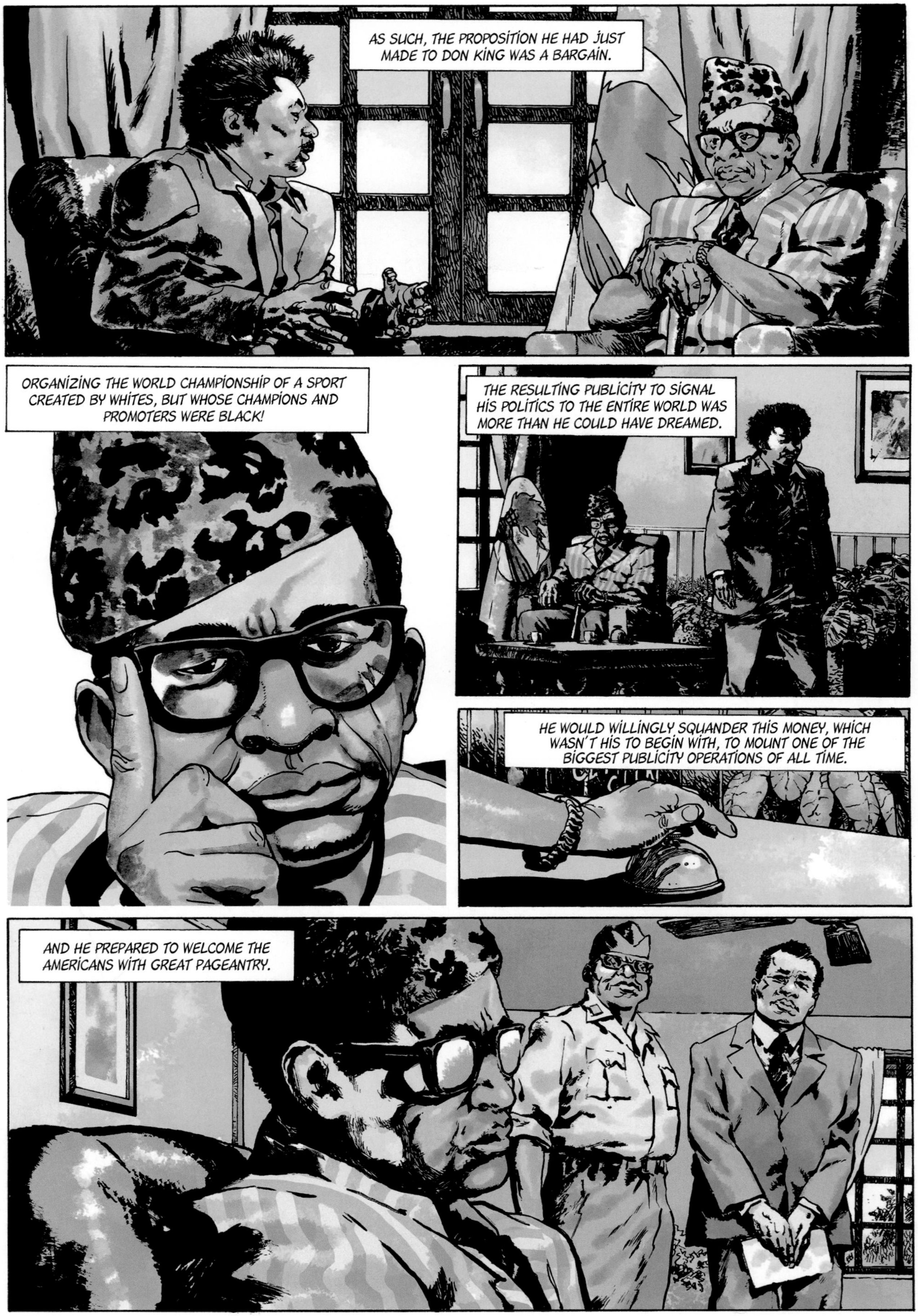
AS SUCH, THE PROPOSITION HE HAD JUST MADE TO DON KING WAS A BARGAIN.
ORGANIZING THE WORLD CHAMPIONSHIP OF A SPORT CREATED BY WHITES, BUT WHOSE CHAMPIONS AND PROMOTERS WERE BLACK!
THE RESULTING PUBLICITY TO SIGNAL HIS POLITICS TO THE ENTIRE WORLD WAS MORE THAN HE COULD HAVE DREAMED.
HE WOULD WILLINGLY SQUANDER THIS MONEY, WHICH WASN'T HIS TO BEGIN WITH, TO MOUNT ONE OF THE BIGGEST PUBLICITY OPERATIONS OF ALL TIME.
AND HE PREPARED TO WELCOME THE AMERICANS WITH GREAT PAGEANTRY.

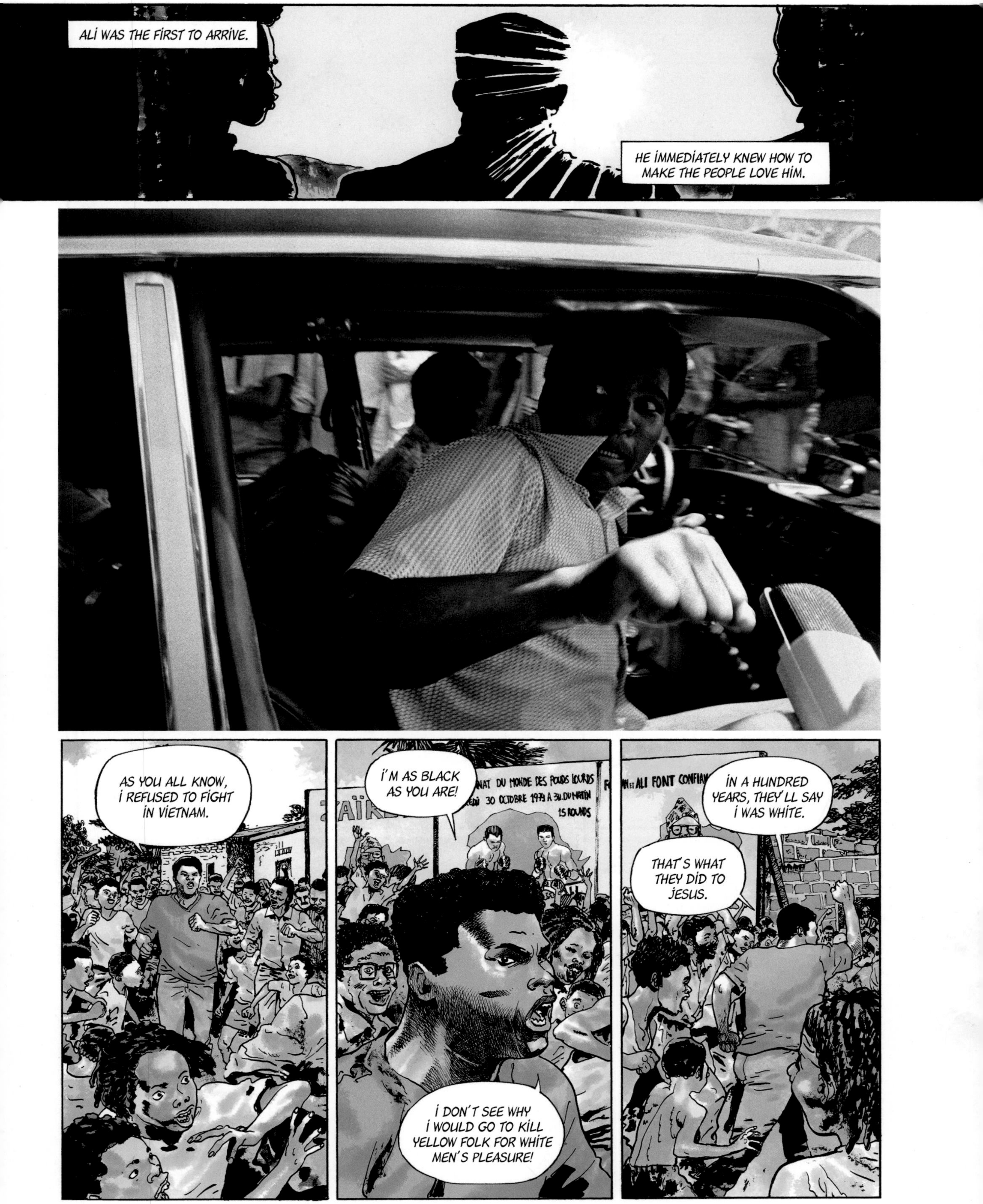
ALI WAS THE FIRST TO ARRIVE.
HE IMMEDIATELY KNEW HOW TO MAKE THE PEOPLE LOVE HIM.
AS YOU ALL KNOW, I REFUSED TO FIGHT IN VIETNAM.
I'M AS BLACK AS YOU ARE!
15 ROUNDS
I DON'T SEE WHY I WOULD GO TO KILL YELLOW FOLK FOR WHITE MEN'S PLEASURE!
IN A HUNDRED YEARS, THEY'LL SAY I WAS WHITE.
THAT'S WHAT THEY DID TO JESUS.

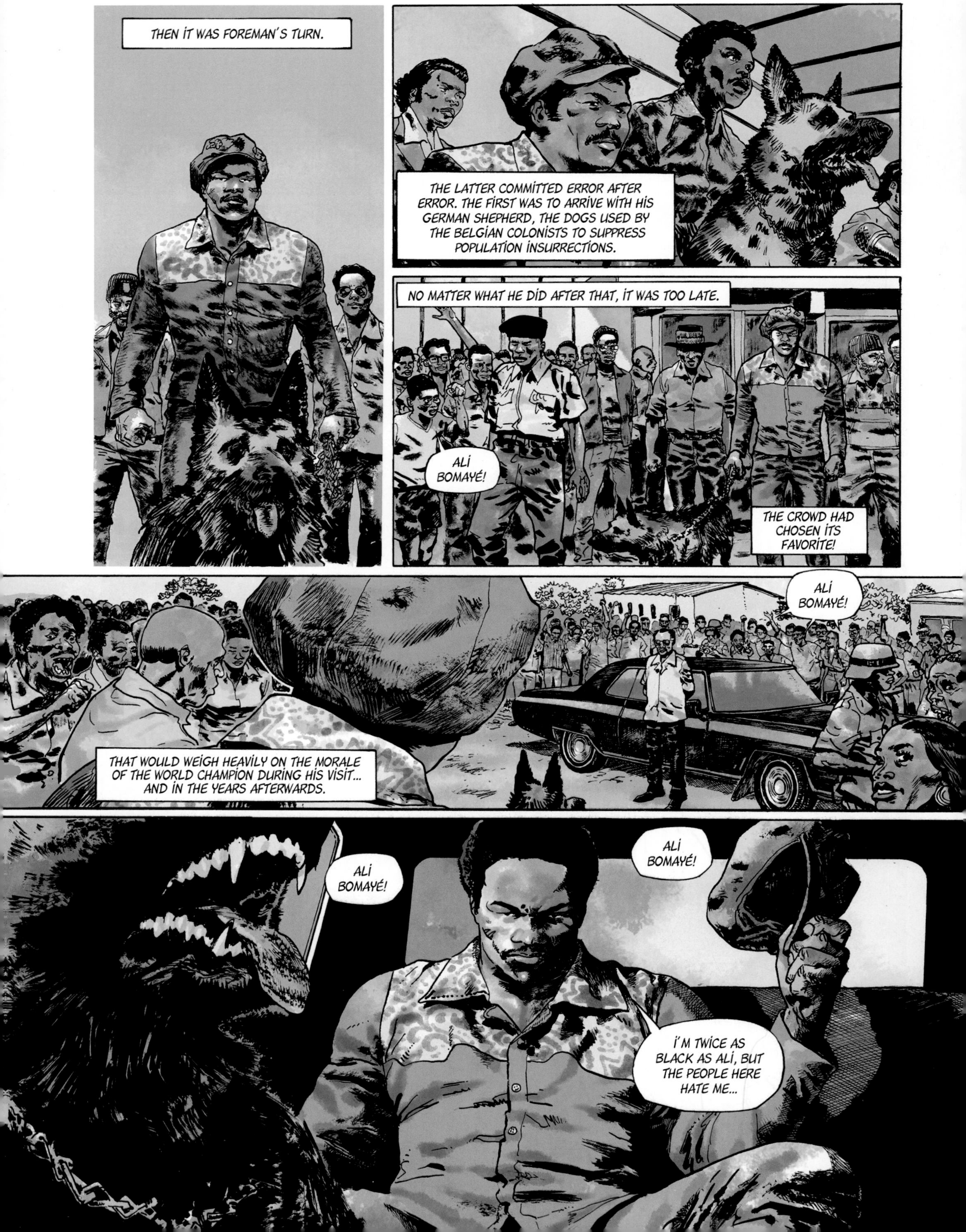
THEN IT WAS FOREMAN'S TURN.
THE LATTER COMMITTED ERROR AFTER ERROR. THE FIRST WAS TO ARRIVE WITH HIS GERMAN SHEPHERD, THE DOGS USED BY THE BELGIAN COLONISTS TO SUPPRESS POPULATION INSURRECTIONS.
NO MATTER WHAT HE DID AFTER THAT, IT WAS TOO LATE.
ALI BOMAYÉ!
THE CROWD HAD CHOSEN ITS FAVORITE!
THAT WOULD WEIGH HEAVILY ON THE MORALE OF THE WORLD CHAMPION DURING HIS VISIT... AND IN THE YEARS AFTERWARDS.
ALI BOMAYÉ!
ALI BOMAYÉ!
ALI BOMAYÉ!
I'M TWICE AS BLACK AS ALI, BUT THE PEOPLE HERE HATE ME...

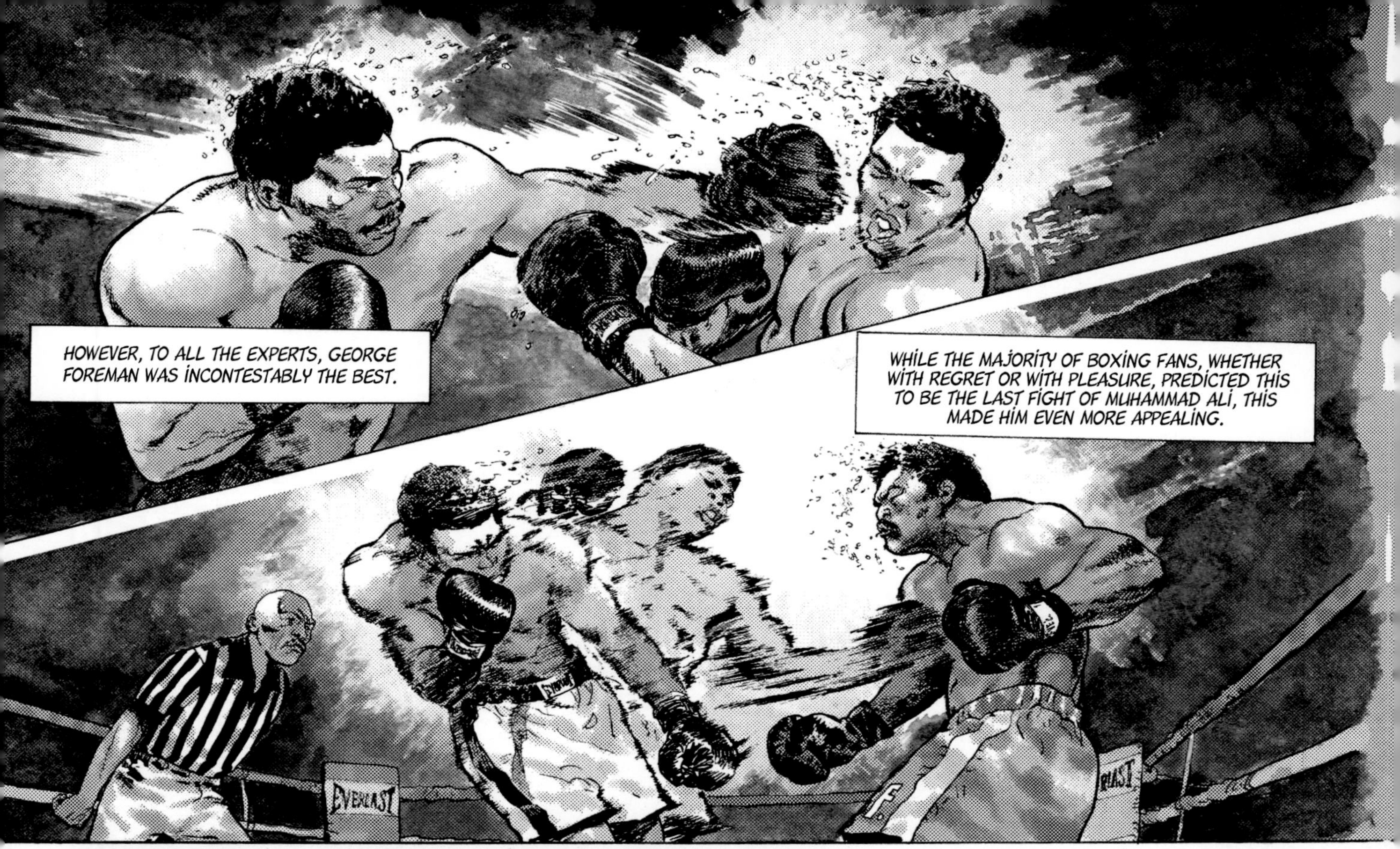
HOWEVER, TO ALL THE EXPERTS, GEORGE FOREMAN WAS INCONTESTABLY THE BEST.
WHILE THE MAJORITY OF BOXING FANS, WHETHER WITH REGRET OR WITH PLEASURE, PREDICTED THIS TO BE THE LAST FIGHT OF MUHAMMAD ALI, THIS MADE HIM EVEN MORE APPEALING.

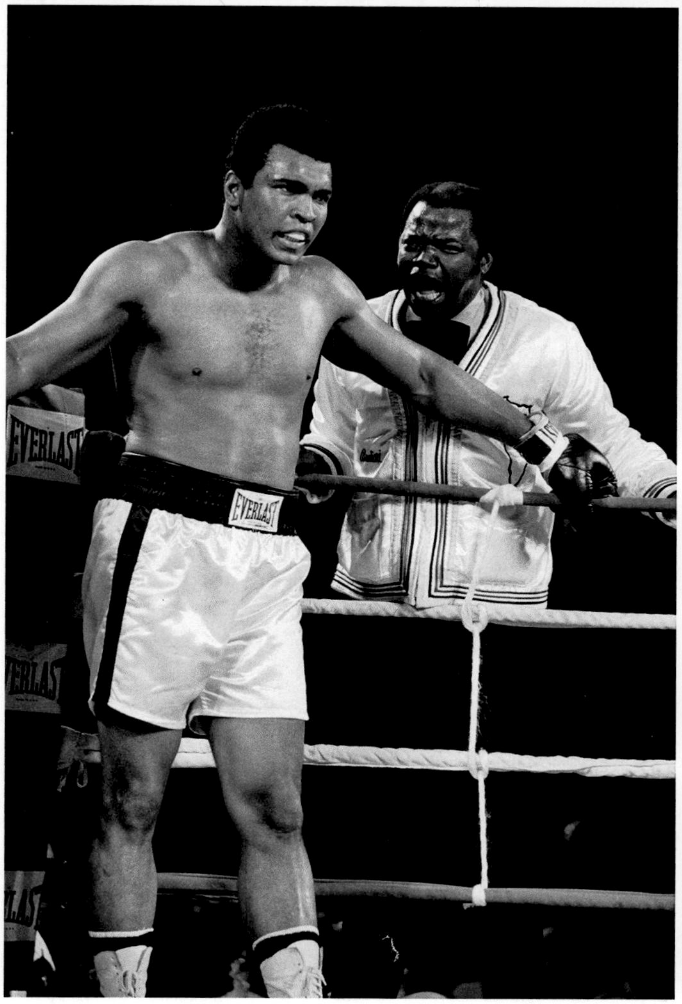

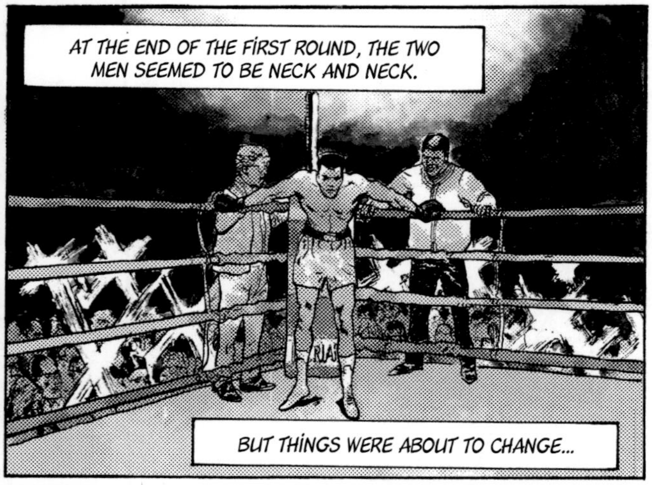
AT THE END OF THE FIRST ROUND, THE TWO MEN SEEMED TO BE NECK AND NECK.
BUT THINGS WERE ABOUT TO CHANGE...

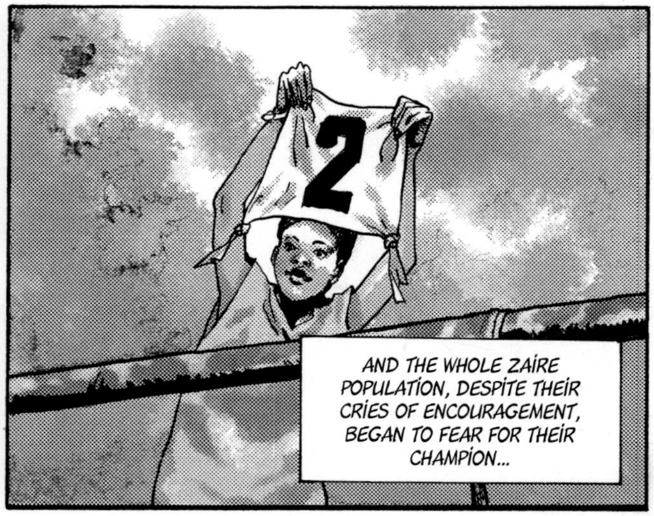
2
AND THE WHOLE ZAIRE POPULATION, DESPITE THEIR CRIES OF ENCOURAGEMENT, BEGAN TO FEAR FOR THEIR CHAMPION...

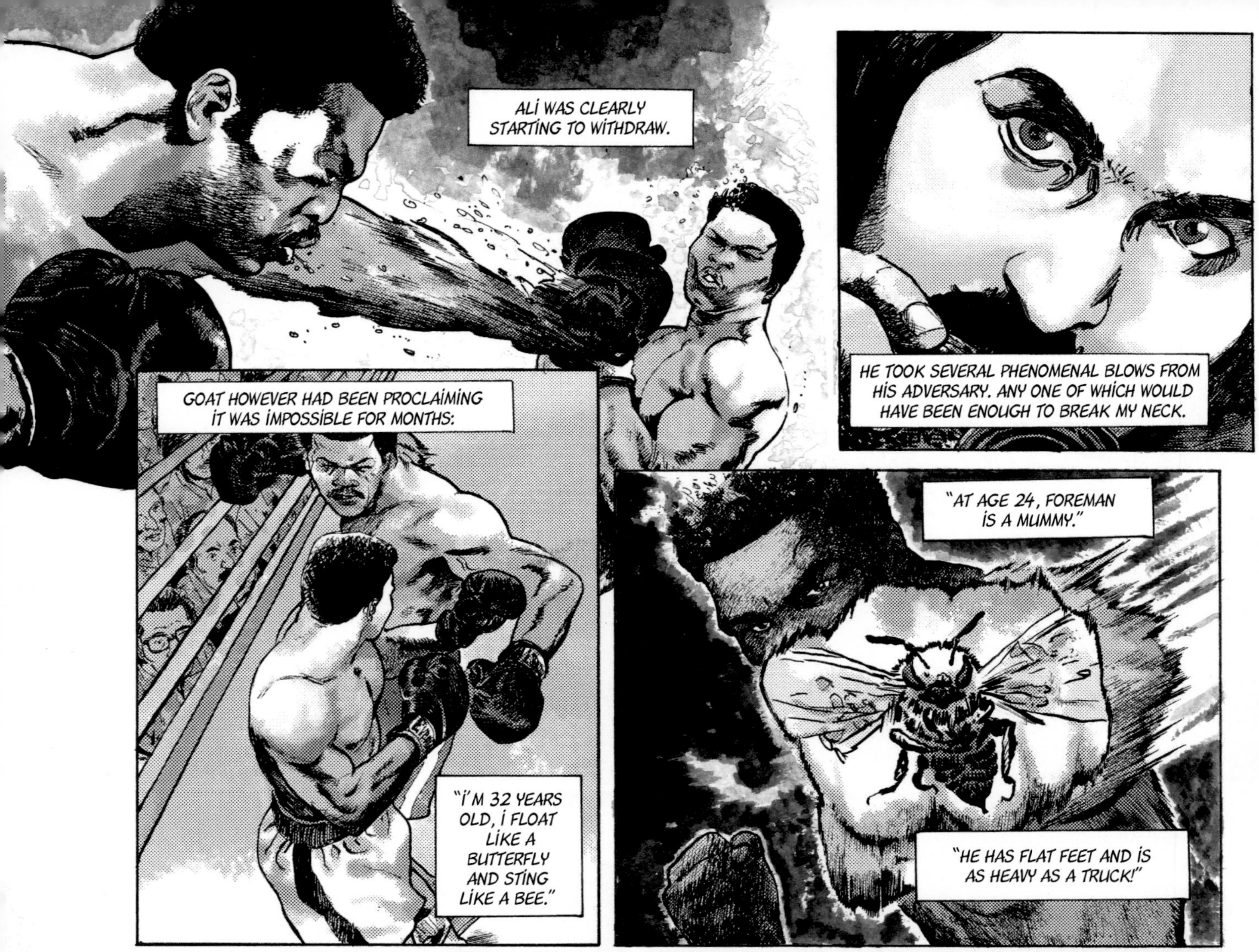
ALI WAS CLEARLY STARTING TO WITHDRAW.
HE TOOK SEVERAL PHENOMENAL BLOWS FROM HIS ADVERSARY. ANY ONE OF WHICH WOULD HAVE BEEN ENOUGH TO BREAK MY NECK.
GOAT HOWEVER HAD BEEN PROCLAIMING IT WAS IMPOSSIBLE FOR MONTHS:
"I'M 32 YEARS OLD, I FLOAT LIKE A BUTTERFLY AND STING LIKE A BEE."
"AT AGE 24, FOREMAN IS A MUMMY."
"HE HAS FLAT FEET AND IS AS HEAVY AS A TRUCK!"

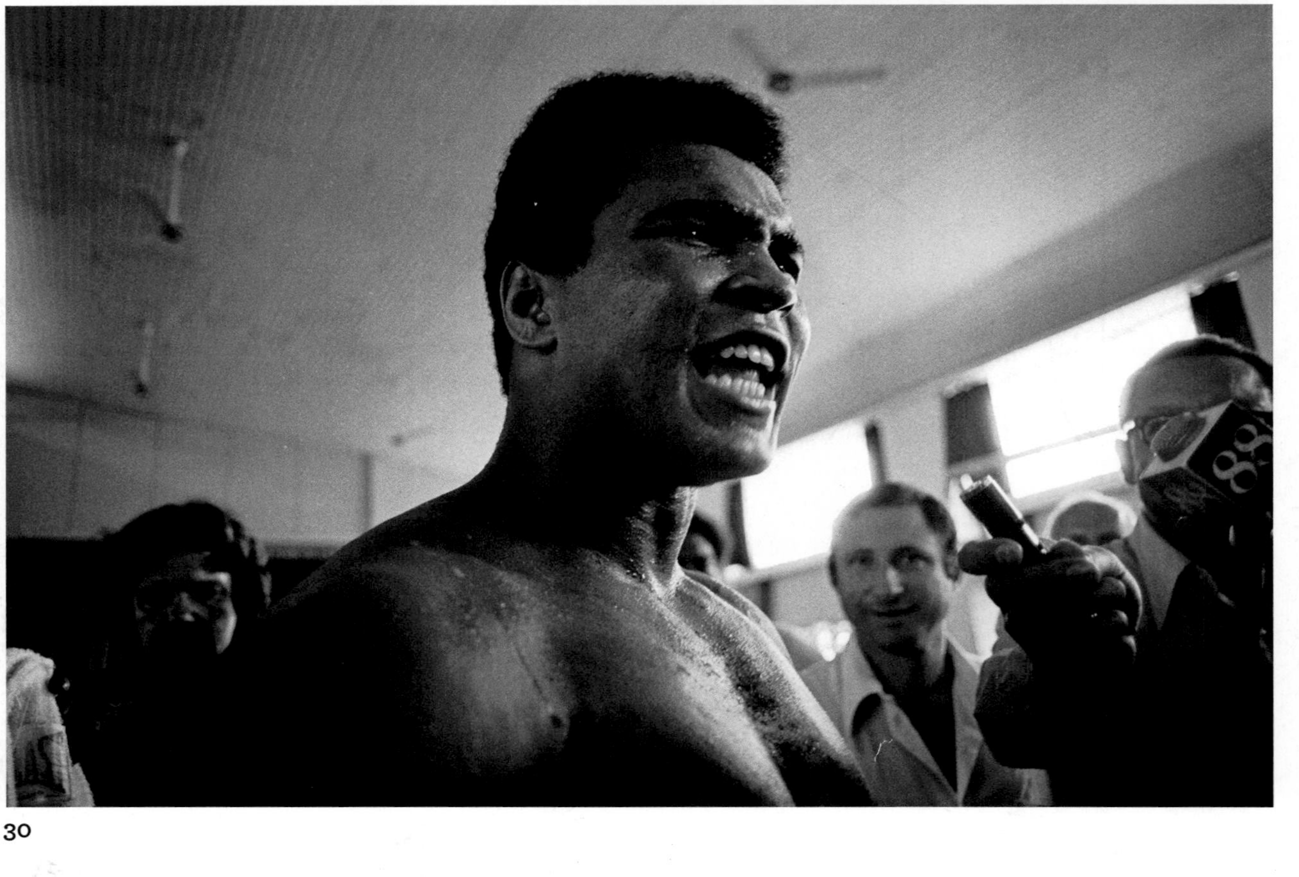

"I'M GOING TO PUT THE WORLD HEAVYWEIGHT CHAMPION INTO RETIREMENT."

"AND THE WORLD WILL BE JUST AS STUNNED AS HIM!"

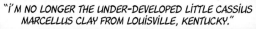

"I'M NO LONGER THE UNDER-DEVELOPED LITTLE CASSIUS MARCELLUS CLAY FROM LOUISVILLE, KENTUCKY."

"EVEN THOUGH HE BEAT THE LAST TWO BOXERS WHO BEAT ME, I HAVE BAD NEWS FOR GEORGE."

"TODAY I'M A BETTER BOXER!"

"I'M EXPERIENCED NOW."

"JAW'S BEEN BROKE. I'VE BEEN LOST, BEEN KNOCKED DOWN A COUPLE OF TIMES..."

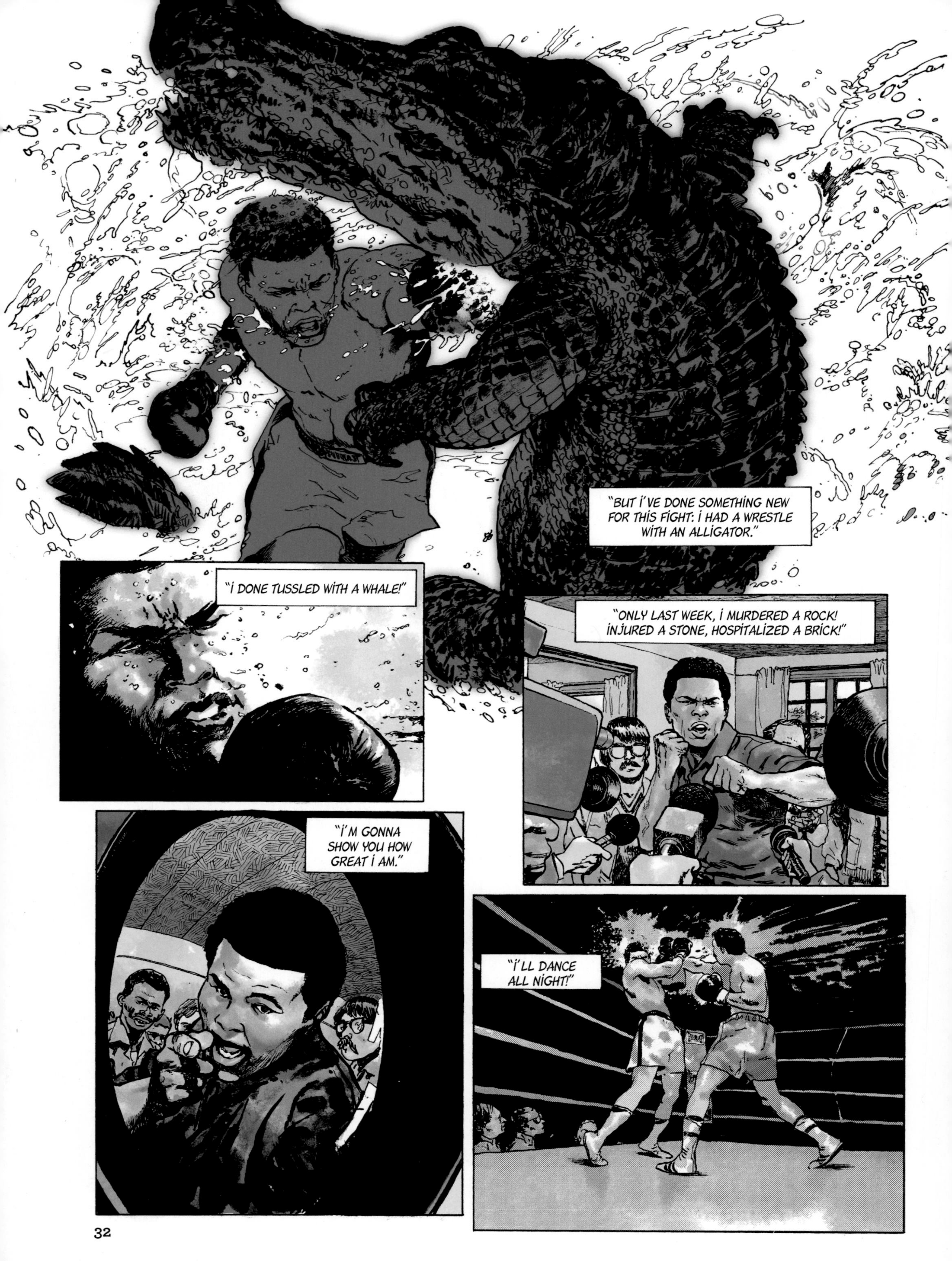
"BUT I'VE DONE SOMETHING NEW FOR THIS FIGHT: I HAD A WRESTLE WITH AN ALLIGATOR."
"I DONE TUSSLED WITH A WHALE!"
"ONLY LAST WEEK, I MURDERED A ROCK! INJURED A STONE, HOSPITALIZED A BRICK!"
"I'M GONNA SHOW YOU HOW GREAT I AM."
"I'LL DANCE ALL NIGHT!"

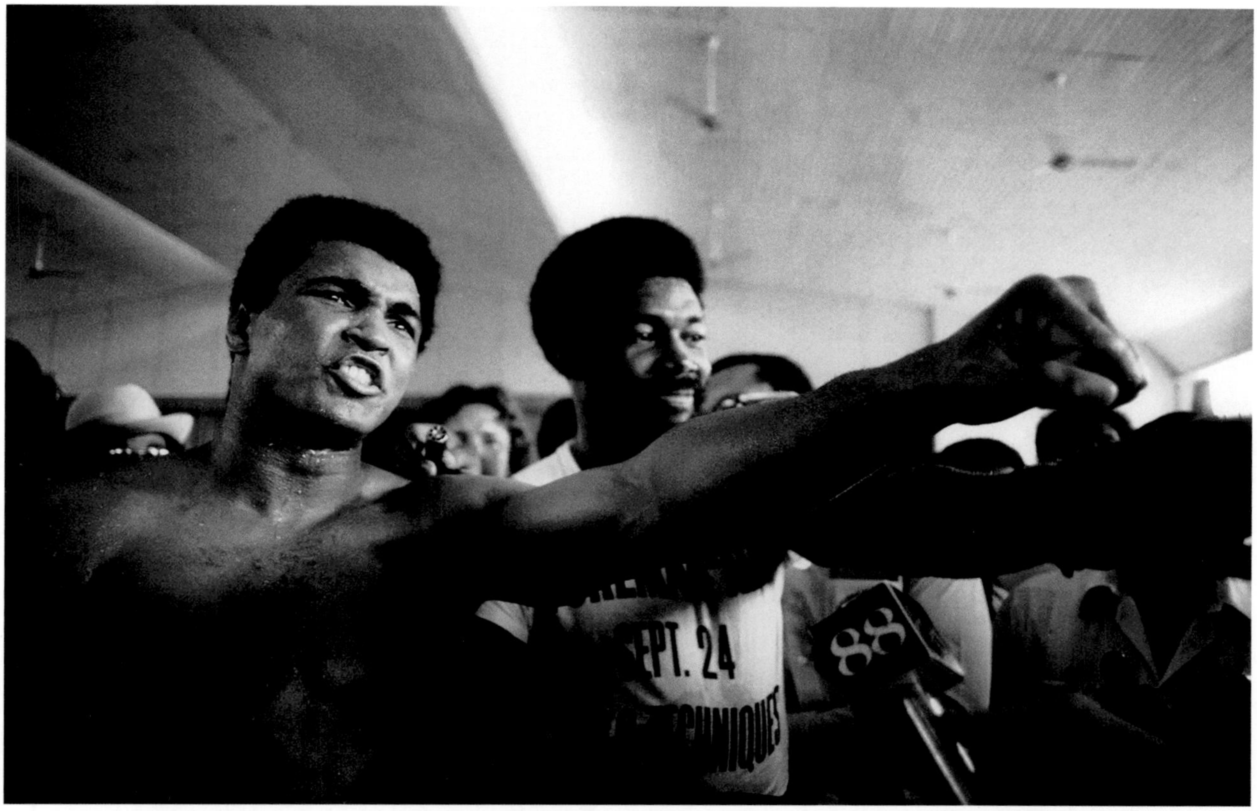

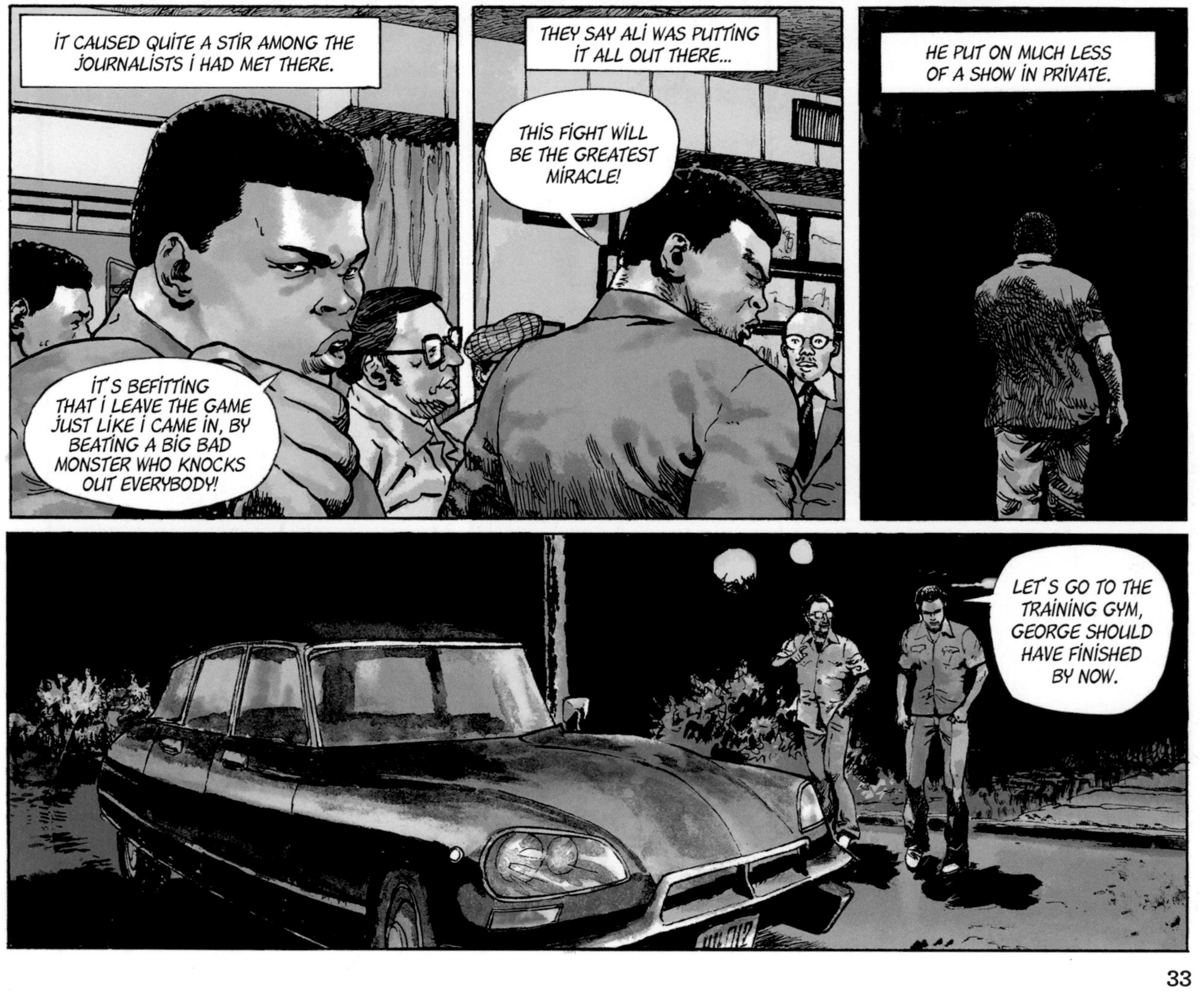
IT CAUSED QUITE A STIR AMONG THE JOURNALISTS I HAD MET THERE.
IT'S BEFITTING THAT I LEAVE THE GAME JUST LIKE I CAME IN, BY BEATING A BIG BAD MONSTER WHO KNOCKS OUT EVERYBODY!
THEY SAY ALI WAS PUTTING IT ALL OUT THERE...
THIS FIGHT WILL BE THE GREATEST MIRACLE!
HE PUT ON MUCH LESS OF A SHOW IN PRIVATE.
LET'S GO TO THE TRAINING GYM, GEORGE SHOULD HAVE FINISHED BY NOW.

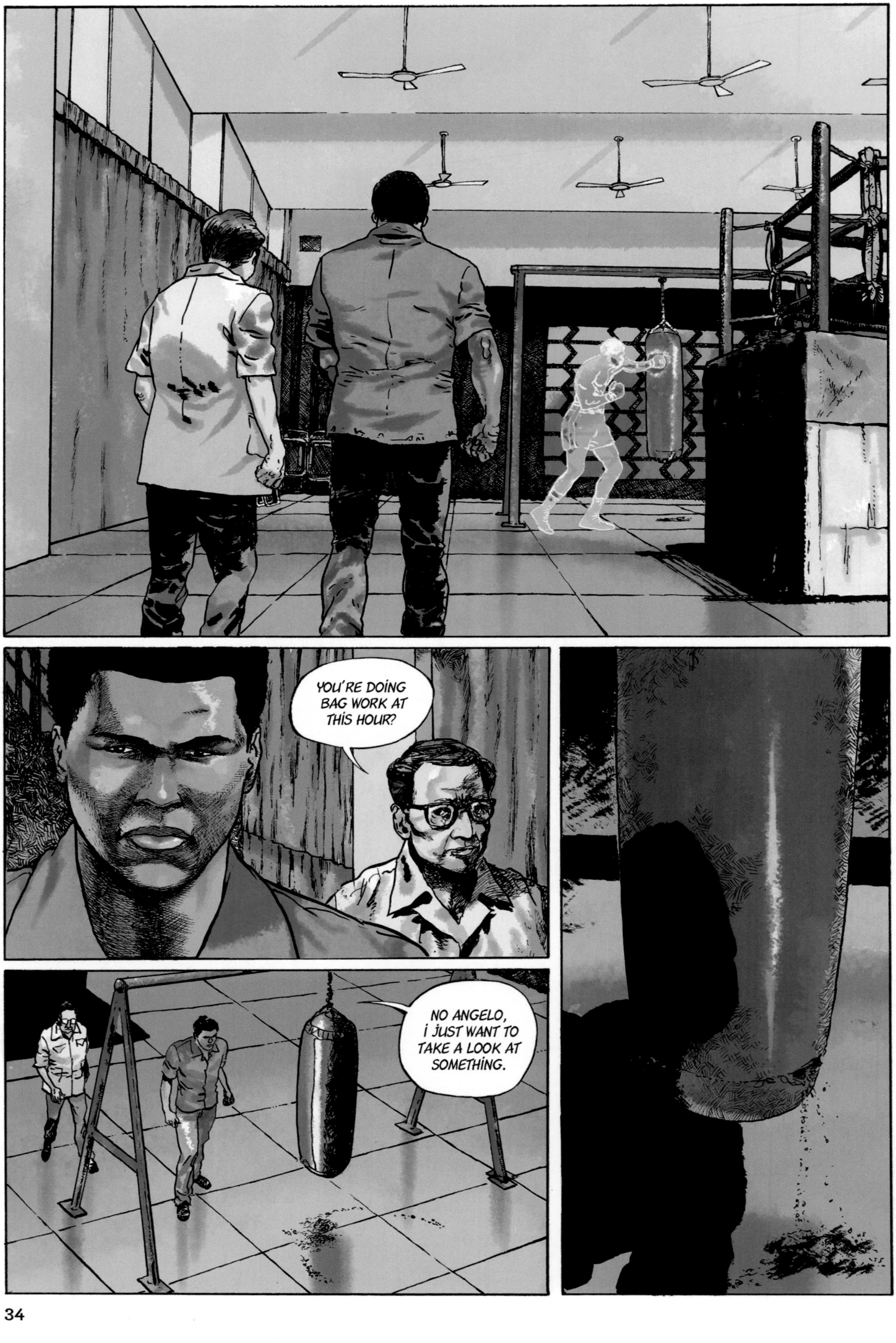
YOU'RE DOING BAG WORK AT THIS HOUR?
NO ANGELO, I JUST WANT TO TAKE A LOOK AT SOMETHING.

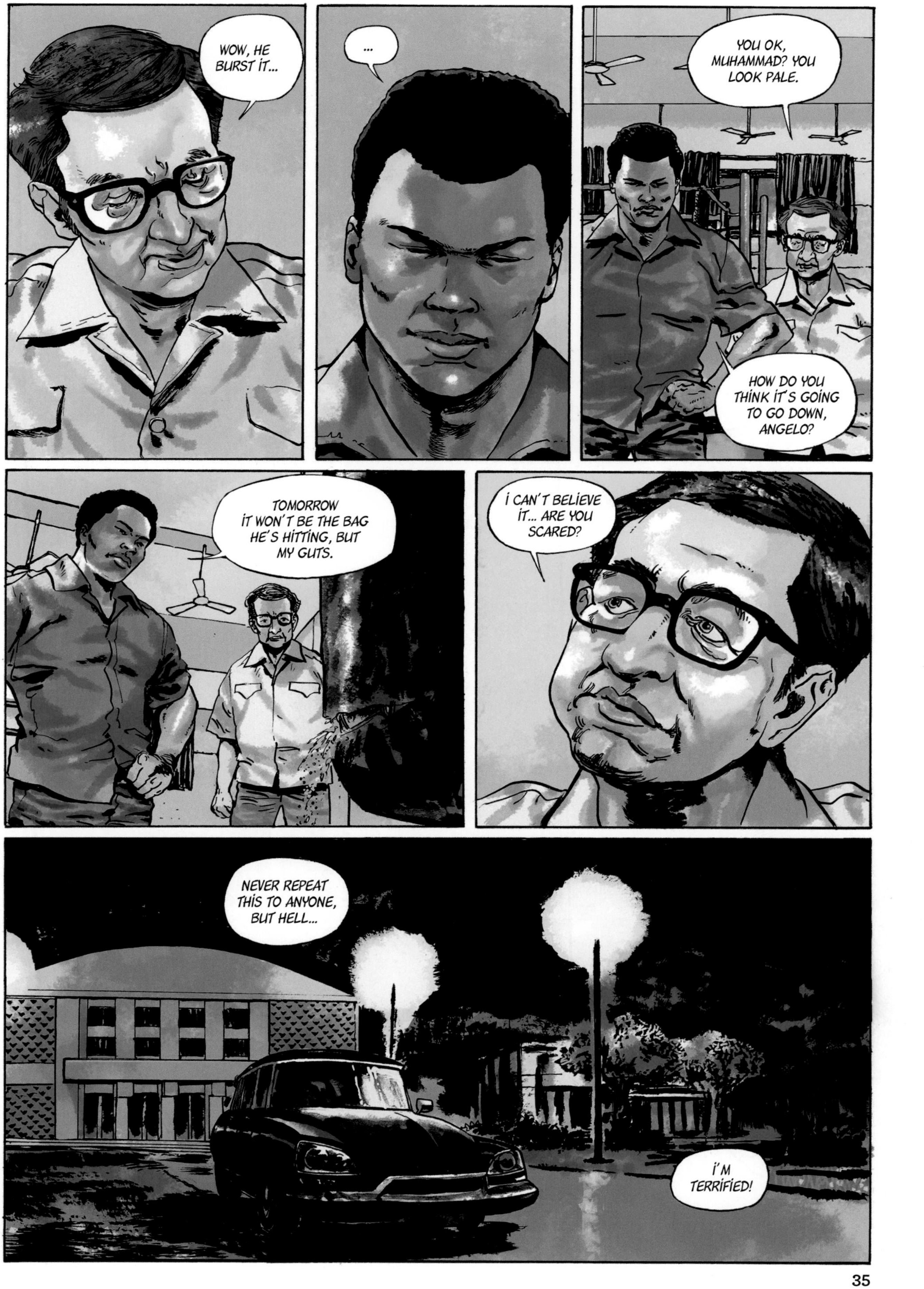
WOW, HE BURST IT...
...
YOU OK, MUHAMMAD? YOU LOOK PALE.
HOW DO YOU THINK IT'S GOING TO GO DOWN, ANGELO?
TOMORROW IT WON'T BE THE BAG HE'S HITTING, BUT MY GUTS.
I CAN'T BELIEVE IT... ARE YOU SCARED?
NEVER REPEAT THIS TO ANYONE, BUT HELL...
I'M TERRIFIED!

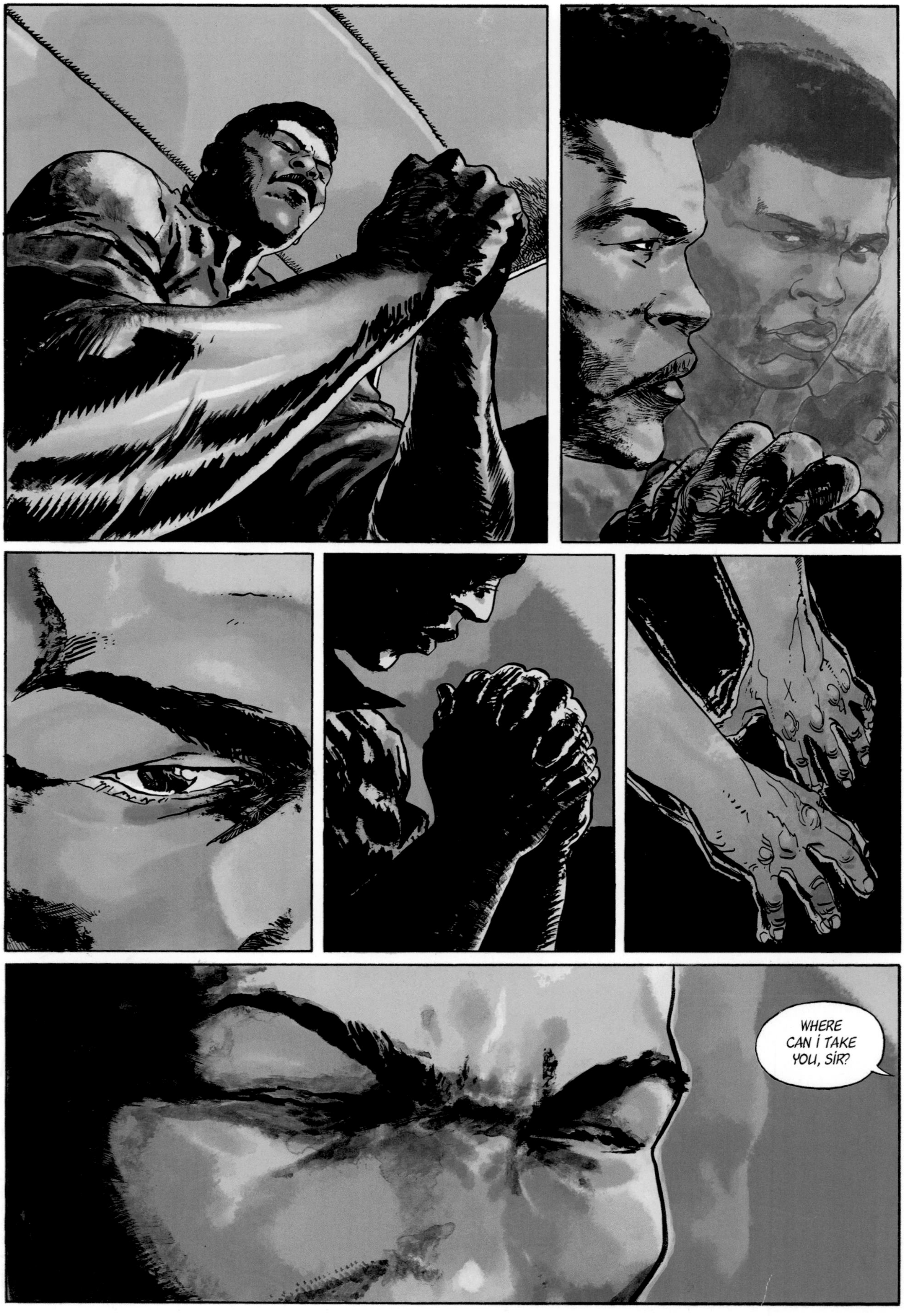
WHERE CAN I TAKE YOU, SIR?

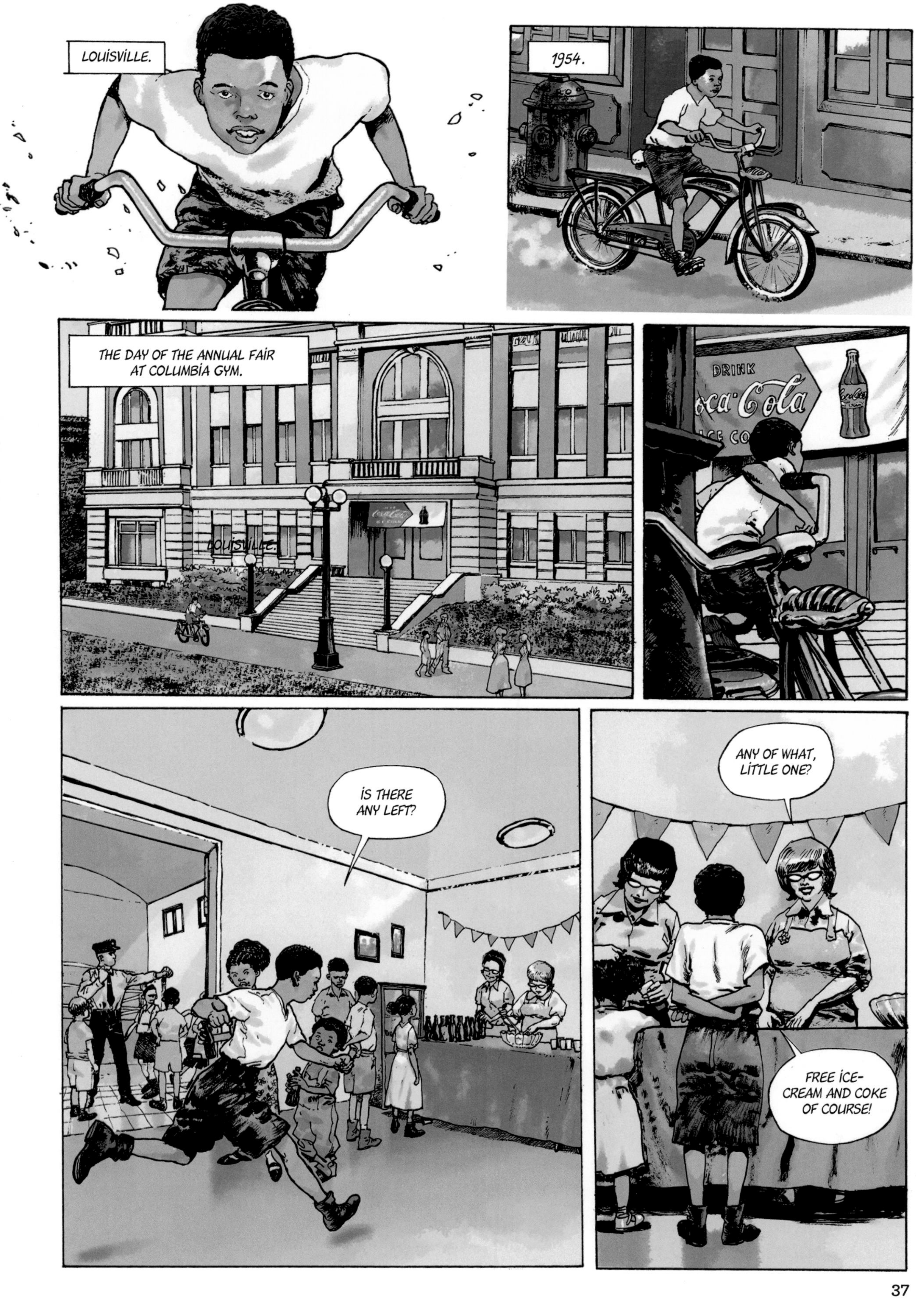
LOUISVILLE.
1954.
THE DAY OF THE ANNUAL FAIR AT COLUMBIA GYM.
LOUISVILLE.
DRINK
IS THERE ANY LEFT?
ANY OF WHAT, LITTLE ONE?
FREE ICE-CREAM AND COKE OF COURSE!

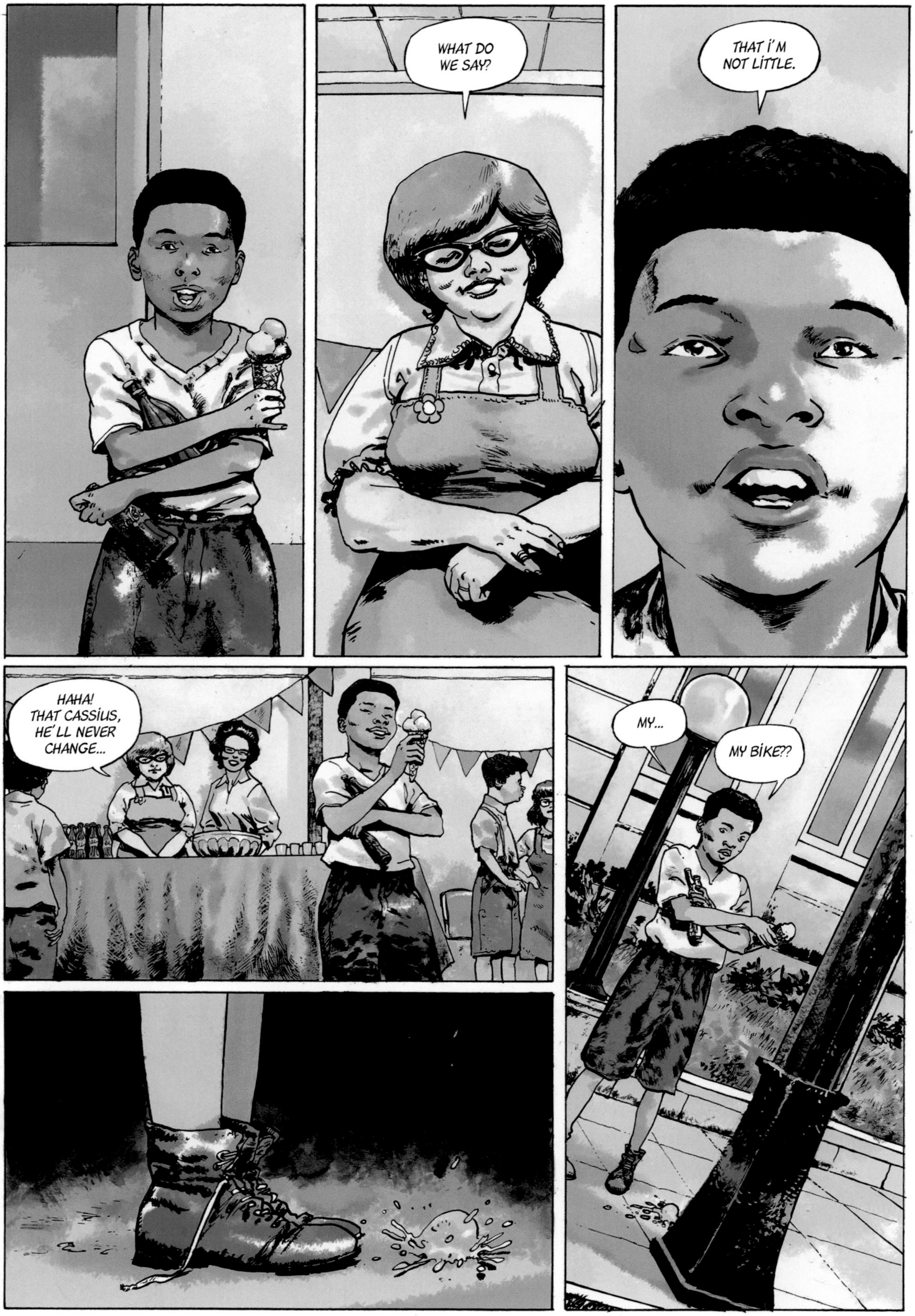
WHAT DO WE SAY?
THAT I'M NOT LITTLE.
HAHA! THAT CASSIUS, HE'LL NEVER CHANGE...
MY...
MY BIKE??

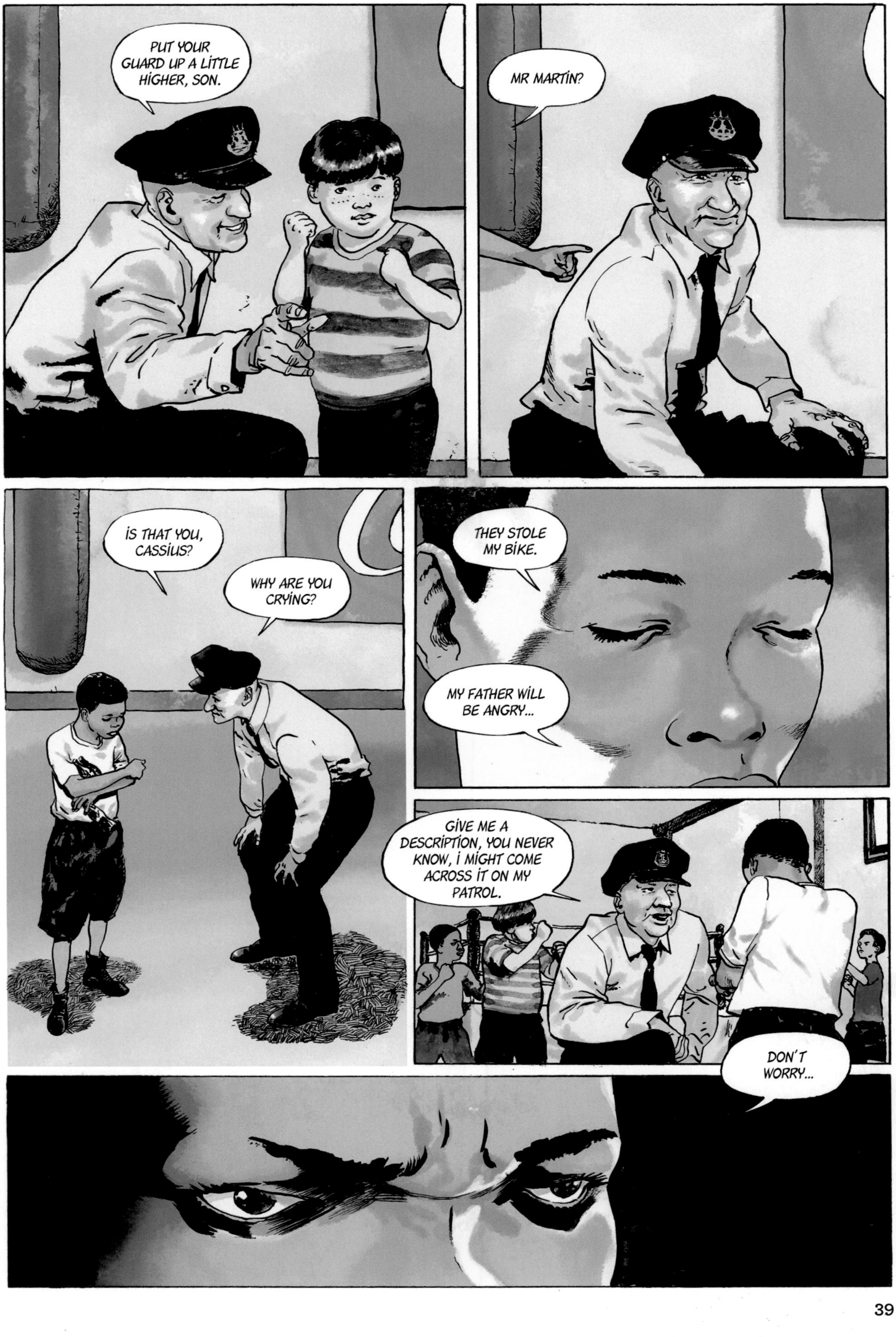
PUT YOUR GUARD UP A LITTLE HIGHER, SON.
MR MARTIN?
IS THAT YOU, CASSIUS?
WHY ARE YOU CRYING?
THEY STOLE MY BIKE.
MY FATHER WILL BE ANGRY...
GIVE ME A DESCRIPTION, YOU NEVER KNOW, I MIGHT COME ACROSS IT ON MY PATROL.
DON'T WORRY...

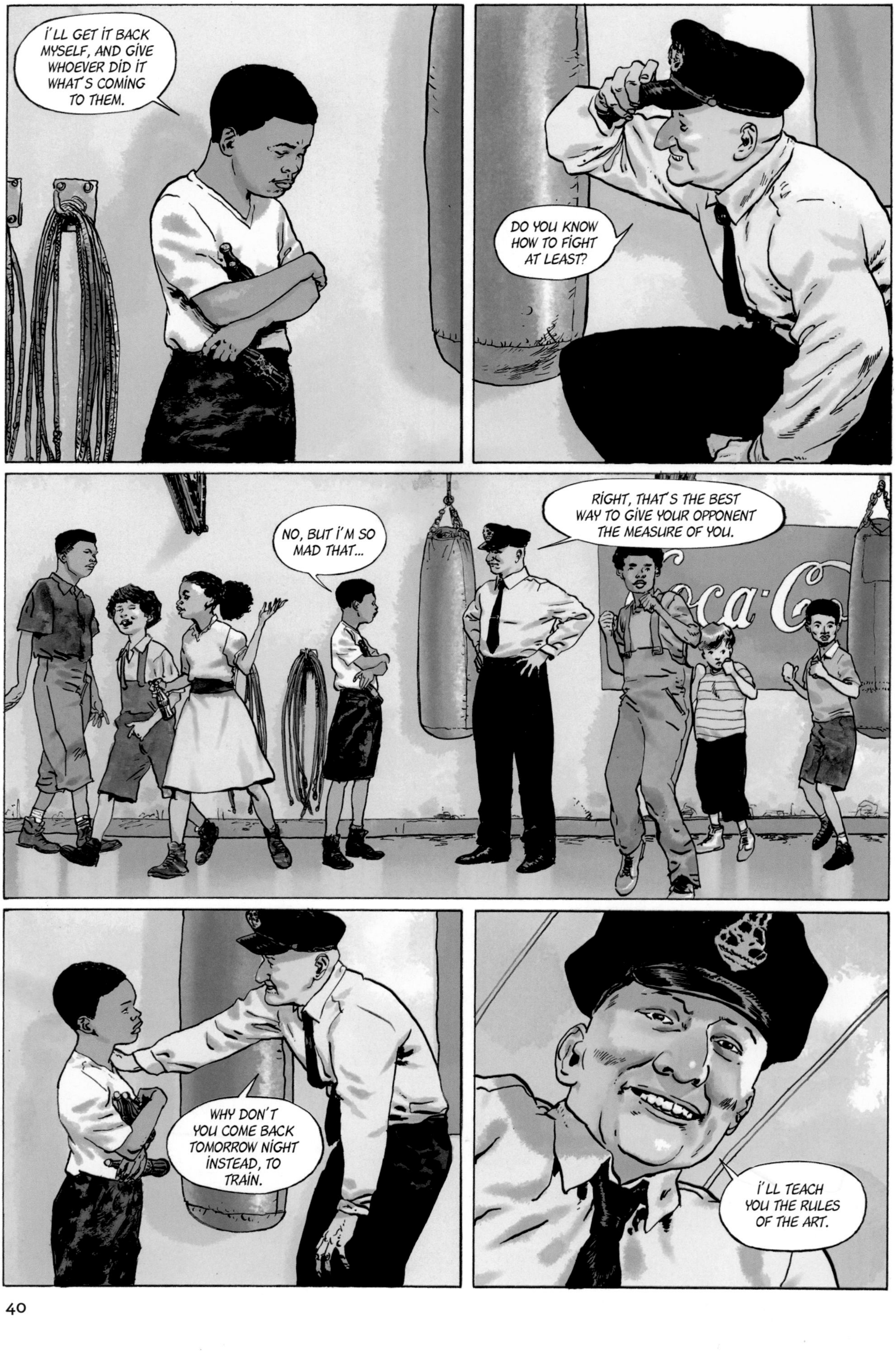
I'LL GET IT BACK MYSELF, AND GIVE WHOEVER DID IT WHAT'S COMING TO THEM.
DO YOU KNOW HOW TO FIGHT AT LEAST?
NO, BUT I'M SO MAD THAT...
RIGHT, THAT'S THE BEST WAY TO GIVE YOUR OPPONENT THE MEASURE OF YOU.
WHY DON'T YOU COME BACK TOMORROW NIGHT INSTEAD, TO TRAIN.
I'LL TEACH YOU THE RULES OF THE ART.

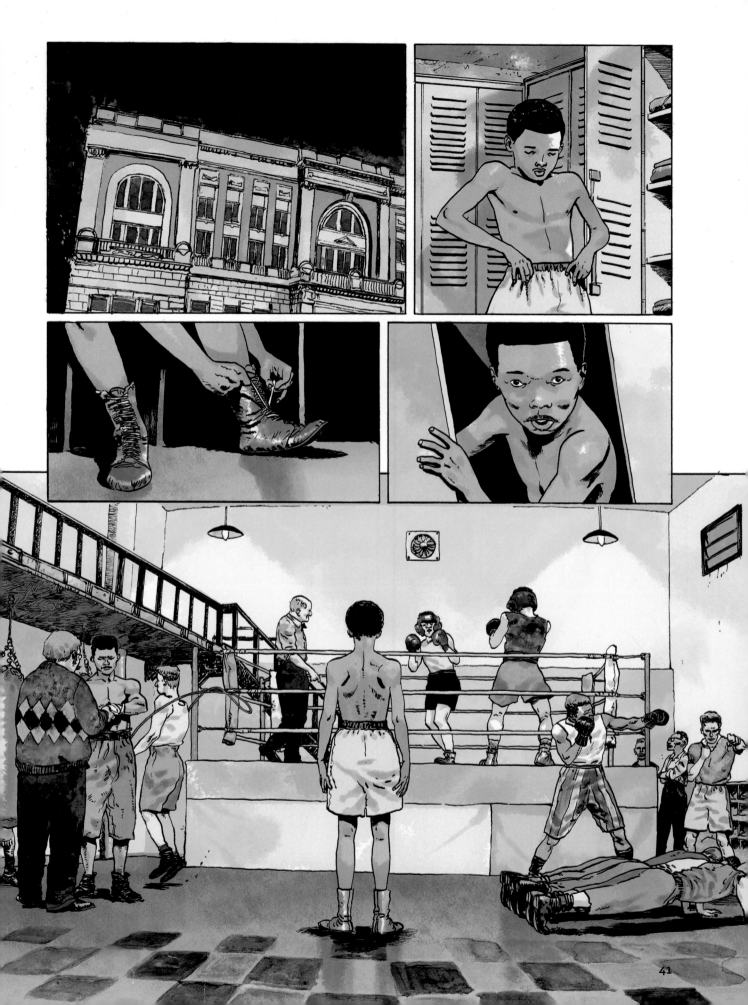

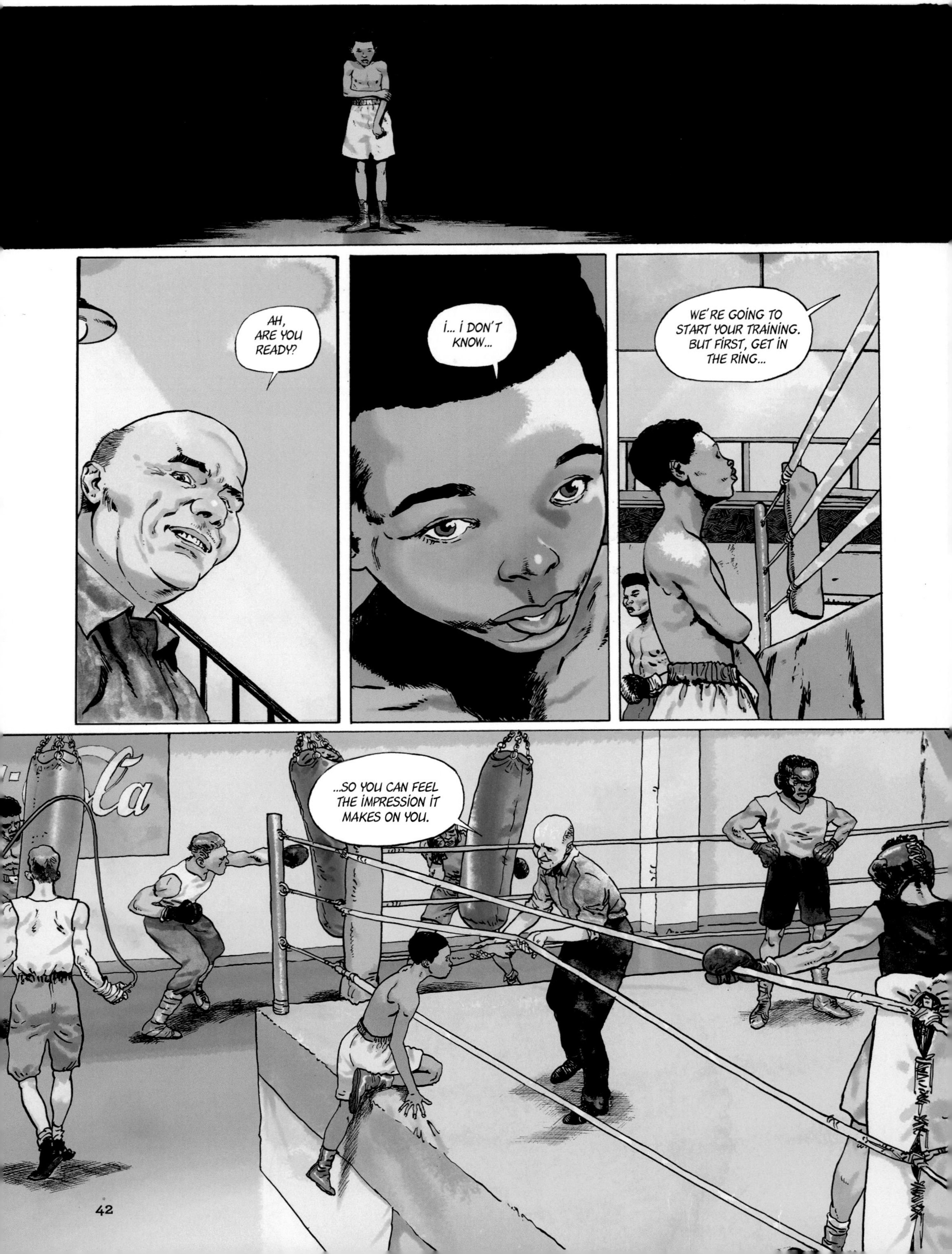
AH, ARE YOU READY?
I... I DON'T KNOW...
WE'RE GOING TO START YOUR TRAINING. BUT FIRST, GET IN THE RING...
...SO YOU CAN FEEL THE IMPRESSION IT MAKES ON YOU.

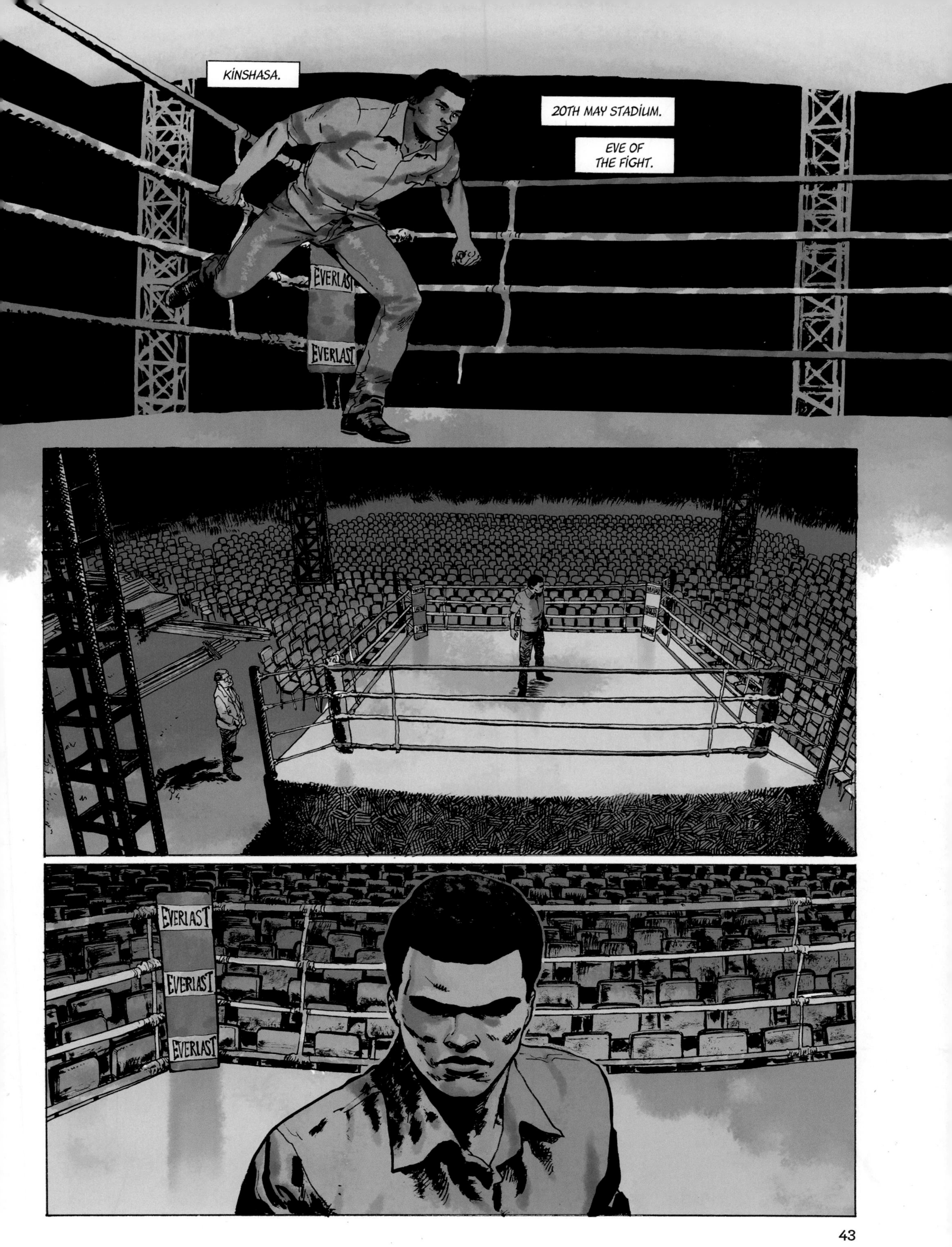
KINSHASA.
20TH MAY STADIUM.
EVE OF THE FIGHT.
EVERLAST
EVERLAST
EVERLAST
EVERLAST
EVERLAST

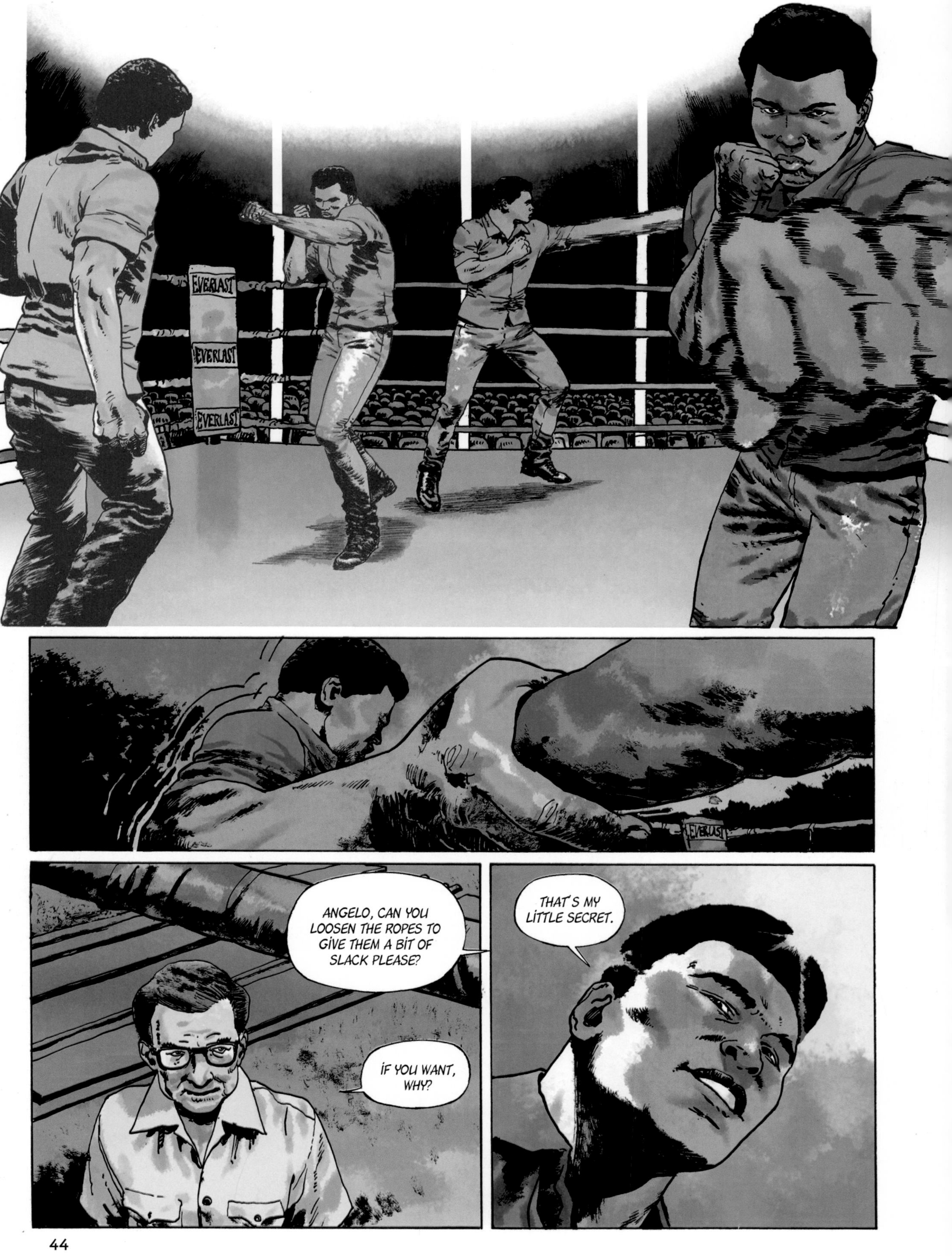
EVERLAST
EVERLAST
EVERLAST
EVERLAST
ANGELO, CAN YOU LOOSEN THE ROPES TO GIVE THEM A BIT OF SLACK PLEASE?
IF YOU WANT, WHY?
THAT'S MY LITTLE SECRET.

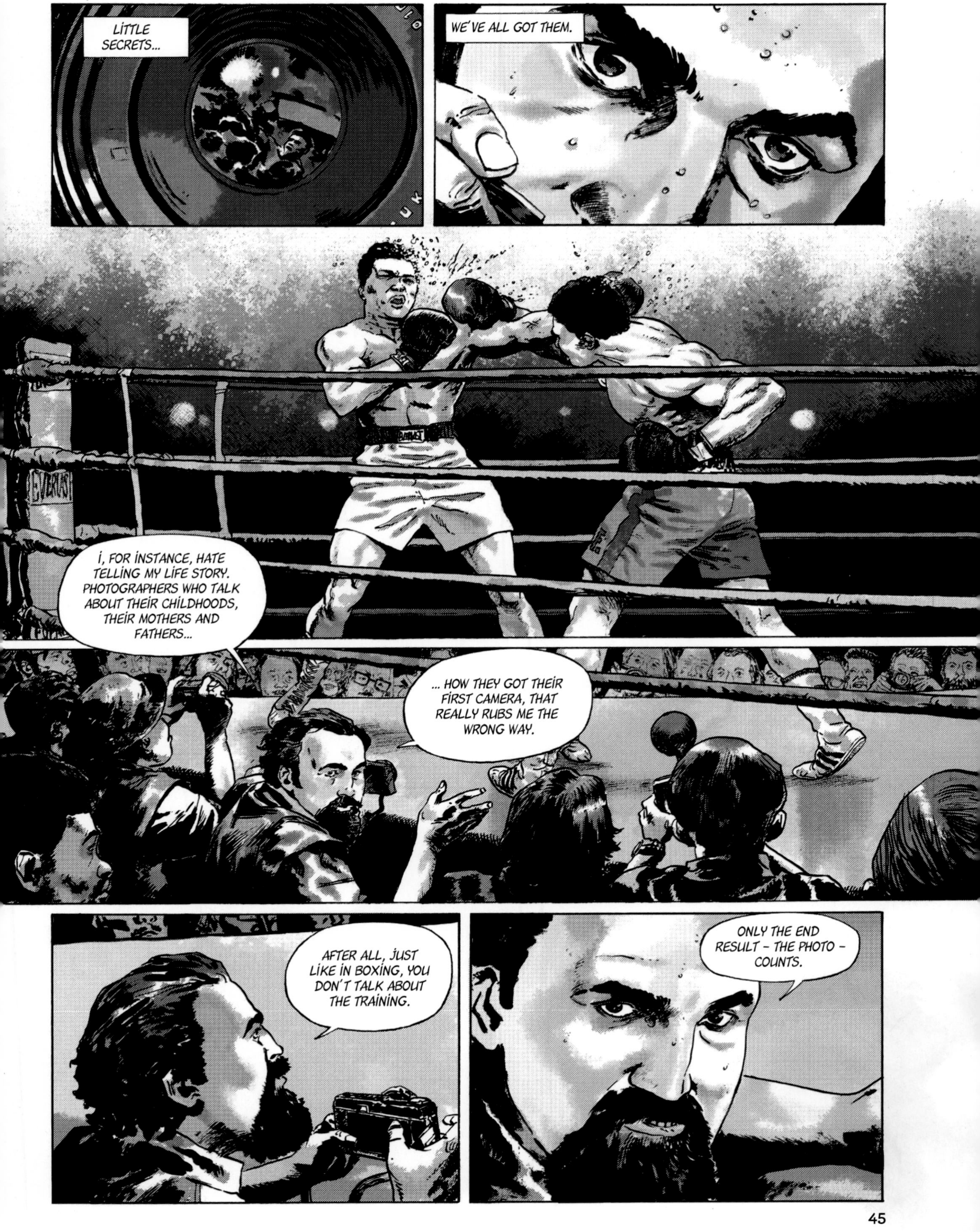
LITTLE SECRETS...
WE'VE ALL GOT THEM.
I, FOR INSTANCE, HATE TELLING MY LIFE STORY. PHOTOGRAPHERS WHO TALK ABOUT THEIR CHILDHOODS, THEIR MOTHERS AND FATHERS...
... HOW THEY GOT THEIR FIRST CAMERA, THAT REALLY RUBS ME THE WRONG WAY.
AFTER ALL, JUST LIKE IN BOXING, YOU DON'T TALK ABOUT THE TRAINING.
ONLY THE END RESULT – THE PHOTO – COUNTS.

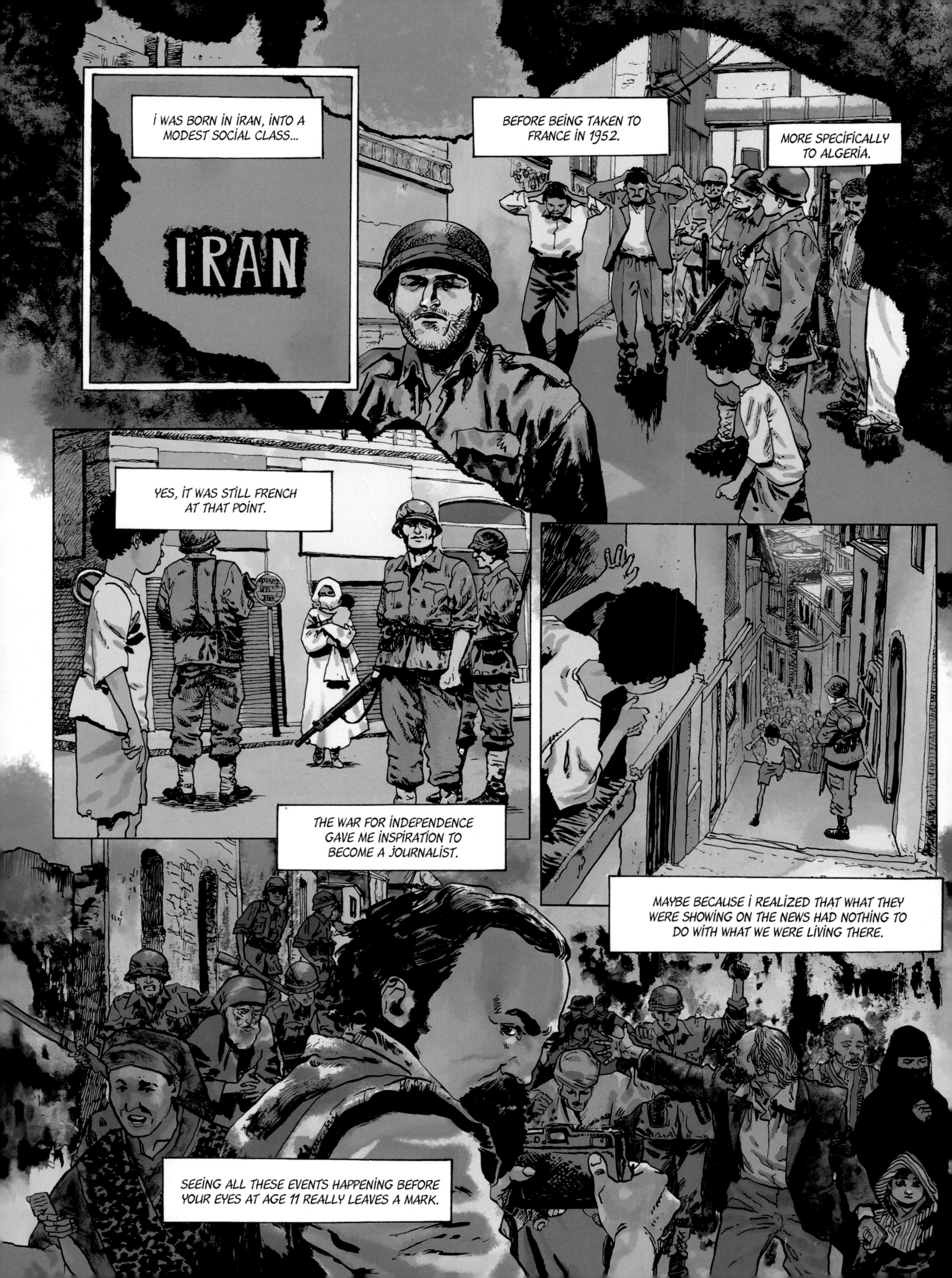
I WAS BORN IN IRAN, INTO A MODEST SOCIAL CLASS...
IRAN
BEFORE BEING TAKEN TO FRANCE IN 1952.
MORE SPECIFICALLY TO ALGERIA.
YES, IT WAS STILL FRENCH AT THAT POINT.
THE WAR FOR INDEPENDENCE GAVE ME INSPIRATION TO BECOME A JOURNALIST.
MAYBE BECAUSE I REALIZED THAT WHAT THEY WERE SHOWING ON THE NEWS HAD NOTHING TO DO WITH WHAT WE WERE LIVING THERE.
SEEING ALL THESE EVENTS HAPPENING BEFORE YOUR EYES AT AGE 11 REALLY LEAVES A MARK.

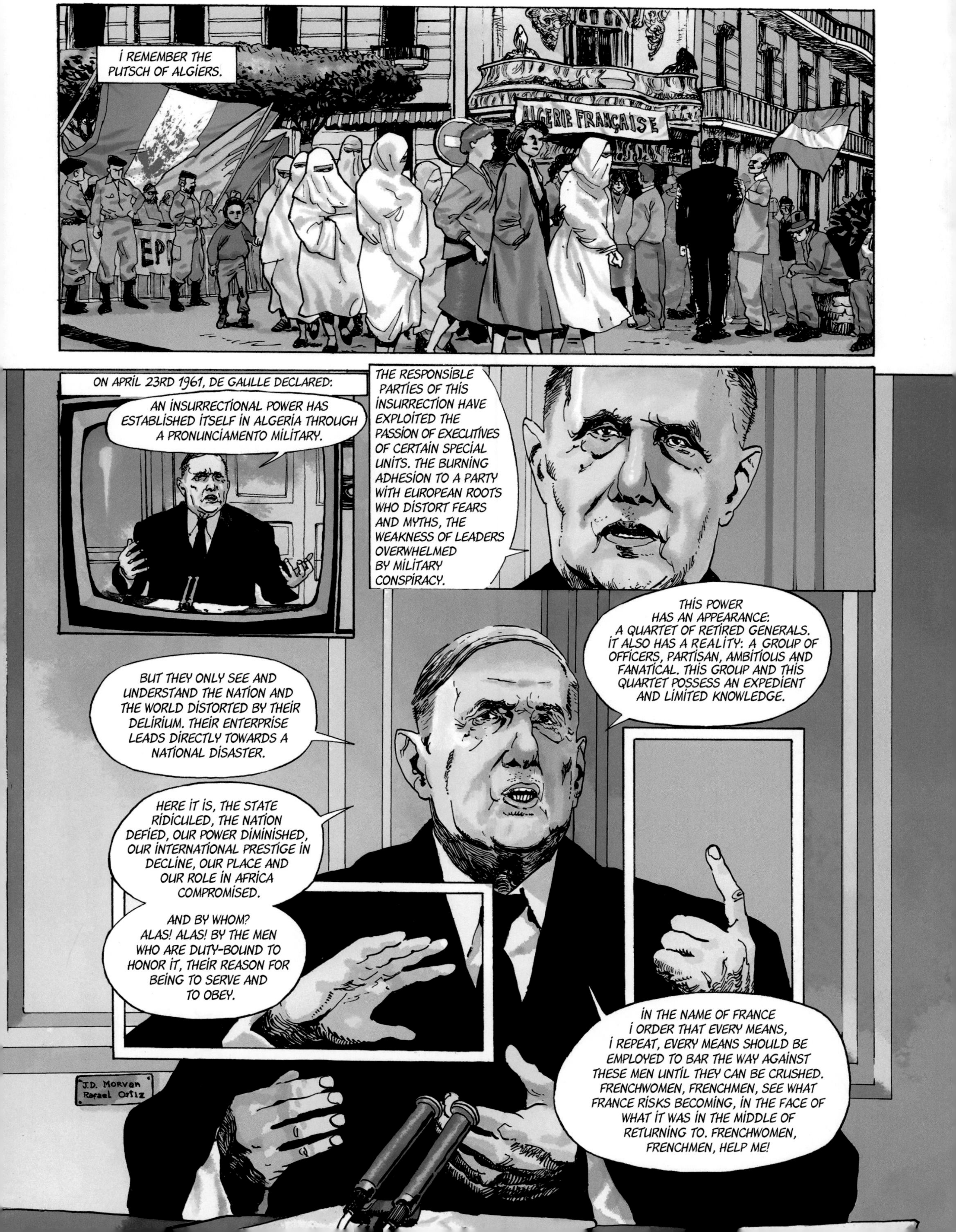

I REMEMBER THE PUTSCH OF ALGIERS.

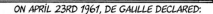

ON APRIL 23RD 1961, DE GAULLE DECLARED:

AN INSURRECTIONAL POWER HAS ESTABLISHED ITSELF IN ALGERIA THROUGH A PRONUNCIAMENTO MILITARY.

THE RESPONSIBLE PARTIES OF THIS INSURRECTION HAVE EXPLOITED THE PASSION OF EXECUTIVES OF CERTAIN SPECIAL UNITS. THE BURNING ADHESION TO A PARTY WITH EUROPEAN ROOTS WHO DISTORT FEARS AND MYTHS, THE WEAKNESS OF LEADERS OVERWHELMED BY MILITARY CONSPIRACY.

THIS POWER HAS AN APPEARANCE: A QUARTET OF RETIRED GENERALS. IT ALSO HAS A REALITY: A GROUP OF OFFICERS, PARTISAN, AMBITIOUS AND FANATICAL. THIS GROUP AND THIS QUARTET POSSESS AN EXPEDIENT AND LIMITED KNOWLEDGE.

BUT THEY ONLY SEE AND UNDERSTAND THE NATION AND THE WORLD DISTORTED BY THEIR DELIRIUM. THEIR ENTERPRISE LEADS DIRECTLY TOWARDS A NATIONAL DISASTER.

HERE IT IS, THE STATE RIDICULED, THE NATION DEFIED, OUR POWER DIMINISHED, OUR INTERNATIONAL PRESTIGE IN DECLINE, OUR PLACE AND OUR ROLE IN AFRICA COMPROMISED.

AND BY WHOM? ALAS! ALAS! BY THE MEN WHO ARE DUTY-BOUND TO HONOR IT, THEIR REASON FOR BEING TO SERVE AND TO OBEY.

IN THE NAME OF FRANCE I ORDER THAT EVERY MEANS, I REPEAT, EVERY MEANS SHOULD BE EMPLOYED TO BAR THE WAY AGAINST THESE MEN UNTIL THEY CAN BE CRUSHED. FRENCHWOMEN, FRENCHMEN, SEE WHAT FRANCE RISKS BECOMING, IN THE FACE OF WHAT IT WAS IN THE MIDDLE OF RETURNING TO. FRENCHWOMEN, FRENCHMEN, HELP ME!

J.D. Morvan
Rafael Ortiz

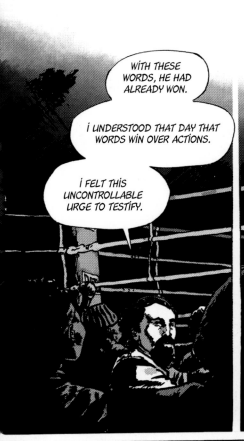

WITH THESE WORDS, HE HAD ALREADY WON.

I UNDERSTOOD THAT DAY THAT WORDS WIN OVER ACTIONS.

I FELT THIS UNCONTROLLABLE URGE TO TESTIFY.

NOWADAYS, EVEN THOUGH I WRITE A SORT OF TRAVEL DIARY FOR MYSELF, I PREFER TO LET MY PHOTOS SPEAK FOR ME.

IT WAS A PHOTO TAKEN IN 1968, SO RIGHT AT THE BEGINNING OF MY CAREER, THAT CONVINCED ME I WAS BORN A PHOTOGRAPHER.

I WAS HITCHHIKING AMERICA FROM NEW YORK TO MEXICO.

ESPLANADE

I STAYED A LITTLE WHILE IN NEW ORLEANS, AND DECIDED TO MAKE A REAL GO AT A REPORT ON THE CITY.

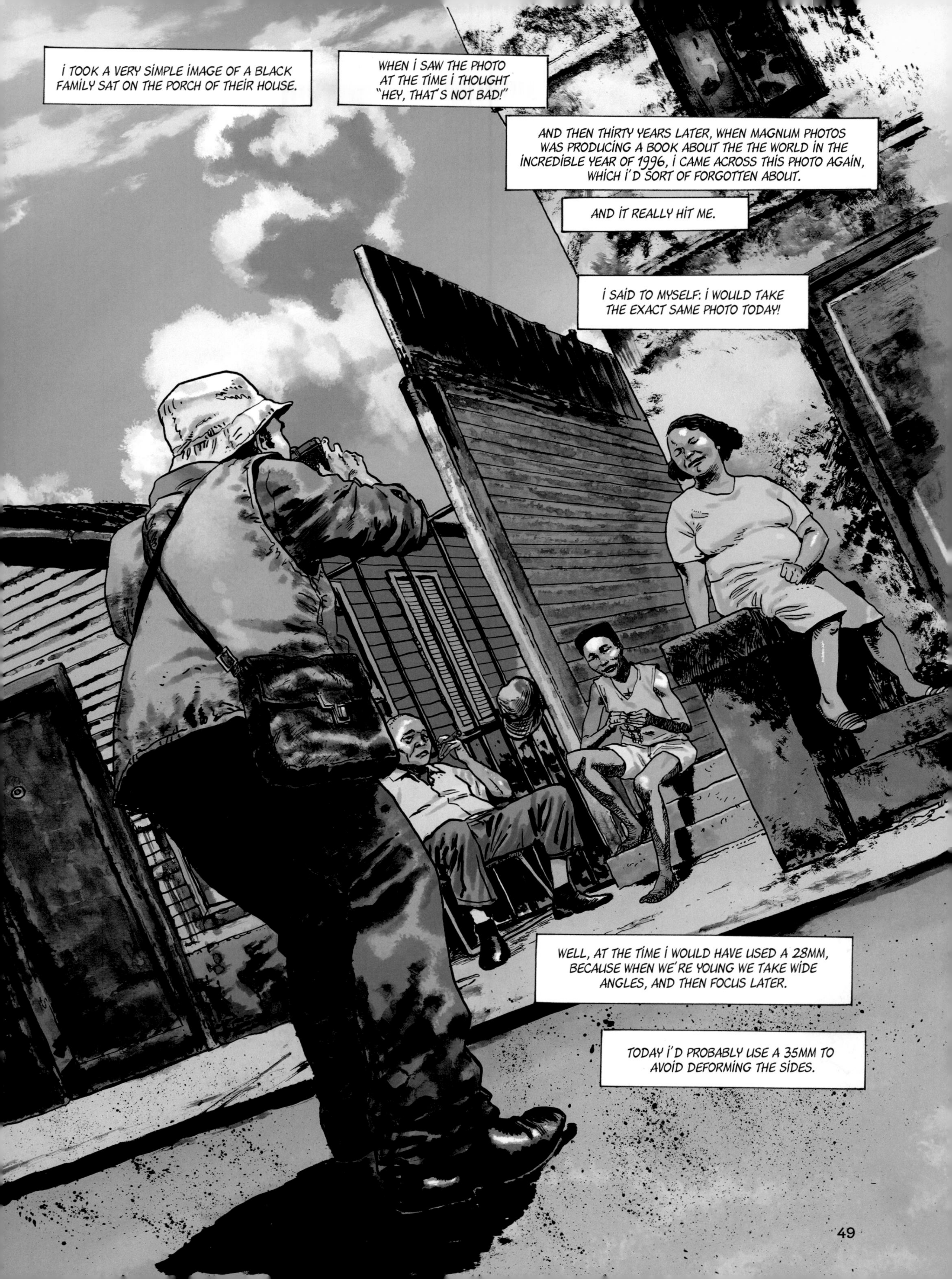
I TOOK A VERY SIMPLE IMAGE OF A BLACK FAMILY SAT ON THE PORCH OF THEIR HOUSE.
WHEN I SAW THE PHOTO AT THE TIME I THOUGHT "HEY, THAT'S NOT BAD!"
AND THEN THIRTY YEARS LATER, WHEN MAGNUM PHOTOS WAS PRODUCING A BOOK ABOUT THE THE WORLD IN THE INCREDIBLE YEAR OF 1996, I CAME ACROSS THIS PHOTO AGAIN, WHICH I'D SORT OF FORGOTTEN ABOUT.
AND IT REALLY HIT ME.
I SAID TO MYSELF: I WOULD TAKE THE EXACT SAME PHOTO TODAY!
WELL, AT THE TIME I WOULD HAVE USED A 28MM, BECAUSE WHEN WE'RE YOUNG WE TAKE WIDE ANGLES, AND THEN FOCUS LATER.
TODAY I'D PROBABLY USE A 35MM TO AVOID DEFORMING THE SIDES.

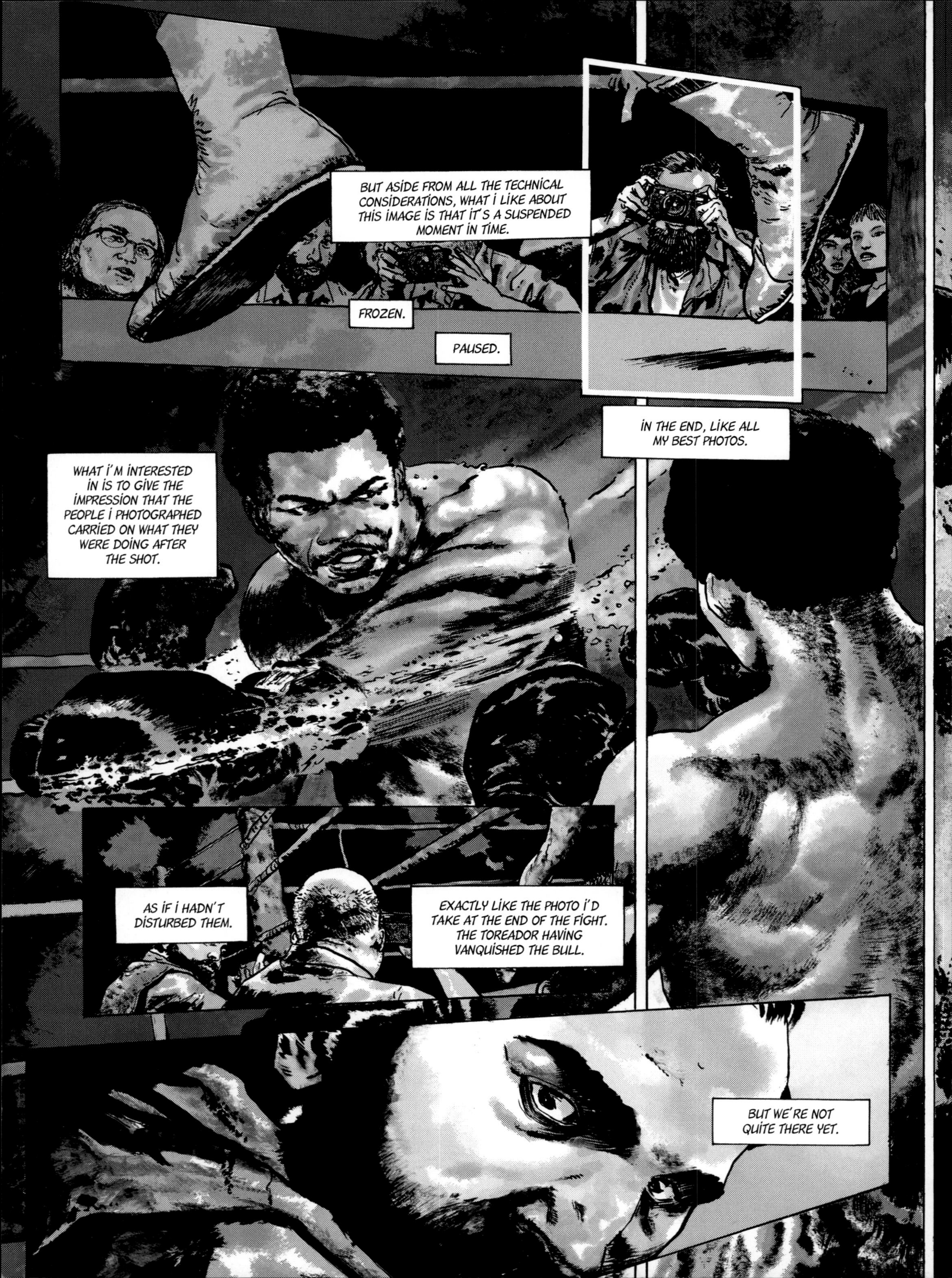
BUT ASIDE FROM ALL THE TECHNICAL CONSIDERATIONS, WHAT I LIKE ABOUT THIS IMAGE IS THAT IT'S A SUSPENDED MOMENT IN TIME.
FROZEN.
PAUSED.
IN THE END, LIKE ALL MY BEST PHOTOS.
WHAT I'M INTERESTED IN IS TO GIVE THE IMPRESSION THAT THE PEOPLE I PHOTOGRAPHED CARRIED ON WHAT THEY WERE DOING AFTER THE SHOT.
AS IF I HADN'T DISTURBED THEM.
EXACTLY LIKE THE PHOTO I'D TAKE AT THE END OF THE FIGHT. THE TOREADOR HAVING VANQUISHED THE BULL.
BUT WE'RE NOT QUITE THERE YET.

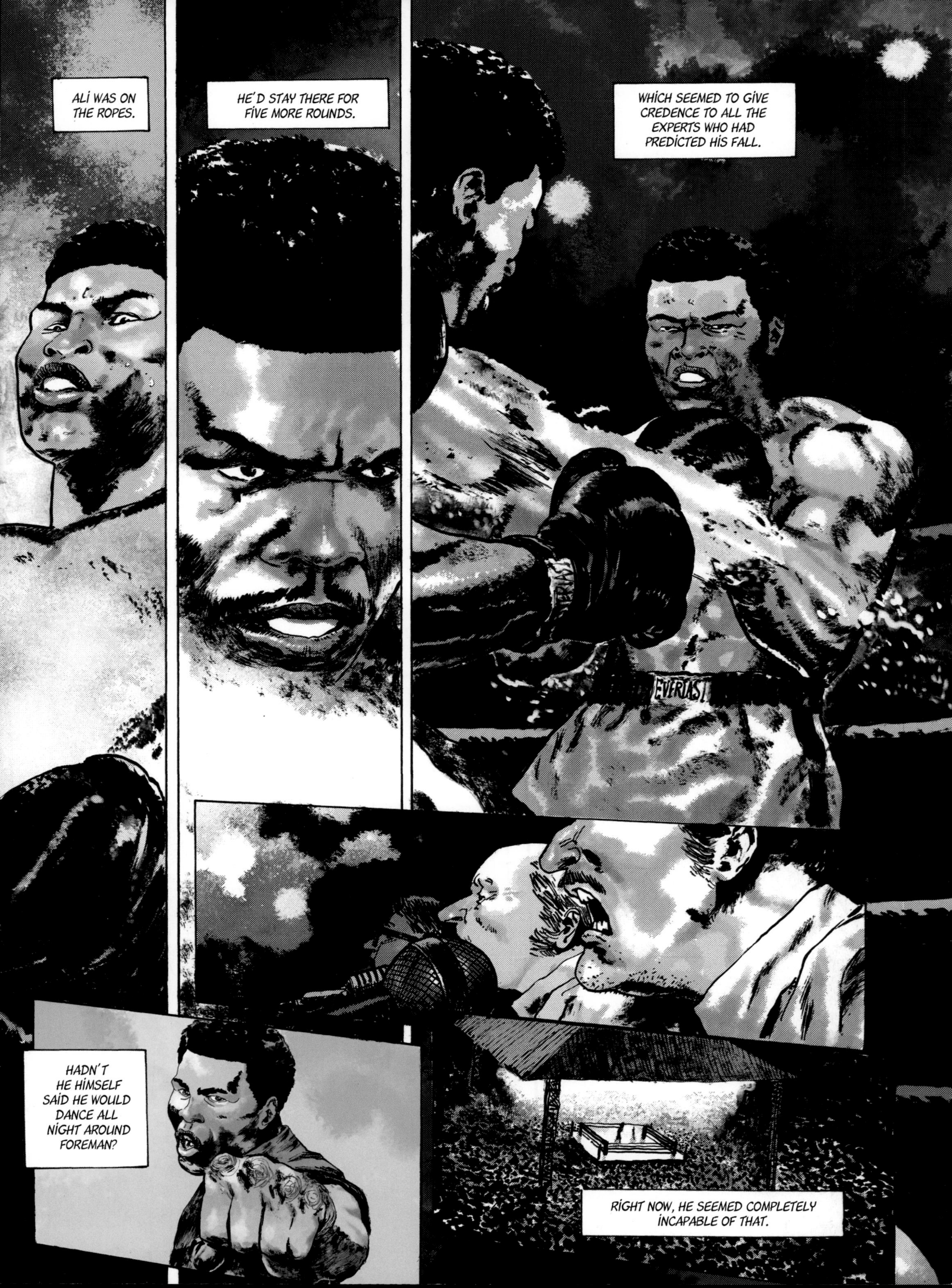
ALI WAS ON THE ROPES.
HE'D STAY THERE FOR FIVE MORE ROUNDS.
WHICH SEEMED TO GIVE CREDENCE TO ALL THE EXPERTS WHO HAD PREDICTED HIS FALL.
EVERLAST
HADN'T HE HIMSELF SAID HE WOULD DANCE ALL NIGHT AROUND FOREMAN?
RIGHT NOW, HE SEEMED COMPLETELY INCAPABLE OF THAT.

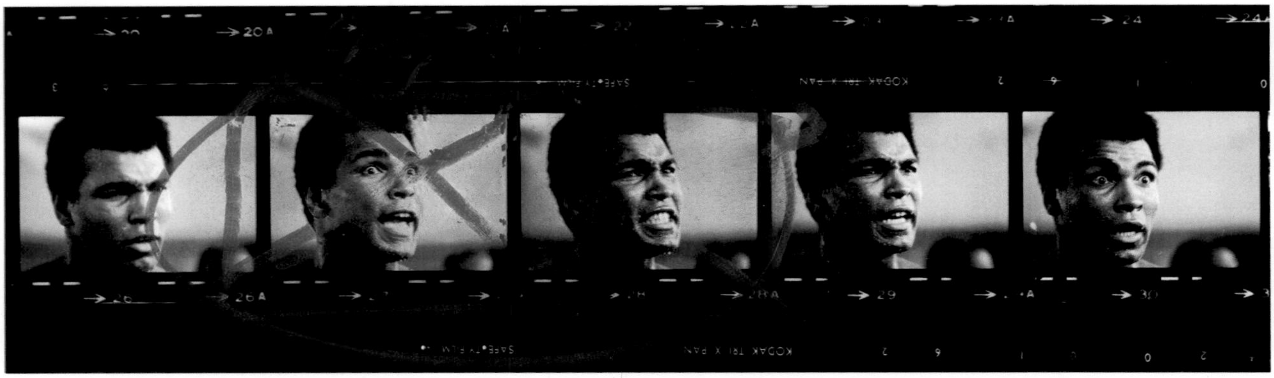

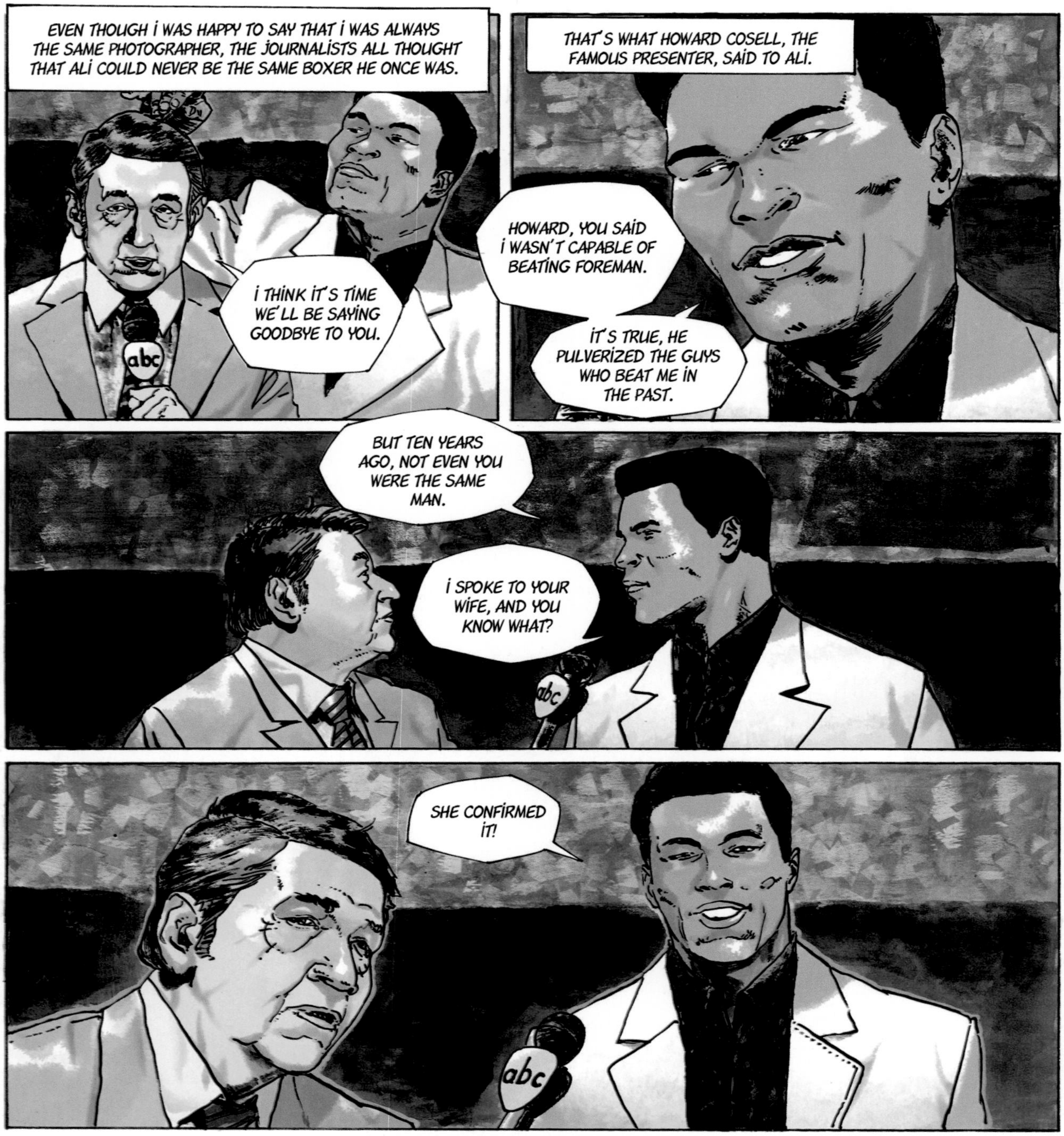
EVEN THOUGH I WAS HAPPY TO SAY THAT I WAS ALWAYS THE SAME PHOTOGRAPHER, THE JOURNALISTS ALL THOUGHT THAT ALI COULD NEVER BE THE SAME BOXER HE ONCE WAS.
I THINK IT'S TIME WE'LL BE SAYING GOODBYE TO YOU.
abc
THAT'S WHAT HOWARD COSELL, THE FAMOUS PRESENTER, SAID TO ALI.
HOWARD, YOU SAID I WASN'T CAPABLE OF BEATING FOREMAN.
IT'S TRUE, HE PULVERIZED THE GUYS WHO BEAT ME IN THE PAST.
BUT TEN YEARS AGO, NOT EVEN YOU WERE THE SAME MAN.
I SPOKE TO YOUR WIFE, AND YOU KNOW WHAT?
abc
SHE CONFIRMED IT!
abc

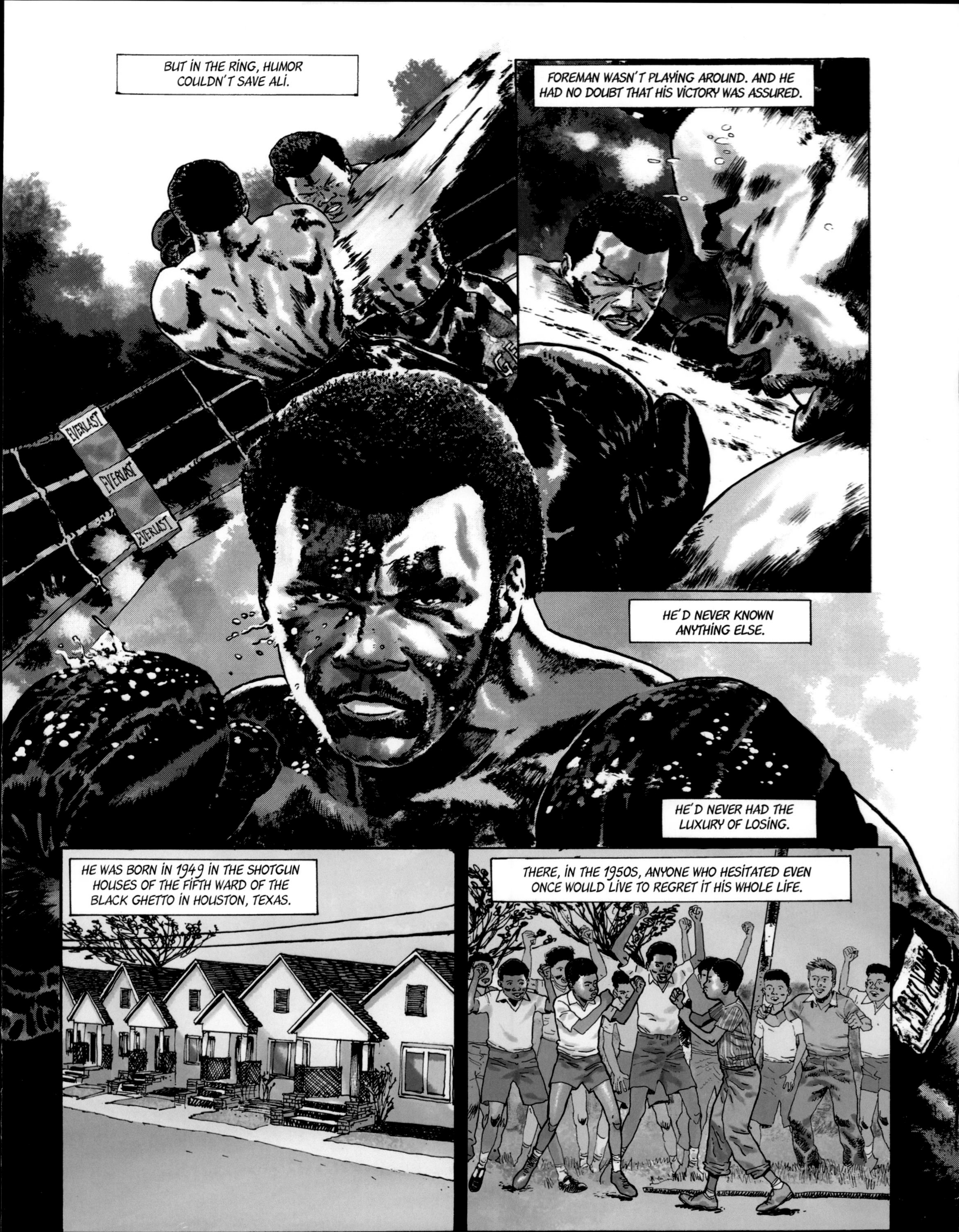
BUT IN THE RING, HUMOR COULDN'T SAVE ALI.
FOREMAN WASN'T PLAYING AROUND. AND HE HAD NO DOUBT THAT HIS VICTORY WAS ASSURED.
EVERLAST
EVERLAST
EVERLAST
HE'D NEVER KNOWN ANYTHING ELSE.
HE'D NEVER HAD THE LUXURY OF LOSING.
HE WAS BORN IN 1949 IN THE SHOTGUN HOUSES OF THE FIFTH WARD OF THE BLACK GHETTO IN HOUSTON, TEXAS.
THERE, IN THE 1950S, ANYONE WHO HESITATED EVEN ONCE WOULD LIVE TO REGRET IT HIS WHOLE LIFE.

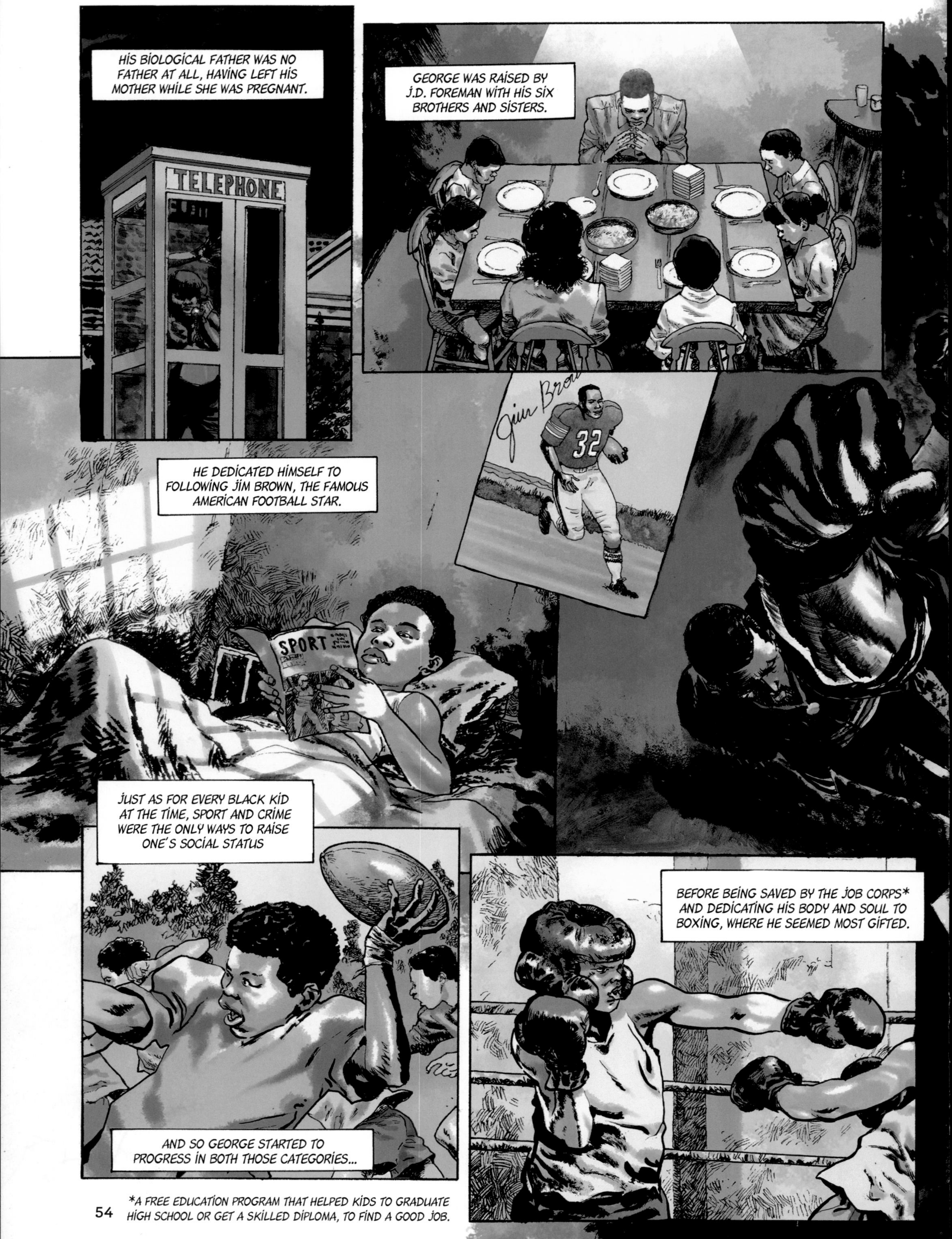
HIS BIOLOGICAL FATHER WAS NO FATHER AT ALL, HAVING LEFT HIS MOTHER WHILE SHE WAS PREGNANT.
TELEPHONE
GEORGE WAS RAISED BY J.D. FOREMAN WITH HIS SIX BROTHERS AND SISTERS.
HE DEDICATED HIMSELF TO FOLLOWING JIM BROWN, THE FAMOUS AMERICAN FOOTBALL STAR.
32
SPORT
JUST AS FOR EVERY BLACK KID AT THE TIME, SPORT AND CRIME WERE THE ONLY WAYS TO RAISE ONE'S SOCIAL STATUS
AND SO GEORGE STARTED TO PROGRESS IN BOTH THOSE CATEGORIES...
BEFORE BEING SAVED BY THE JOB CORPS* AND DEDICATING HIS BODY AND SOUL TO BOXING, WHERE HE SEEMED MOST GIFTED.

*A FREE EDUCATION PROGRAM THAT HELPED KIDS TO GRADUATE HIGH SCHOOL OR GET A SKILLED DIPLOMA, TO FIND A GOOD JOB.

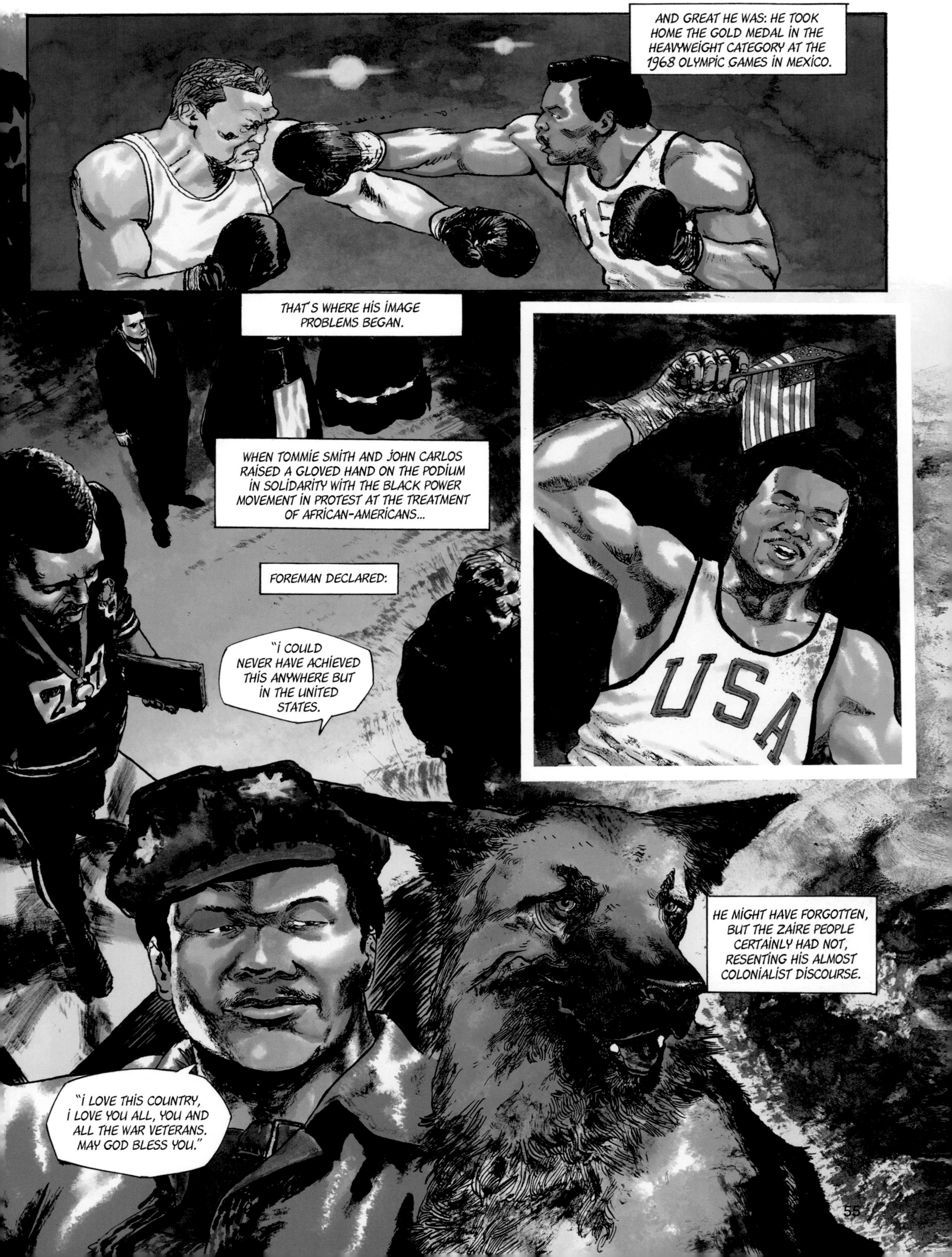

AND GREAT HE WAS: HE TOOK HOME THE GOLD MEDAL IN THE HEAVYWEIGHT CATEGORY AT THE 1968 OLYMPIC GAMES IN MEXICO.
THAT'S WHERE HIS IMAGE PROBLEMS BEGAN.
WHEN TOMMIE SMITH AND JOHN CARLOS RAISED A GLOVED HAND ON THE PODIUM IN SOLIDARITY WITH THE BLACK POWER MOVEMENT IN PROTEST AT THE TREATMENT OF AFRICAN-AMERICANS...
FOREMAN DECLARED:
"I COULD NEVER HAVE ACHIEVED THIS ANYWHERE BUT IN THE UNITED STATES.
USA
HE MIGHT HAVE FORGOTTEN, BUT THE ZAIRE PEOPLE CERTAINLY HAD NOT, RESENTING HIS ALMOST COLONIALIST DISCOURSE.
"I LOVE THIS COUNTRY, I LOVE YOU ALL, YOU AND ALL THE WAR VETERANS. MAY GOD BLESS YOU."

IN SHORT, BIG GEORGE WAS A GIANT HUNK OF MARBLE...

...THAT ALI WAS LOOKING TO CRACK.

AND AGAINST ALL THAT BRUTE FORCE, WHAT COULD BE MORE POWERFUL THAN SARCASM?

ALI DARTED EVERYWHERE, DROPPING INSULTS AND POINTING OUT FLAWS.

RIGHT TO THE POINT OF BREAKING HIS SELF-CONFIDENCE.

FROM THE BEGINNING OF THE MATCH, I WAS WONDERING WHAT I WAS HEARING EVERY TIME FOREMAN PUSHED ALI INTO MY CORNER, SO I LISTENED HARD.

IS THAT ALL YOU'VE GOT FOR ME, GEORGE?

AND I REALIZED THAT EVEN DURING PUNCHES...

ALI DID NOT LET UP ON MOCKING HIS OPPONENT.

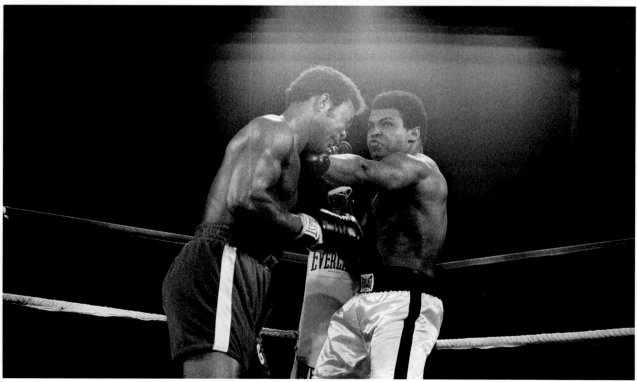

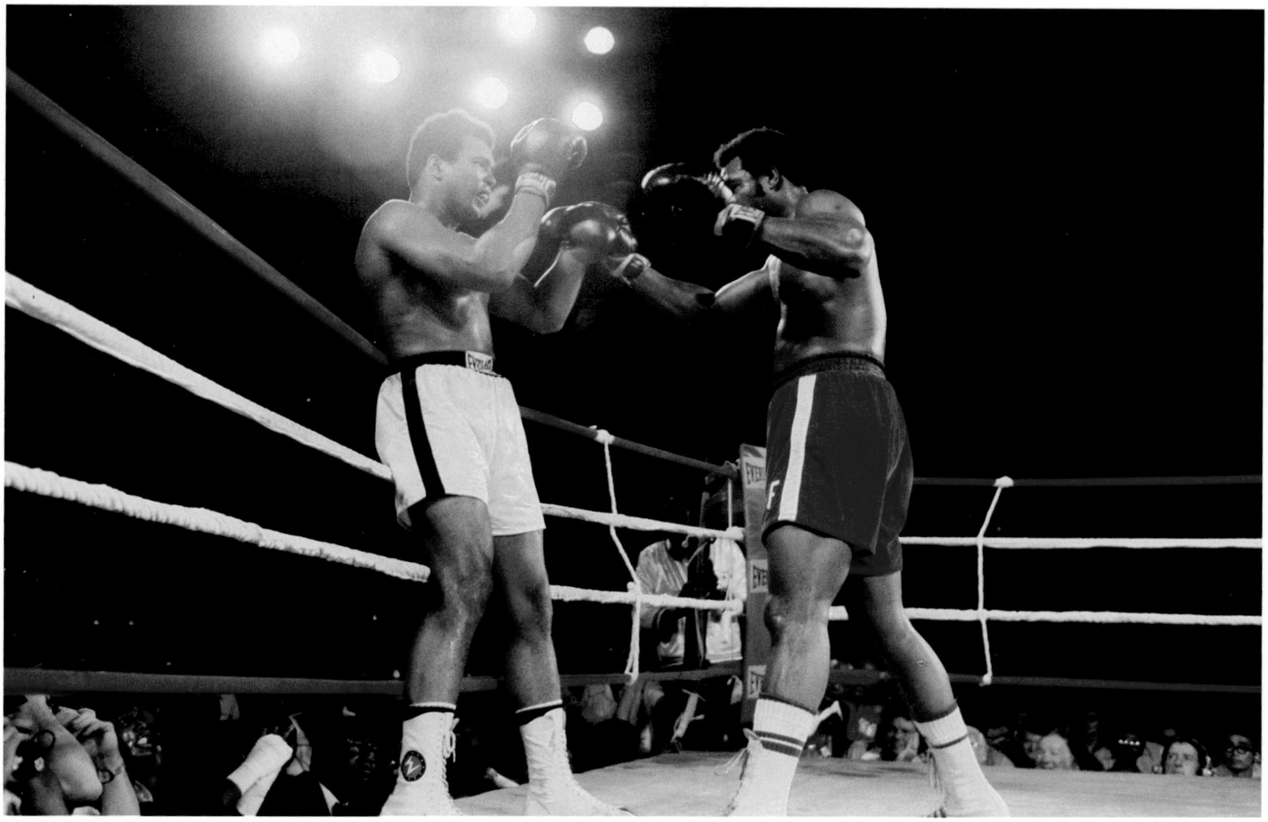

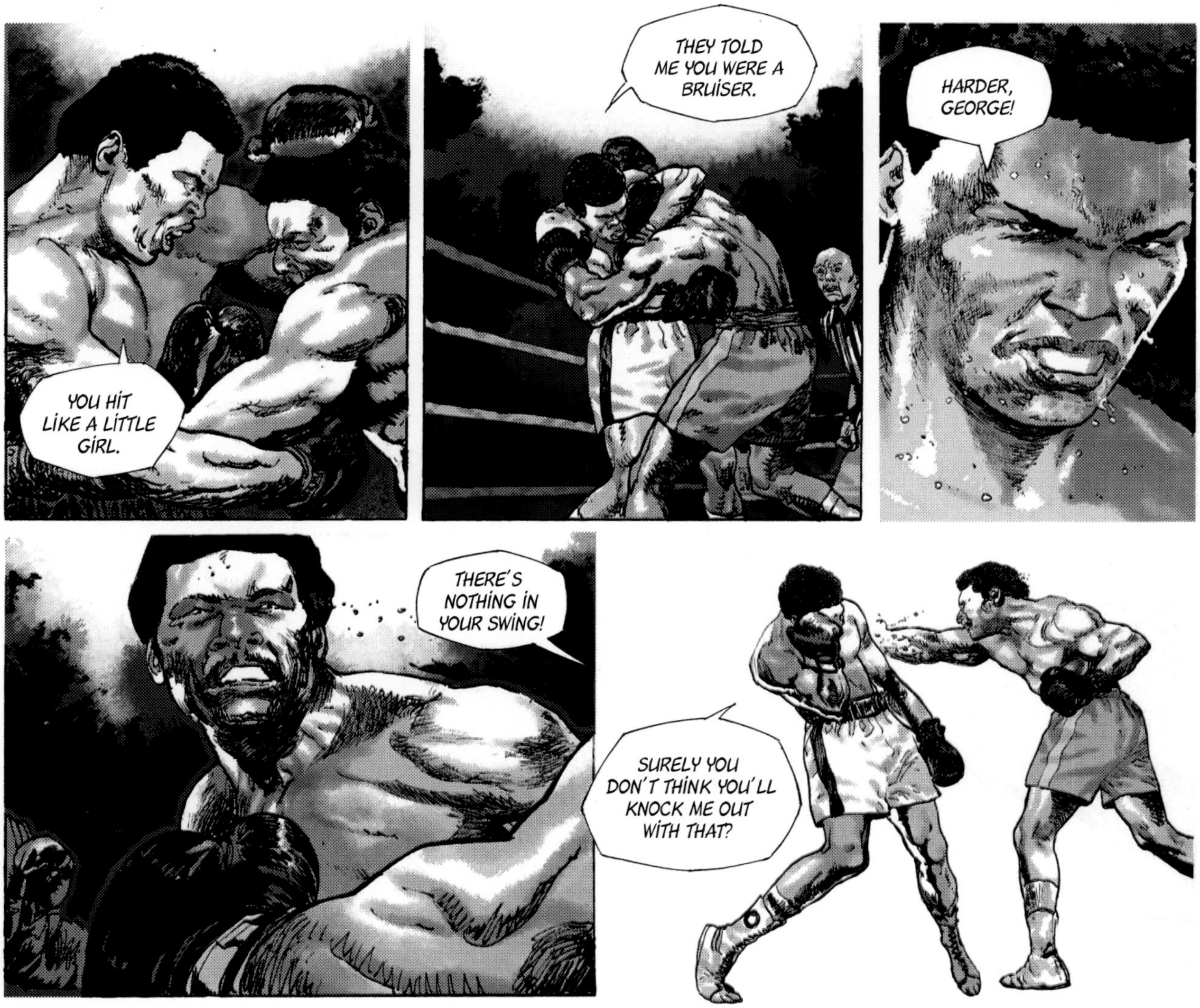

YOU HIT LIKE A LITTLE GIRL.
THEY TOLD ME YOU WERE A BRUISER.
HARDER, GEORGE!
THERE'S NOTHING IN YOUR SWING!
SURELY YOU DON'T THINK YOU'LL KNOCK ME OUT WITH THAT?

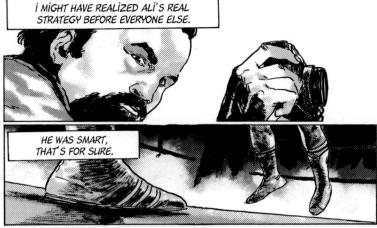

I MIGHT HAVE REALIZED ALI'S REAL STRATEGY BEFORE EVERYONE ELSE.

HE WAS SMART, THAT'S FOR SURE.

HE KNEW FULL WELL HE HAD NO CHANCE IN A PURELY PHYSICAL FIGHT.

THAT WAS PARTICULARLY EVIDENT ON THE DAY OF THE WEIGH-IN...

...IN SEEING THE TWO CHAMPIONS ONE AFTER THE OTHER.

FOREMAN'S BICEPS WERE AS BIG AS MY THIGHS.

EXPLOSIVE POWER JUST OOZED OUT OF HIM.

HIS YOUTH WAS EVIDENT.

EVERYONE THOUGHT HE WOULD MURDER THE POOR ALI, WHO IN COMPARISON LOOKED UNDERDEVELOPED AND... OLD.

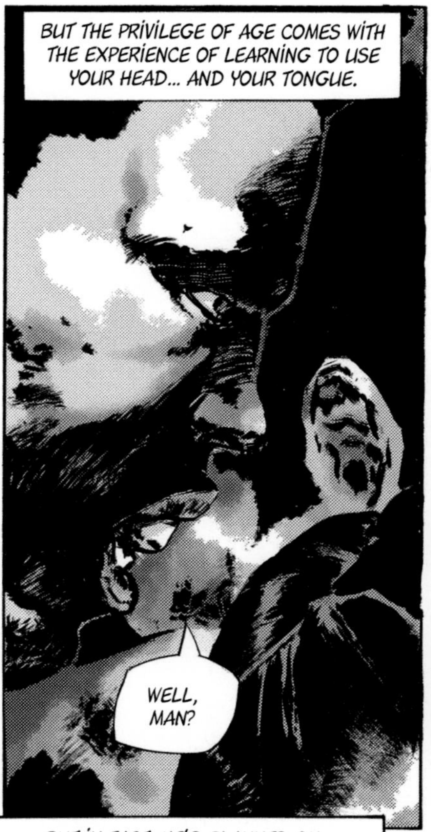
BUT THE PRIVILEGE OF AGE COMES WITH THE EXPERIENCE OF LEARNING TO USE YOUR HEAD... AND YOUR TONGUE.
WELL, MAN?

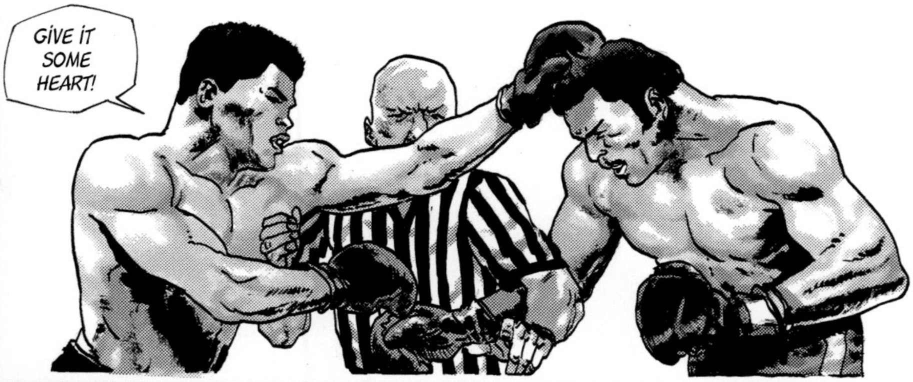
GIVE IT SOME HEART!

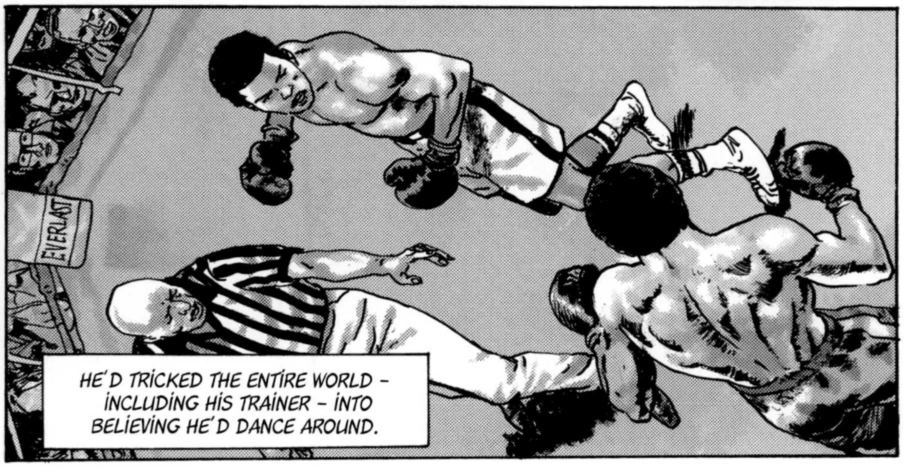
EVERLAST
HE'D TRICKED THE ENTIRE WORLD – INCLUDING HIS TRAINER – INTO BELIEVING HE'D DANCE AROUND.

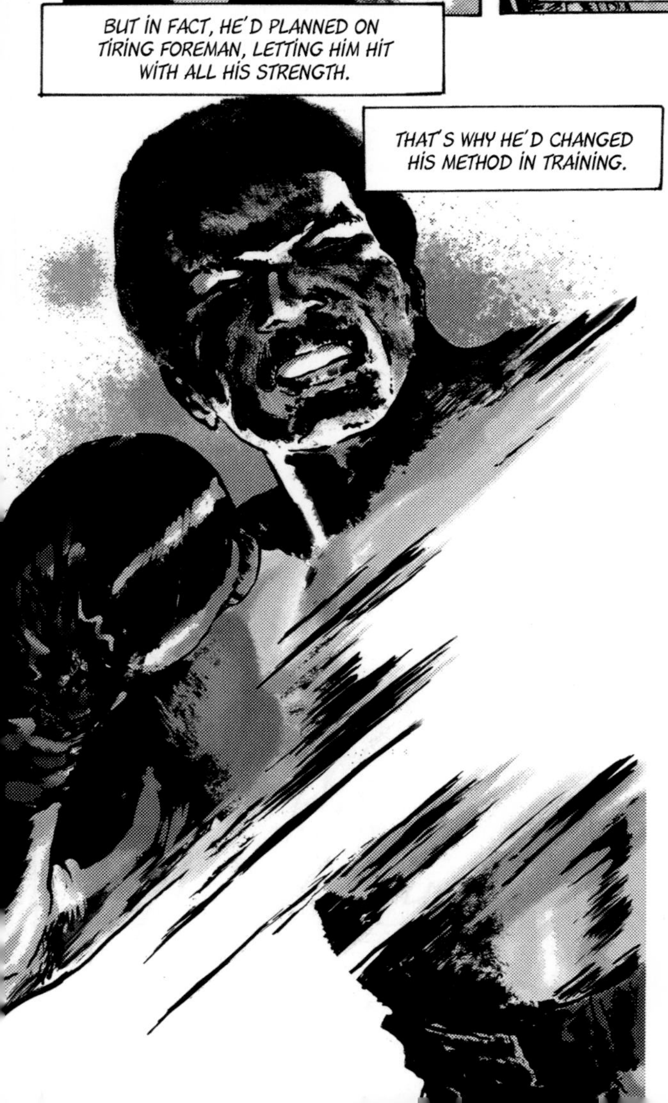
BUT IN FACT, HE'D PLANNED ON TIRING FOREMAN, LETTING HIM HIT WITH ALL HIS STRENGTH.
THAT'S WHY HE'D CHANGED HIS METHOD IN TRAINING.

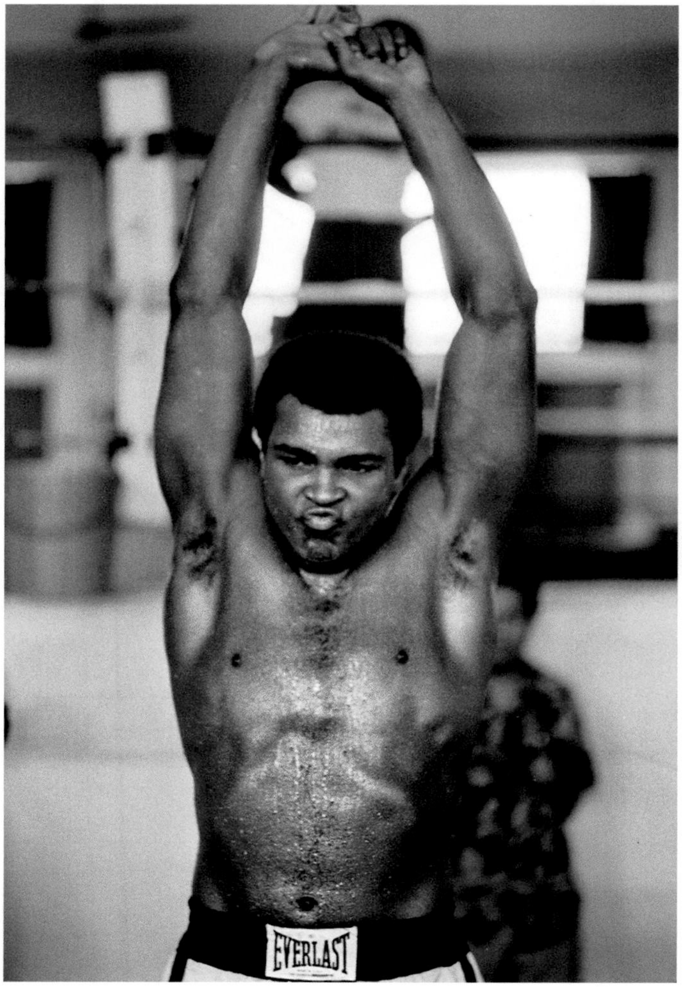
EVERLAST

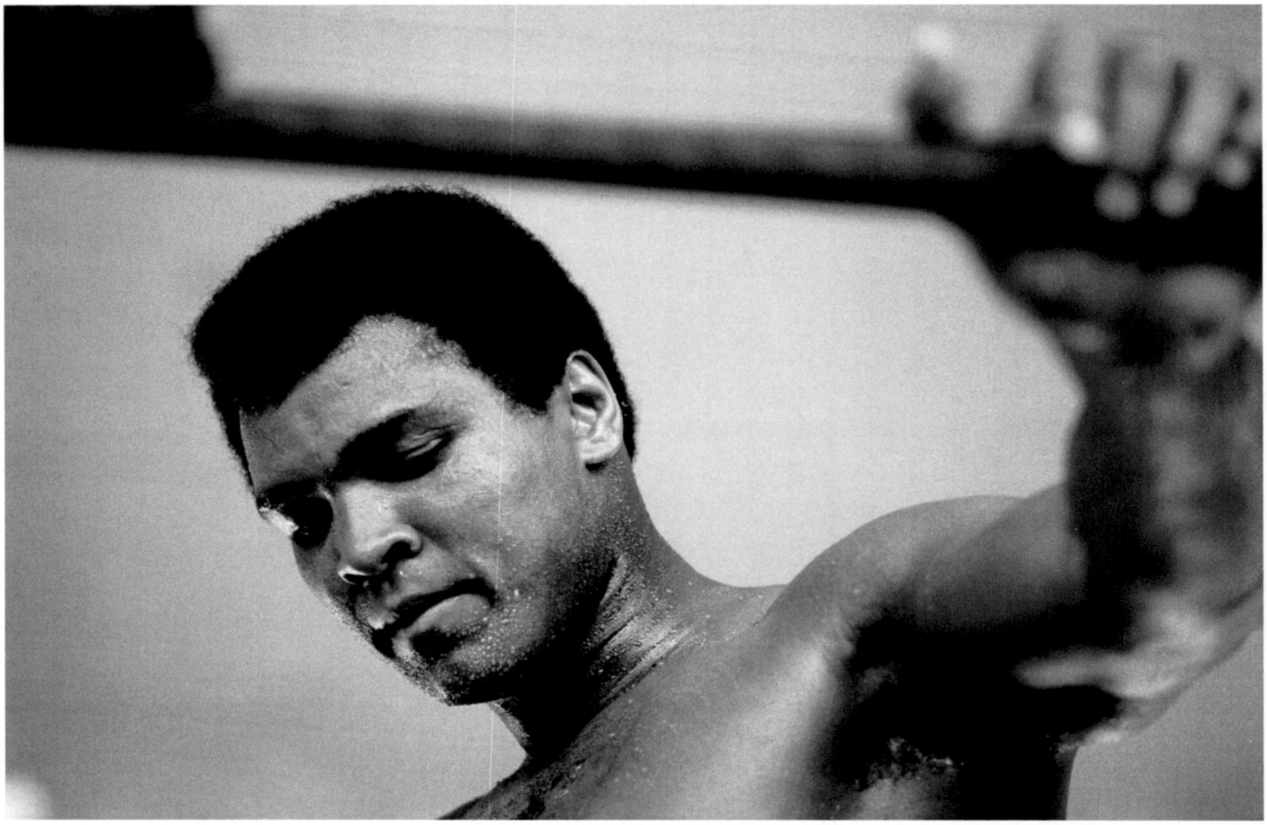

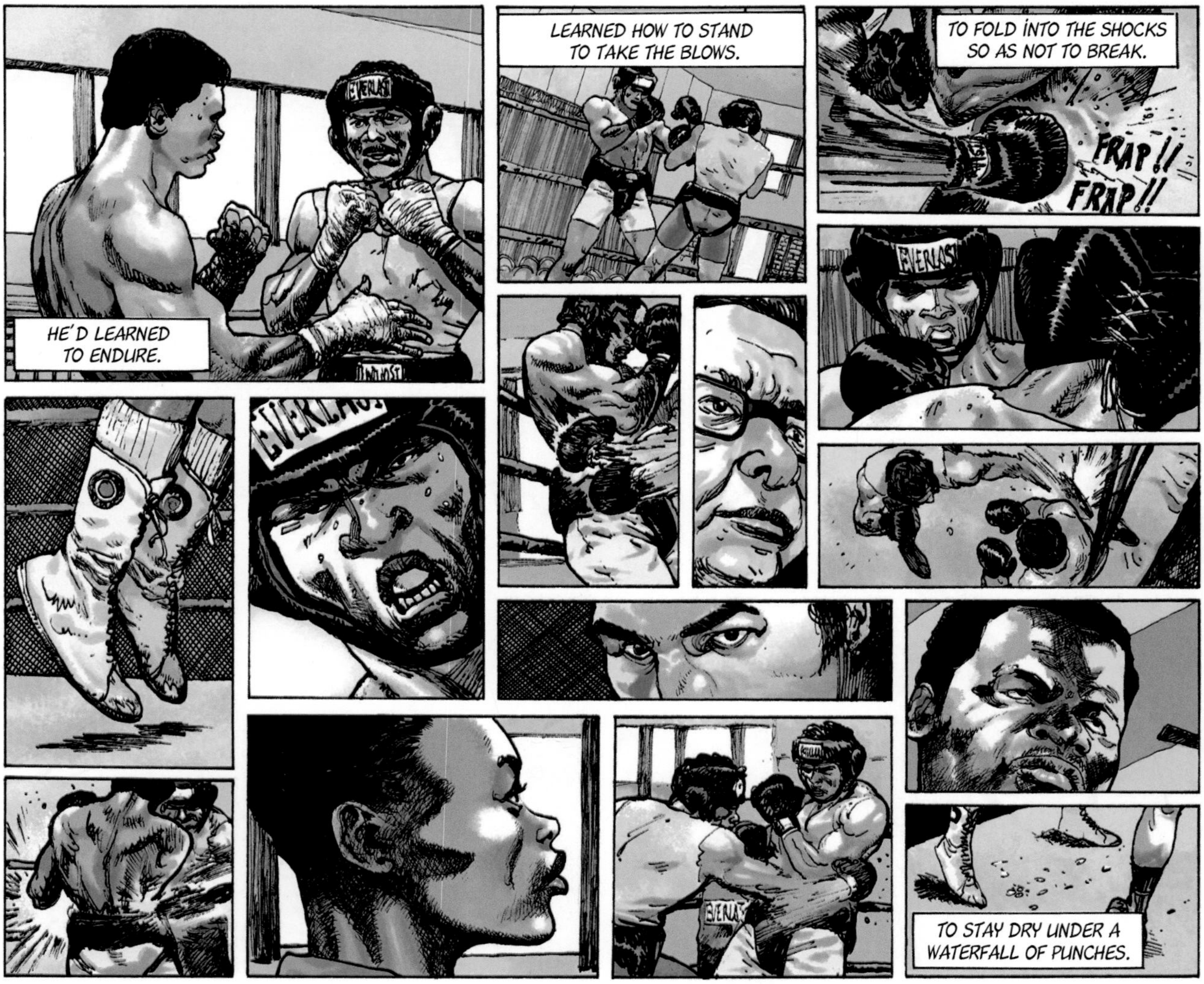
HE'D LEARNED
TO ENDURE.
LEARNED HOW TO STAND
TO TAKE THE BLOWS.
TO FOLD INTO THE SHOCKS
SO AS NOT TO BREAK.
FRAP!!
FRAP!!
TO STAY DRY UNDER A
WATERFALL OF PUNCHES.

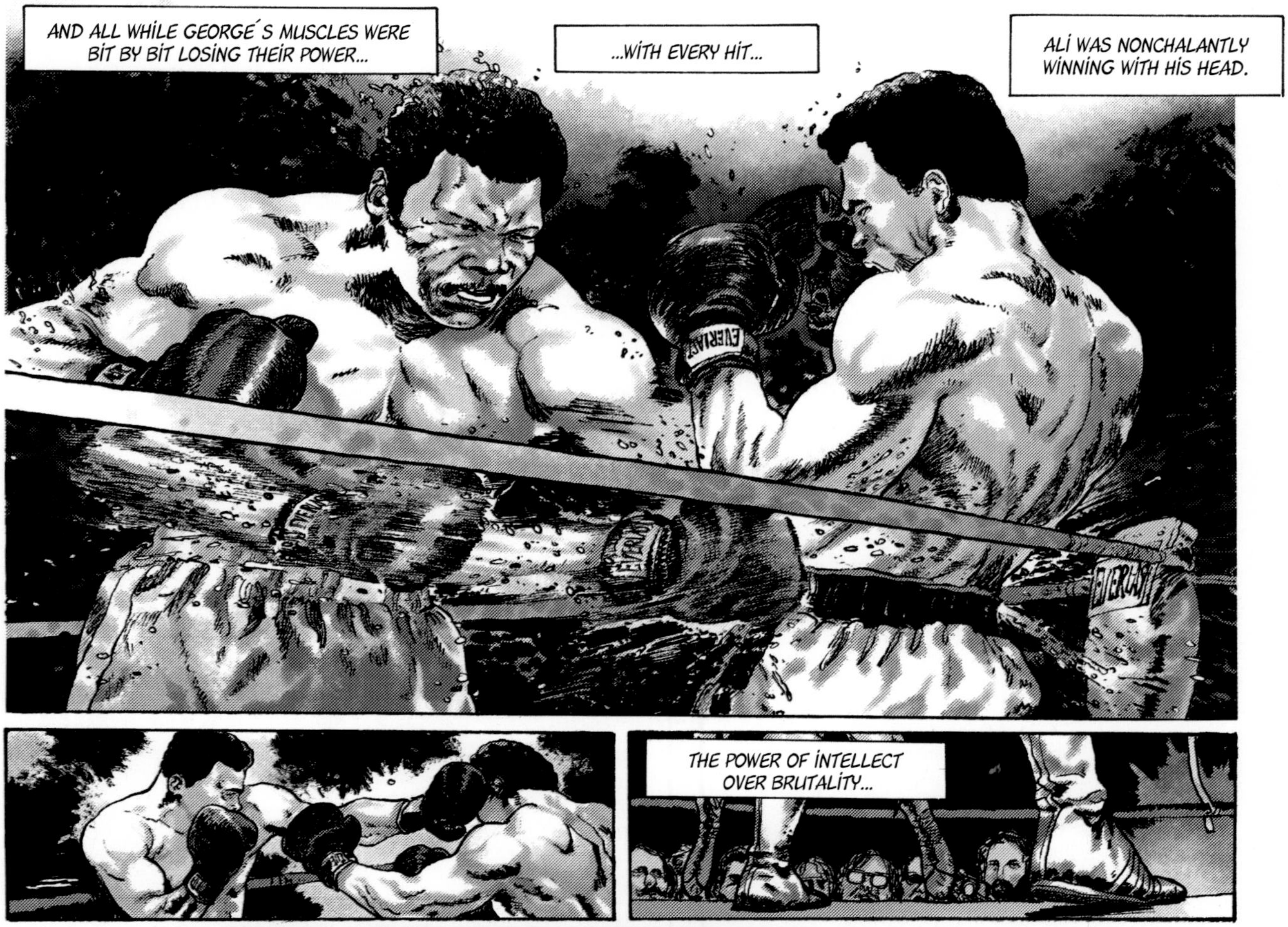
AND ALL WHILE GEORGE´S MUSCLES WERE BIT BY BIT LOSING THEIR POWER...
...WITH EVERY HIT...
ALI WAS NONCHALANTLY WINNING WITH HIS HEAD.
THE POWER OF INTELLECT OVER BRUTALITY...

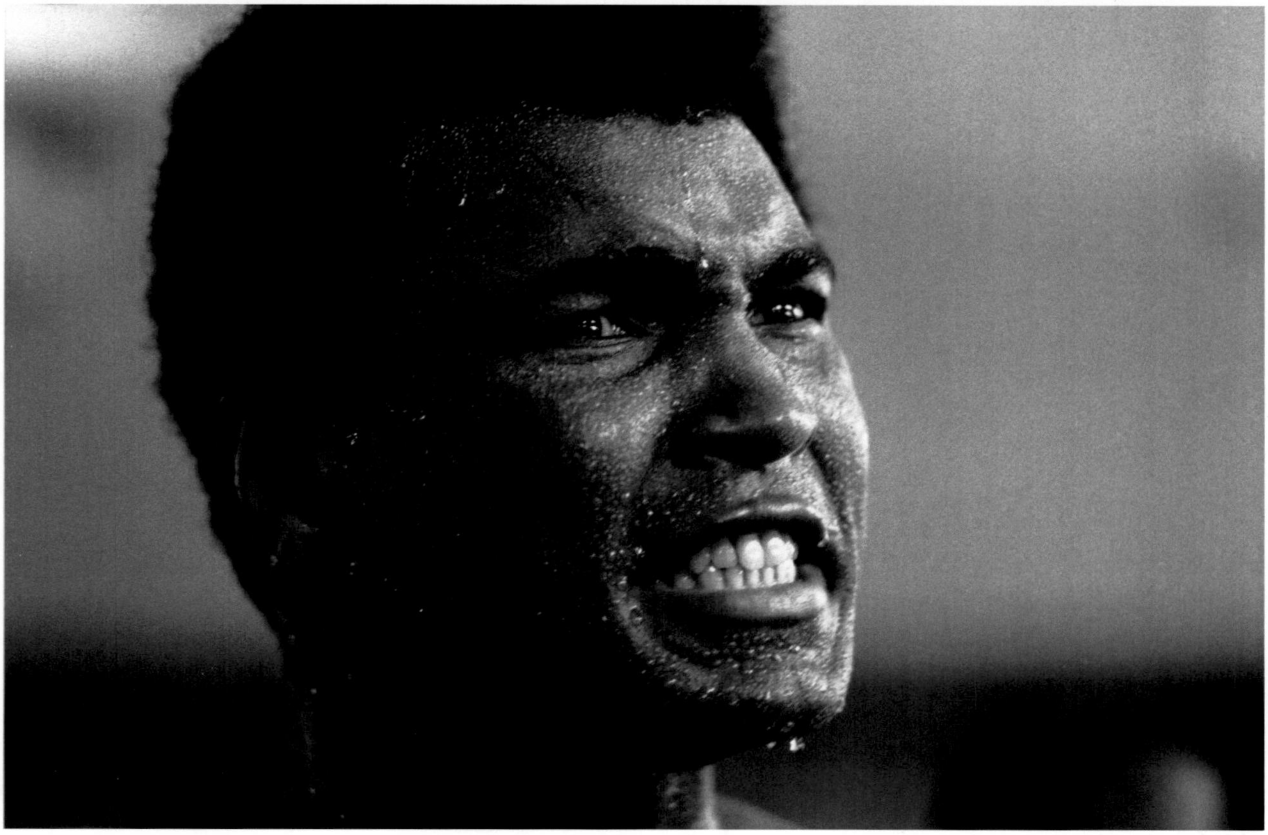

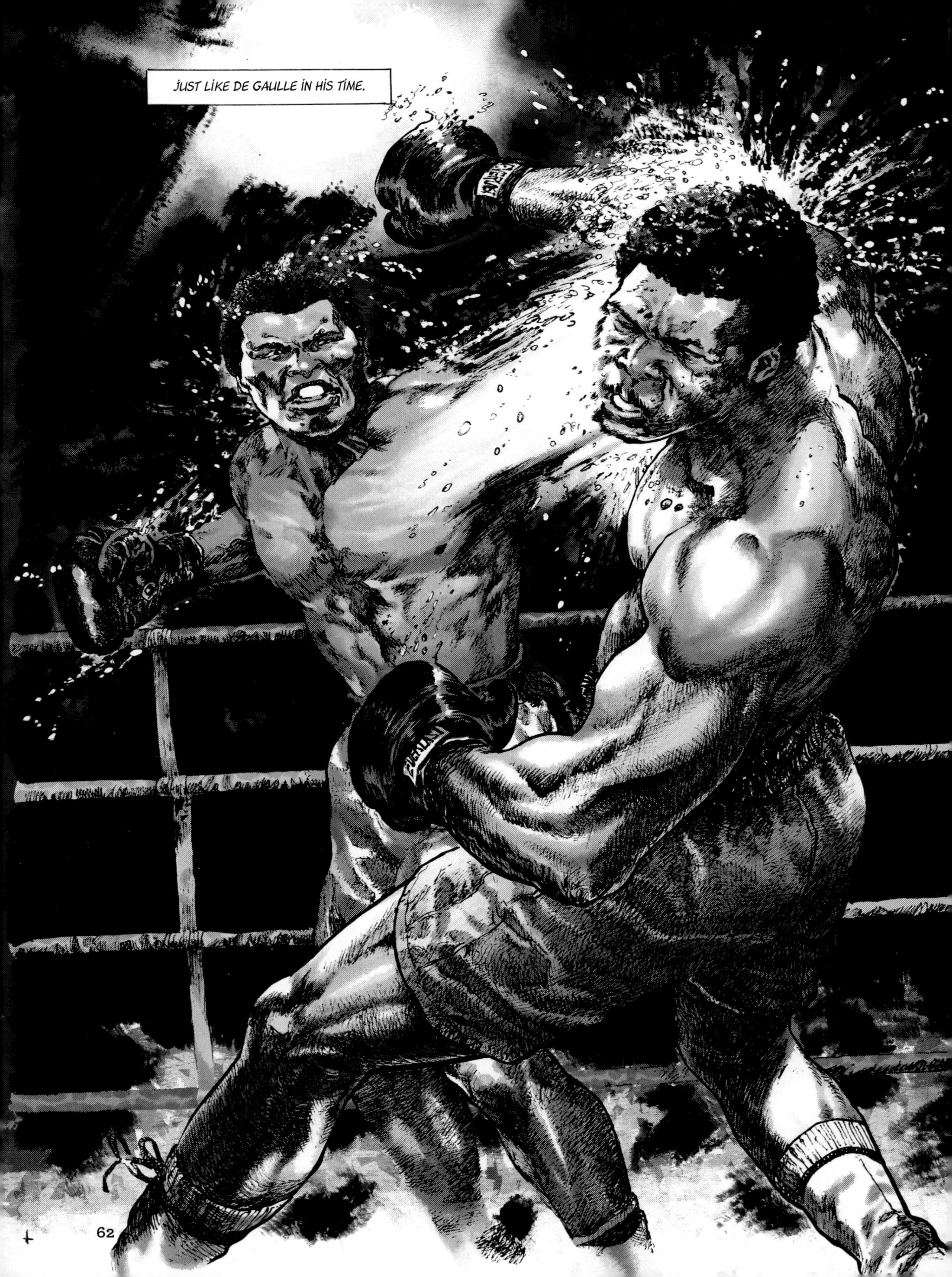
JUST LIKE DE GAULLE IN HIS TIME.

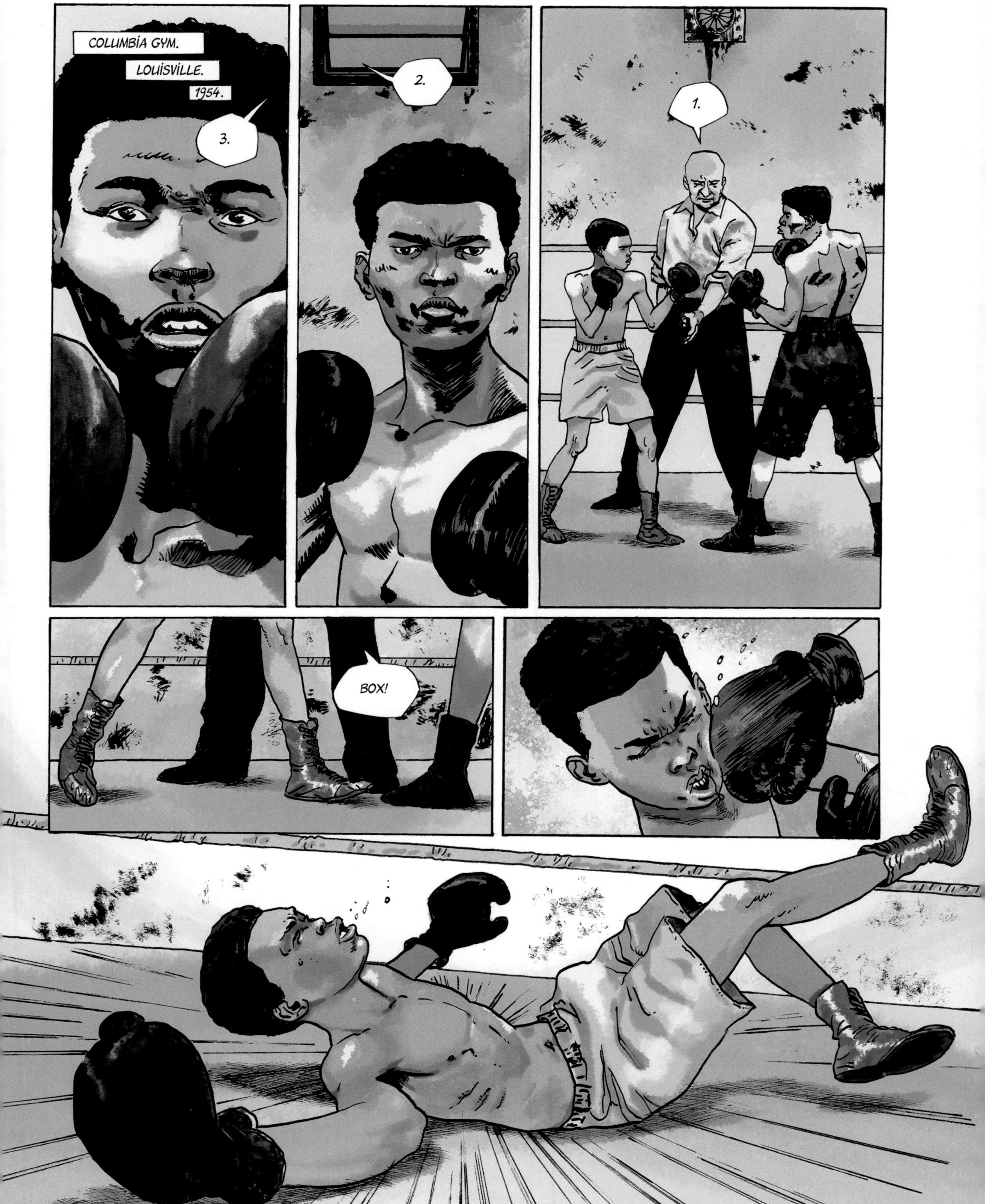
COLUMBIA GYM.
LOUISVILLE.
1954.
3.
2.
1.
BOX!

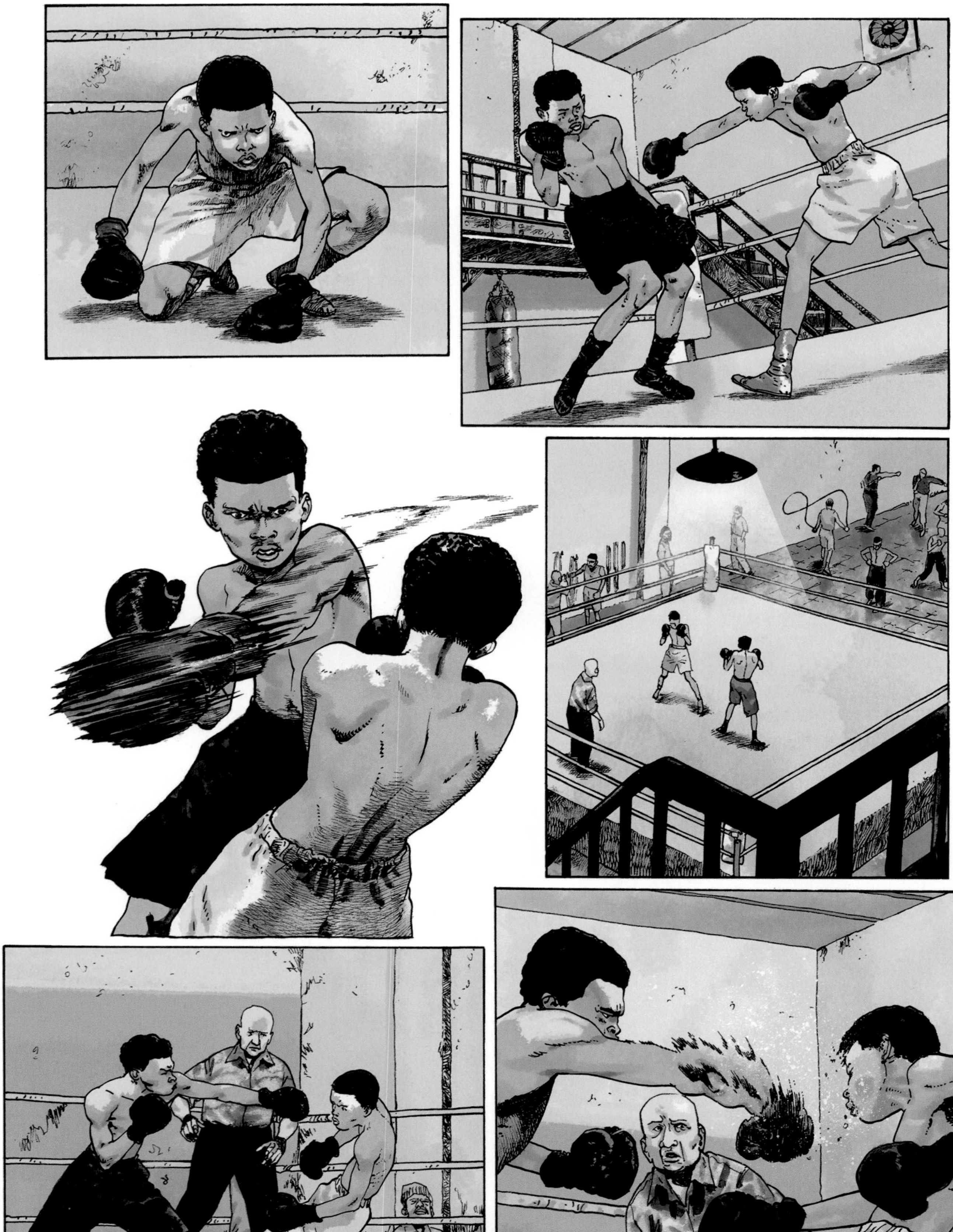

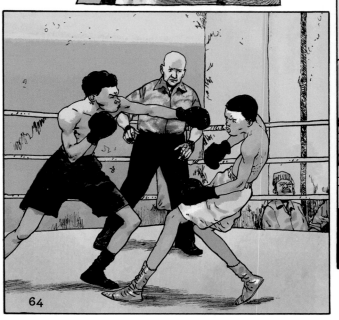

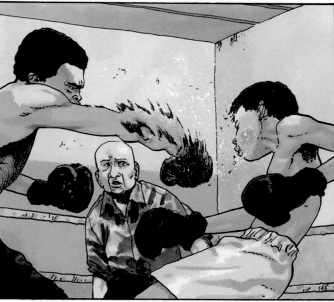

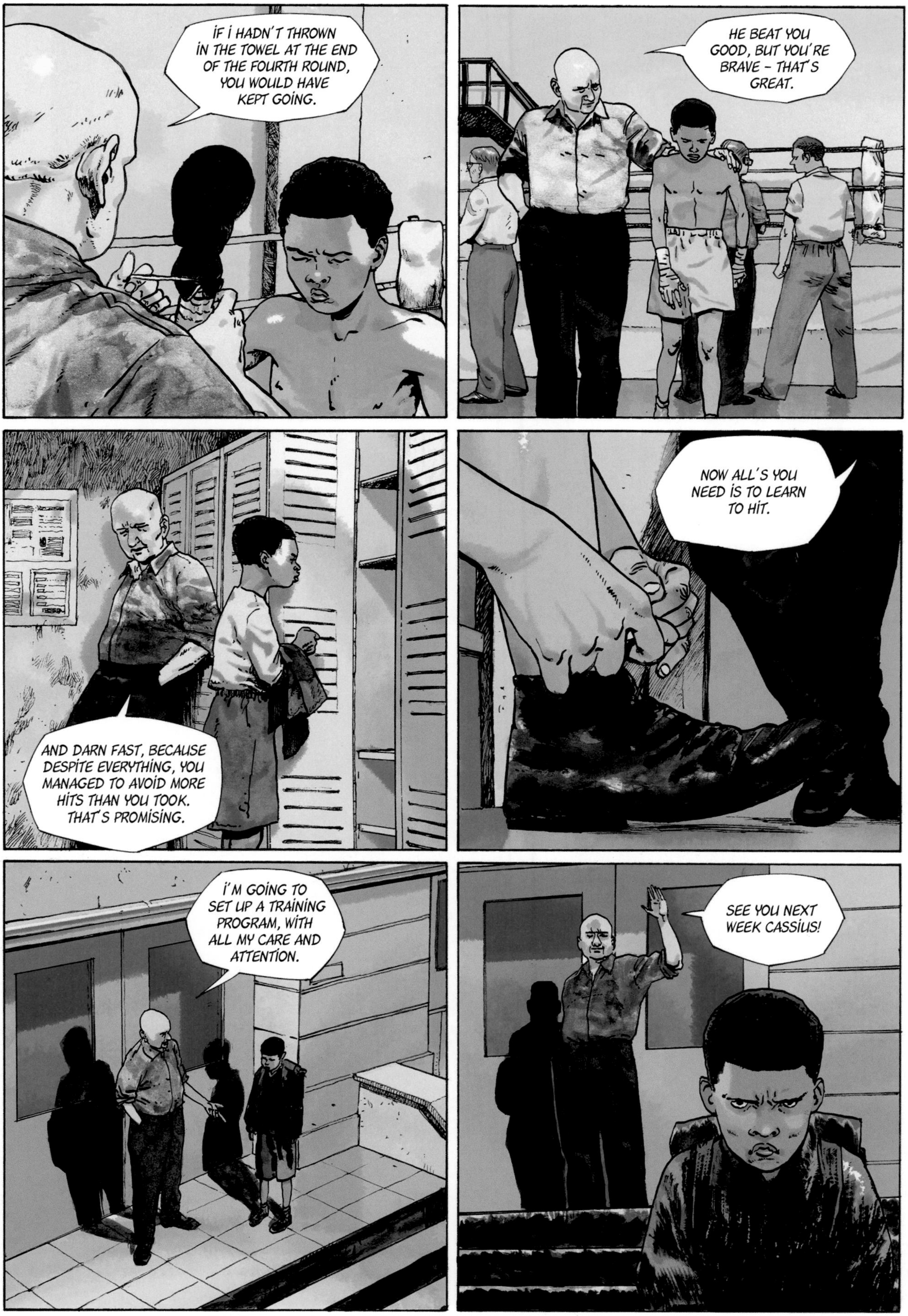
IF I HADN'T THROWN IN THE TOWEL AT THE END OF THE FOURTH ROUND, YOU WOULD HAVE KEPT GOING.
HE BEAT YOU GOOD, BUT YOU'RE BRAVE – THAT'S GREAT.
AND DARN FAST, BECAUSE DESPITE EVERYTHING, YOU MANAGED TO AVOID MORE HITS THAN YOU TOOK. THAT'S PROMISING.
NOW ALL'S YOU NEED IS TO LEARN TO HIT.
I'M GOING TO SET UP A TRAINING PROGRAM, WITH ALL MY CARE AND ATTENTION.
SEE YOU NEXT WEEK CASSIUS!

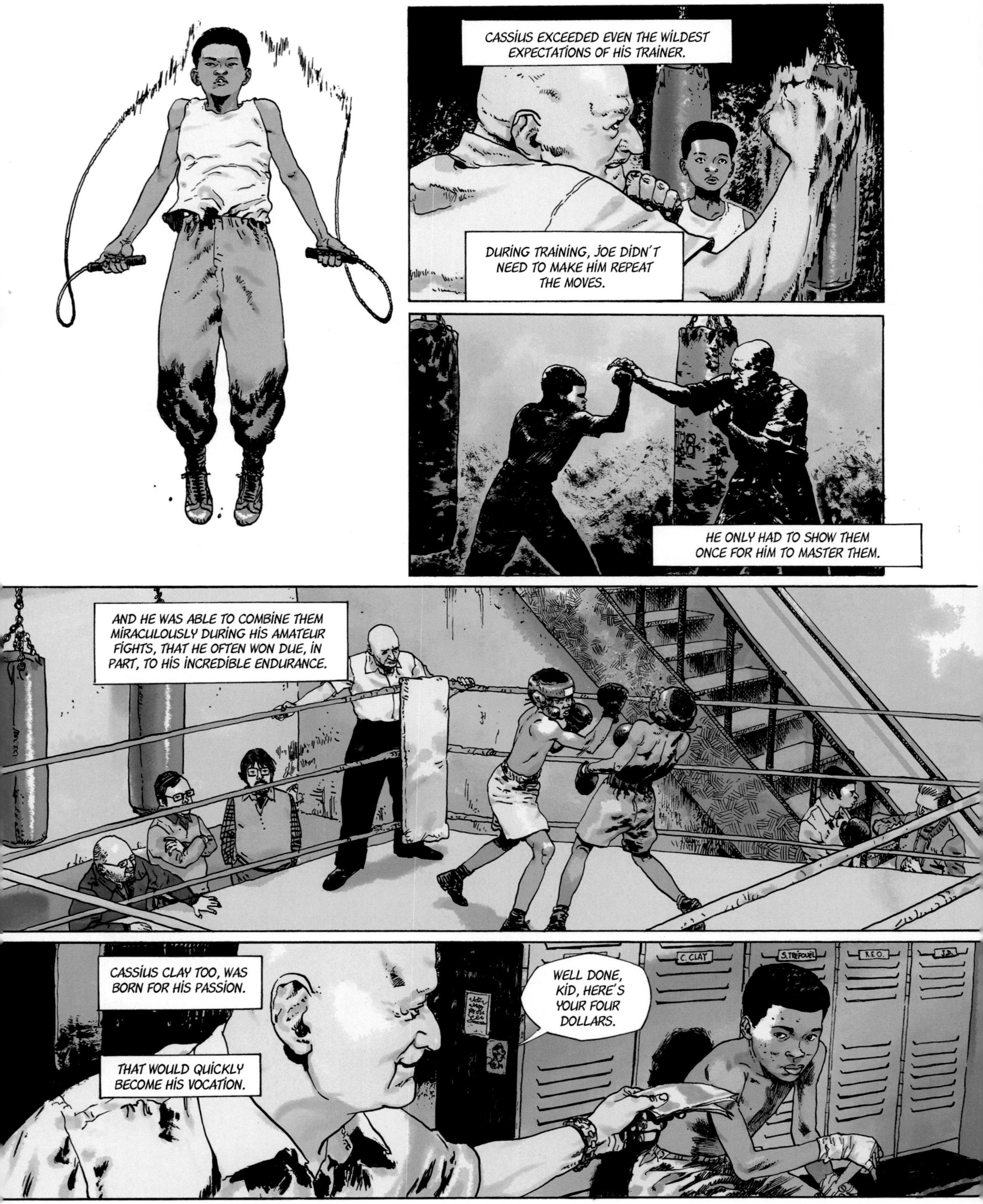
CASSIUS EXCEEDED EVEN THE WILDEST EXPECTATIONS OF HIS TRAINER.
DURING TRAINING, JOE DIDN'T NEED TO MAKE HIM REPEAT THE MOVES.
HE ONLY HAD TO SHOW THEM ONCE FOR HIM TO MASTER THEM.
AND HE WAS ABLE TO COMBINE THEM MIRACULOUSLY DURING HIS AMATEUR FIGHTS, THAT HE OFTEN WON DUE, IN PART, TO HIS INCREDIBLE ENDURANCE.
CASSIUS CLAY TOO, WAS BORN FOR HIS PASSION.
THAT WOULD QUICKLY BECOME HIS VOCATION.
WELL DONE, KID, HERE'S YOUR FOUR DOLLARS.

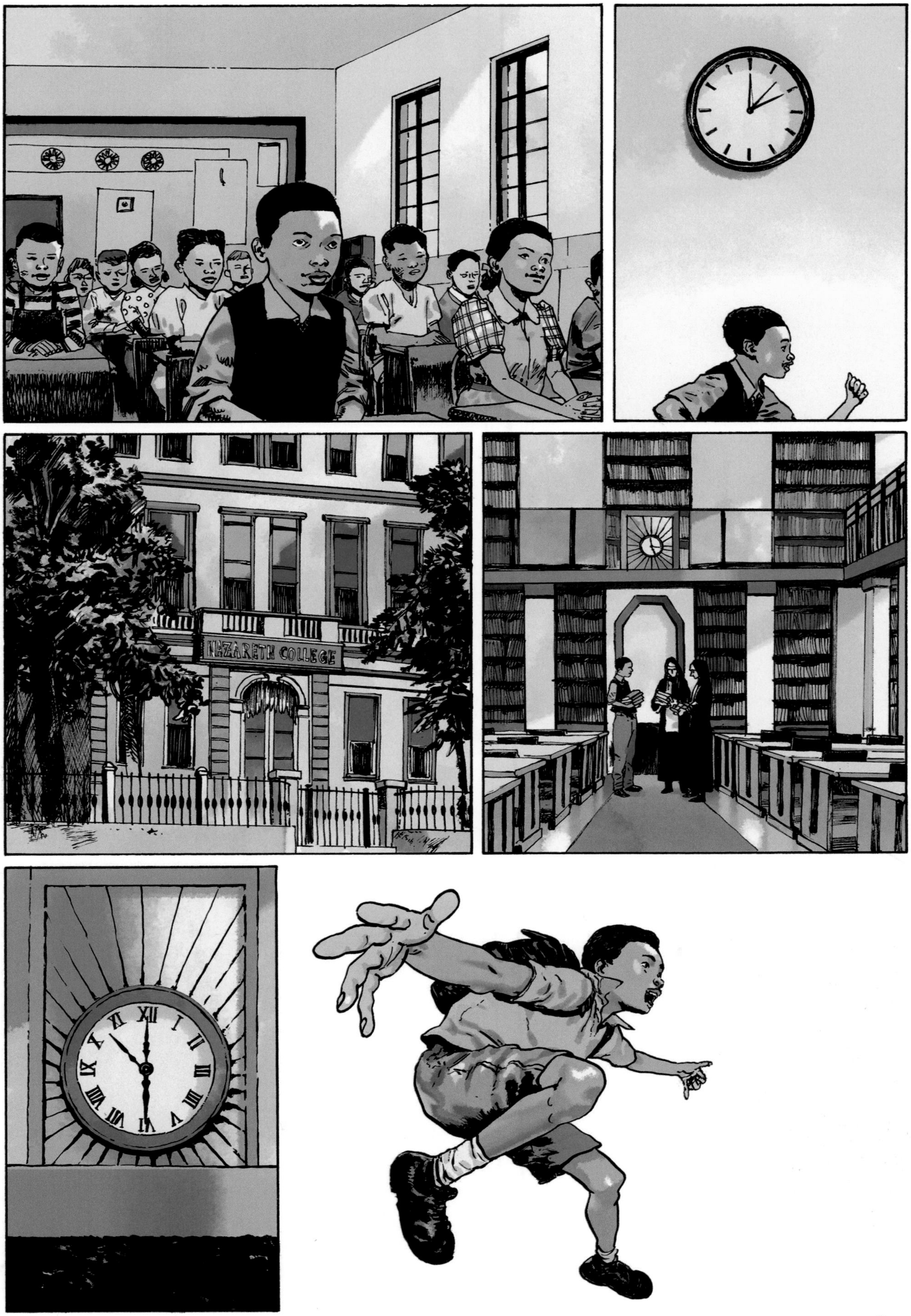
NAZARETH COLLEGE

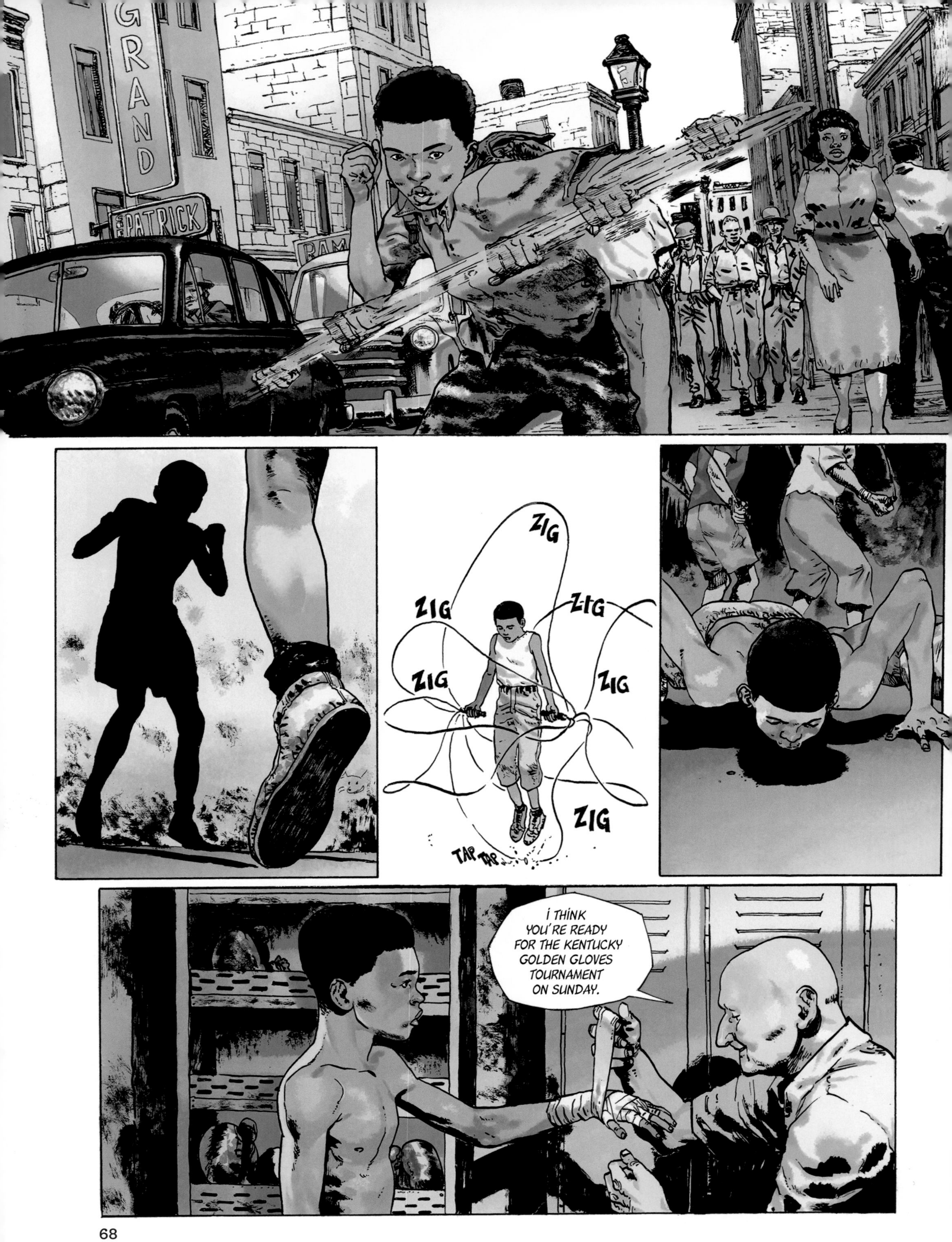
GRAND
PATRICK
ZIG
ZIG
ZIG
ZIG
ZIG
ZIG
TAP TAP
I THINK YOU'RE READY FOR THE KENTUCKY GOLDEN GLOVES TOURNAMENT ON SUNDAY.

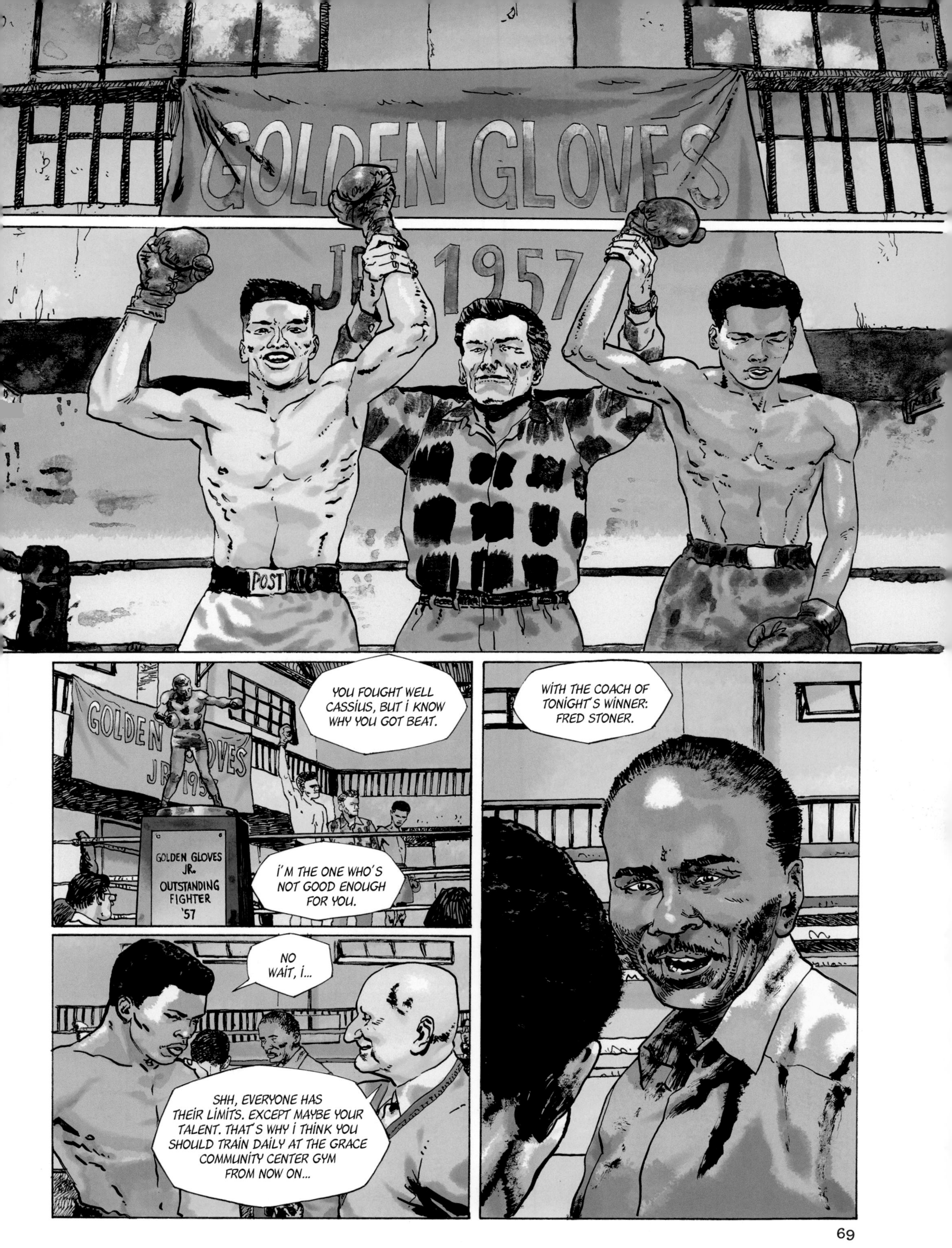
GOLDEN GLOVES
JR 1957
POST
YOU FOUGHT WELL CASSIUS, BUT I KNOW WHY YOU GOT BEAT.
GOLDEN GLOVES JR. OUTSTANDING FIGHTER '57
I'M THE ONE WHO'S NOT GOOD ENOUGH FOR YOU.
WITH THE COACH OF TONIGHT'S WINNER: FRED STONER.
NO WAIT, I...
SHH, EVERYONE HAS THEIR LIMITS. EXCEPT MAYBE YOUR TALENT. THAT'S WHY I THINK YOU SHOULD TRAIN DAILY AT THE GRACE COMMUNITY CENTER GYM FROM NOW ON...

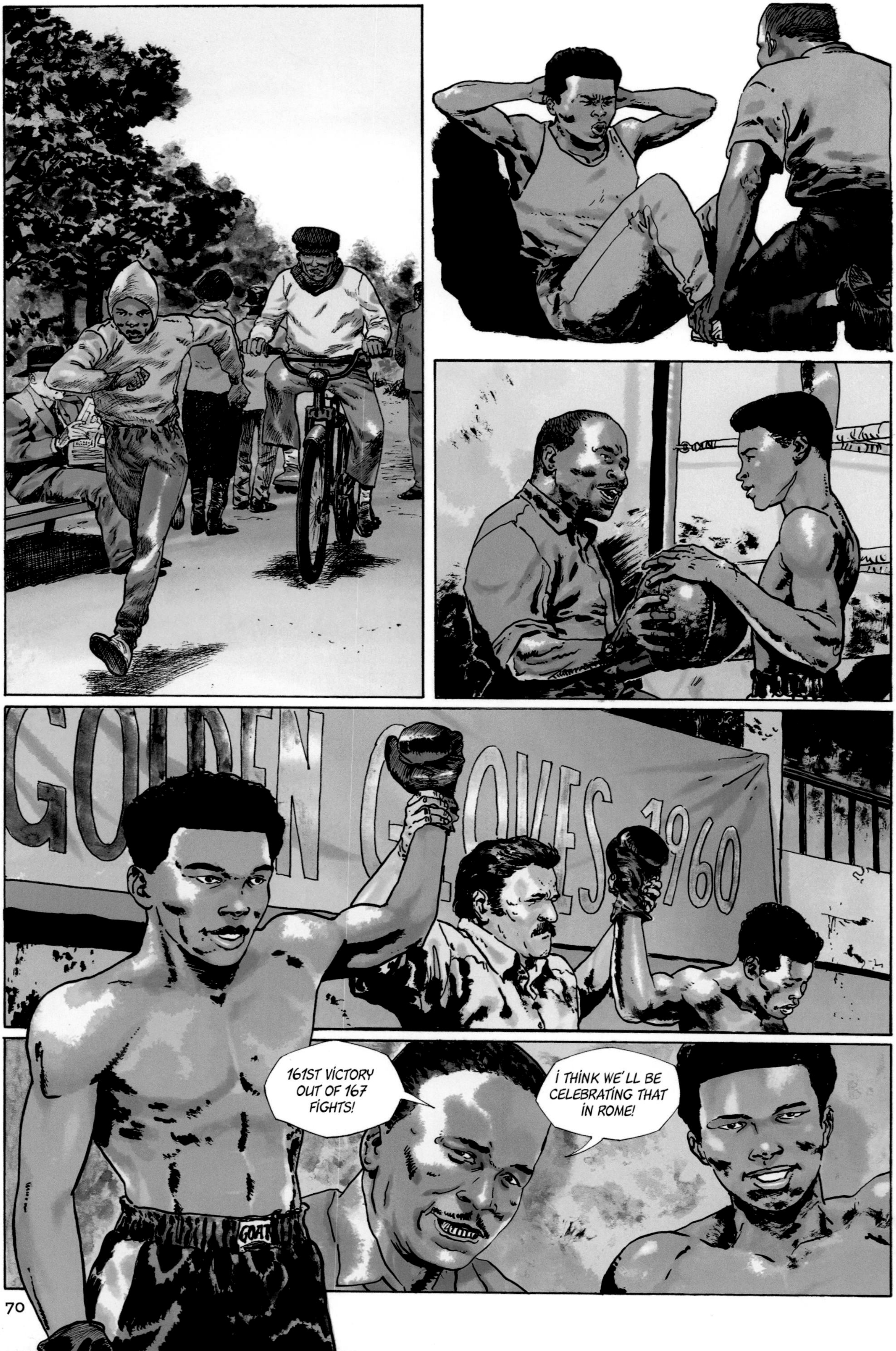
161ST VICTORY OUT OF 167 FIGHTS!
I THINK WE'LL BE CELEBRATING THAT IN ROME!

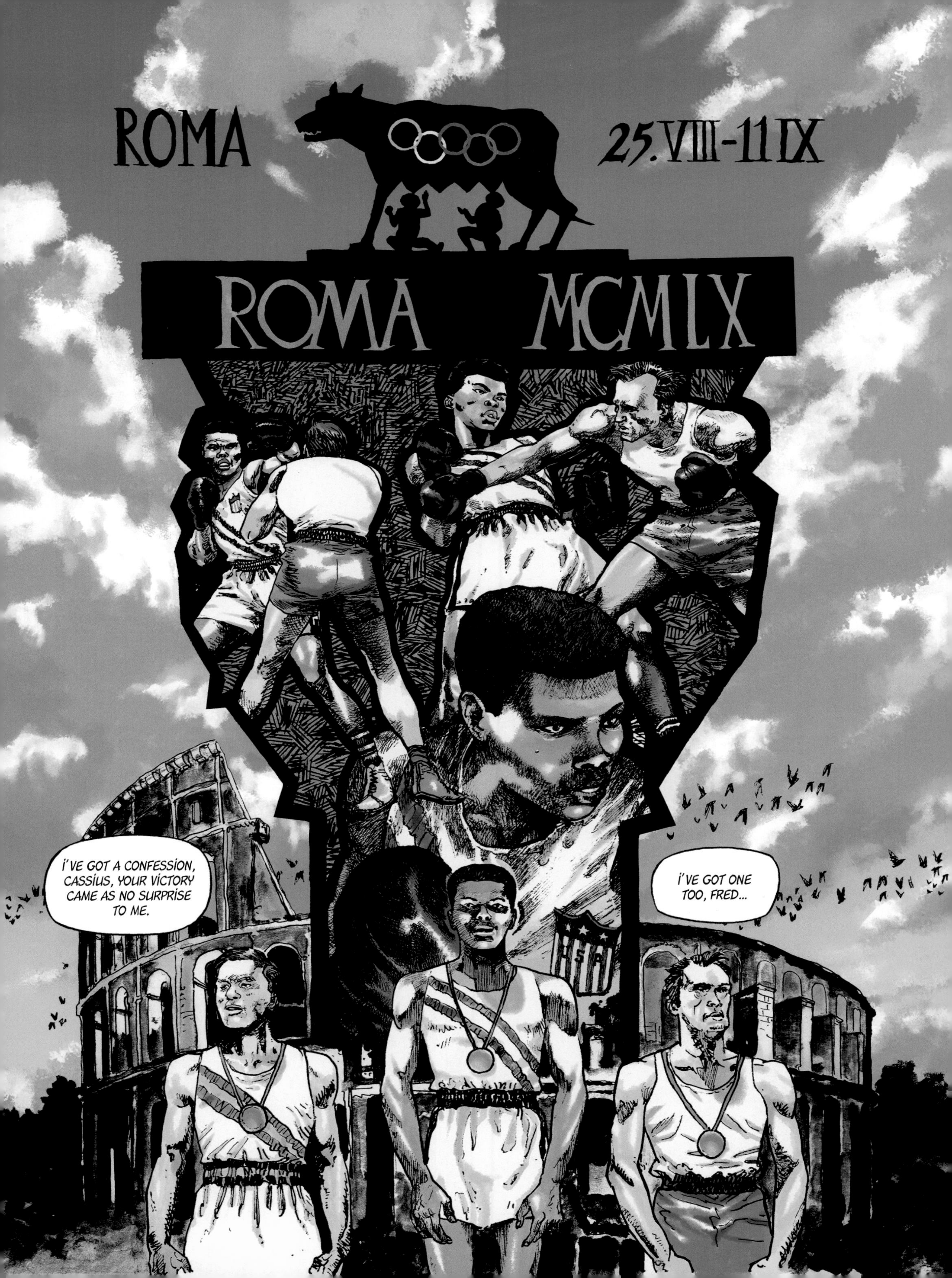
ROMA
25.VIII-11.IX
ROMA MCMLX
I'VE GOT A CONFESSION, CASSIUS, YOUR VICTORY CAME AS NO SURPRISE TO ME.
I'VE GOT ONE TOO, FRED...

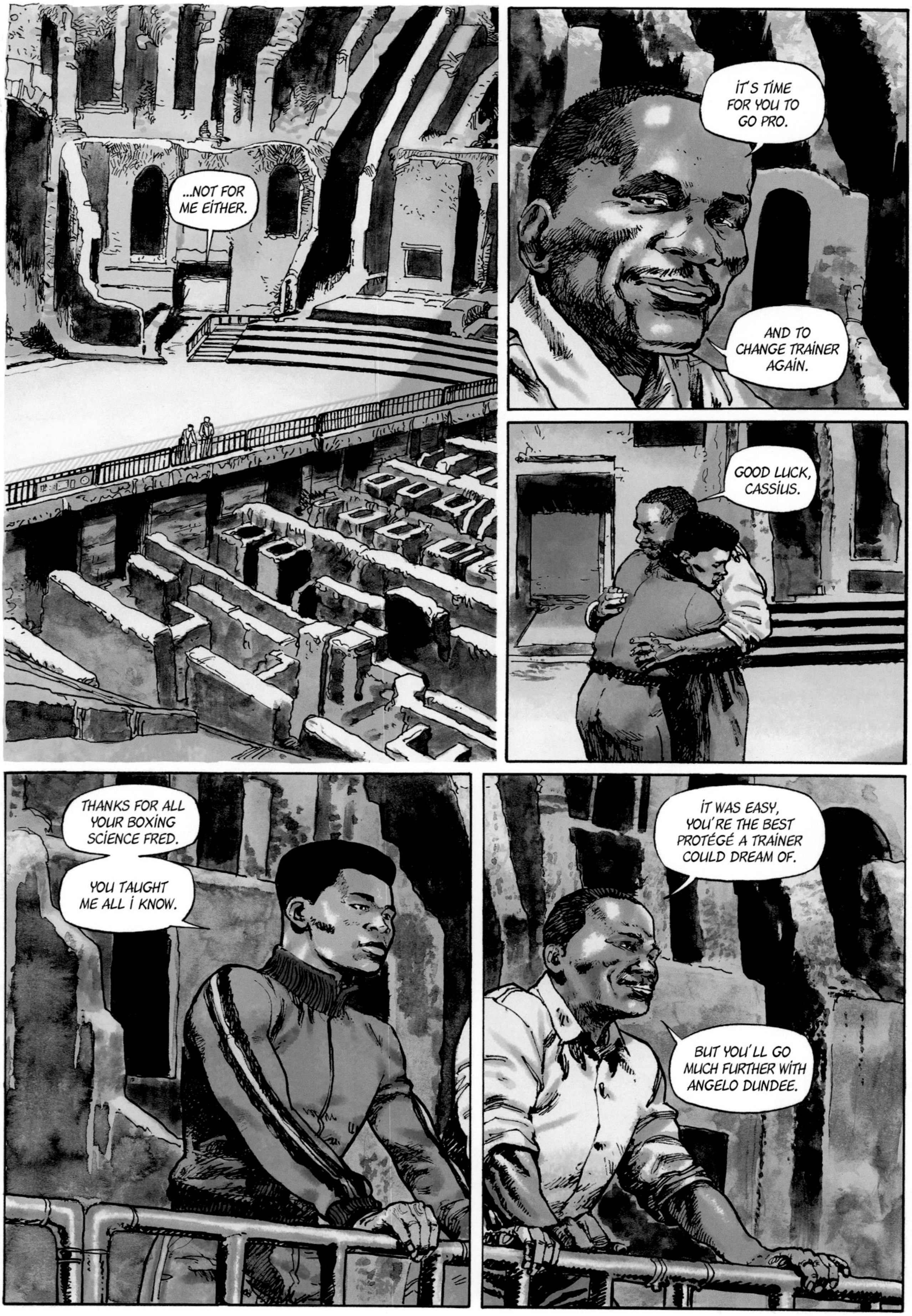
...NOT FOR ME EITHER.
IT'S TIME FOR YOU TO GO PRO.
AND TO CHANGE TRAINER AGAIN.
GOOD LUCK, CASSIUS.
THANKS FOR ALL YOUR BOXING SCIENCE FRED.
YOU TAUGHT ME ALL I KNOW.
IT WAS EASY, YOU'RE THE BEST PROTÉGÉ A TRAINER COULD DREAM OF.
BUT YOU'LL GO MUCH FURTHER WITH ANGELO DUNDEE.

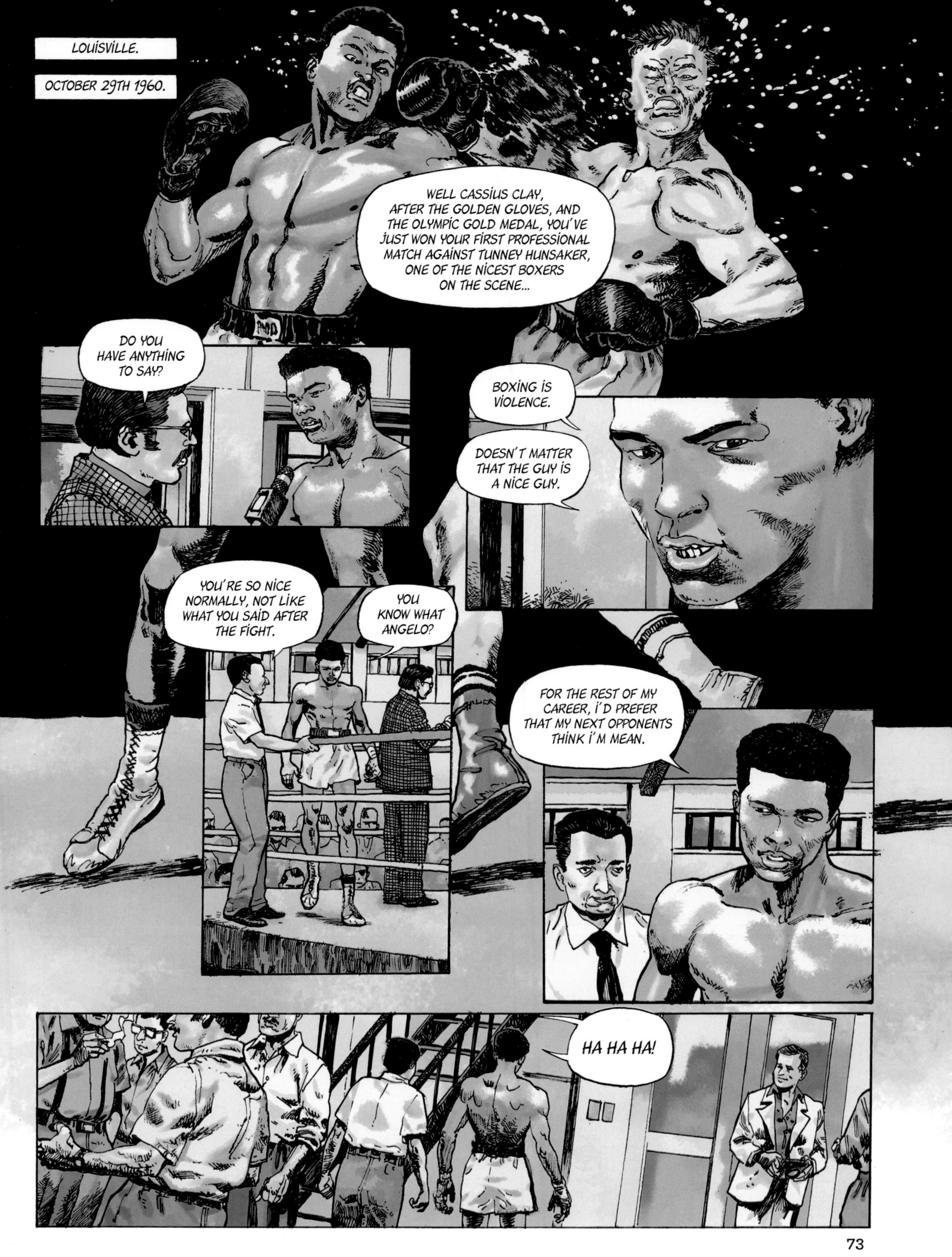
LOUISVILLE.
OCTOBER 29TH 1960.
WELL CASSIUS CLAY, AFTER THE GOLDEN GLOVES, AND THE OLYMPIC GOLD MEDAL, YOU'VE JUST WON YOUR FIRST PROFESSIONAL MATCH AGAINST TUNNEY HUNSAKER, ONE OF THE NICEST BOXERS ON THE SCENE...
DO YOU HAVE ANYTHING TO SAY?
BOXING IS VIOLENCE.
DOESN'T MATTER THAT THE GUY IS A NICE GUY.
YOU'RE SO NICE NORMALLY, NOT LIKE WHAT YOU SAID AFTER THE FIGHT.
YOU KNOW WHAT ANGELO?
FOR THE REST OF MY CAREER, I'D PREFER THAT MY NEXT OPPONENTS THINK I'M MEAN.
HA HA HA!

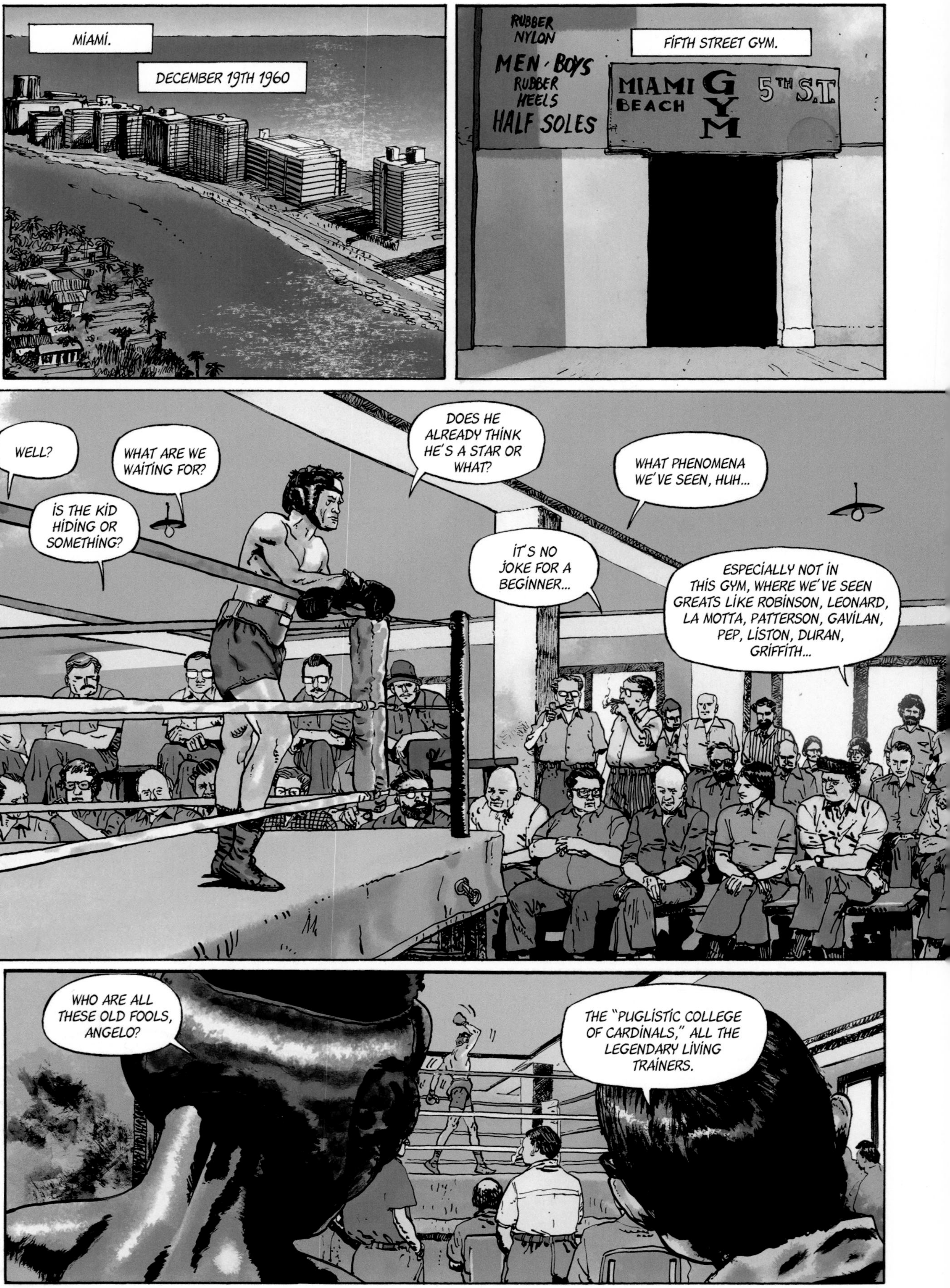
MIAMI.
DECEMBER 19TH 1960
FIFTH STREET GYM.
RUBBER NYLON
MEN · BOYS
RUBBER HEELS
HALF SOLES
MIAMI BEACH GYM 5TH ST
WELL?
WHAT ARE WE WAITING FOR?
IS THE KID HIDING OR SOMETHING?
DOES HE ALREADY THINK HE'S A STAR OR WHAT?
WHAT PHENOMENA WE'VE SEEN, HUH...
IT'S NO JOKE FOR A BEGINNER...
ESPECIALLY NOT IN THIS GYM, WHERE WE'VE SEEN GREATS LIKE ROBINSON, LEONARD, LA MOTTA, PATTERSON, GAVILAN, PEP, LISTON, DURAN, GRIFFITH...
WHO ARE ALL THESE OLD FOOLS, ANGELO?
THE "PUGLISTIC COLLEGE OF CARDINALS," ALL THE LEGENDARY LIVING TRAINERS.

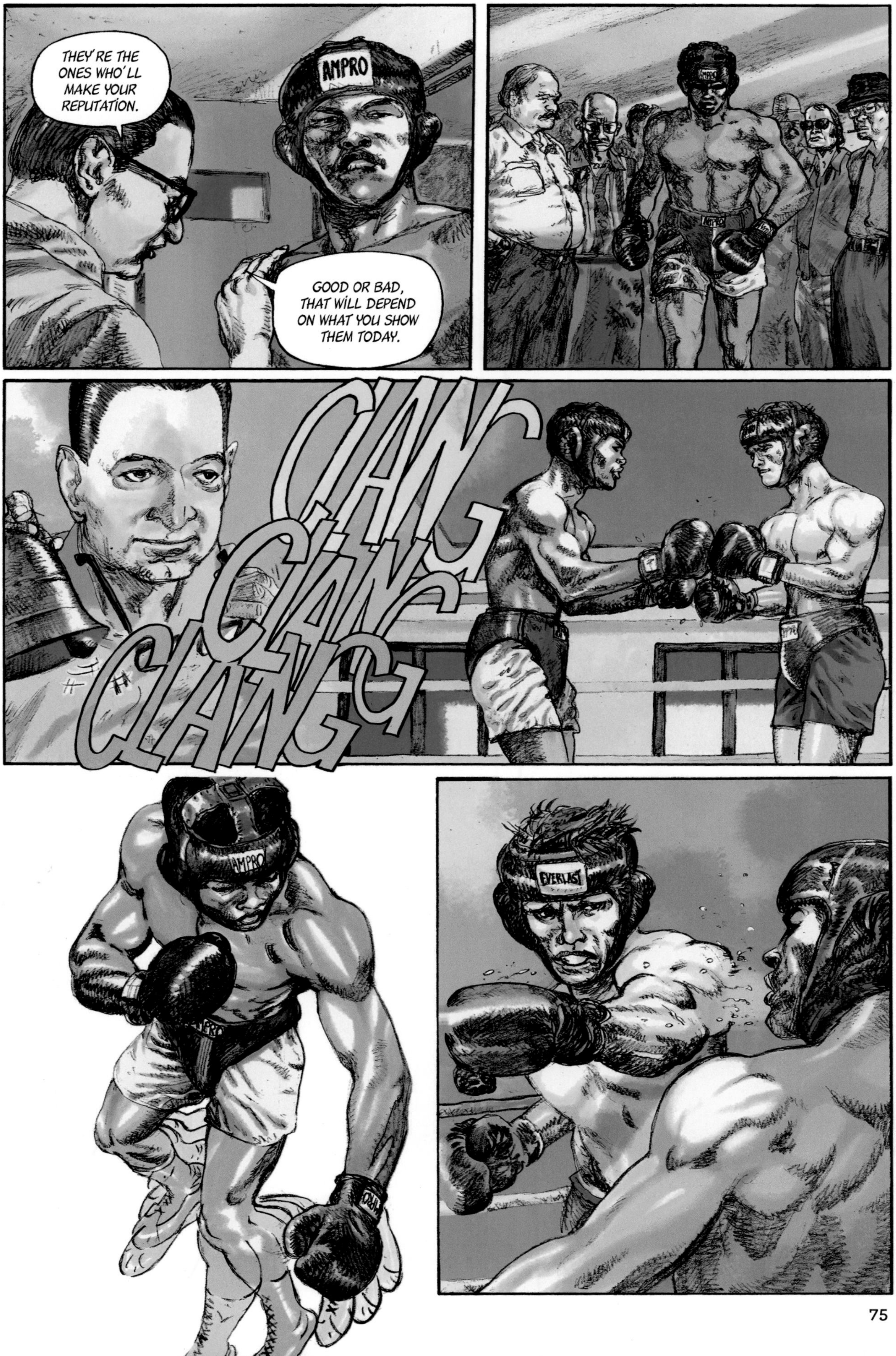
THEY'RE THE ONES WHO'LL MAKE YOUR REPUTATION.
AMPRO
GOOD OR BAD, THAT WILL DEPEND ON WHAT YOU SHOW THEM TODAY.
CLANG
CLANG
CLANG
CLANG
AMPRO
EVERLAST

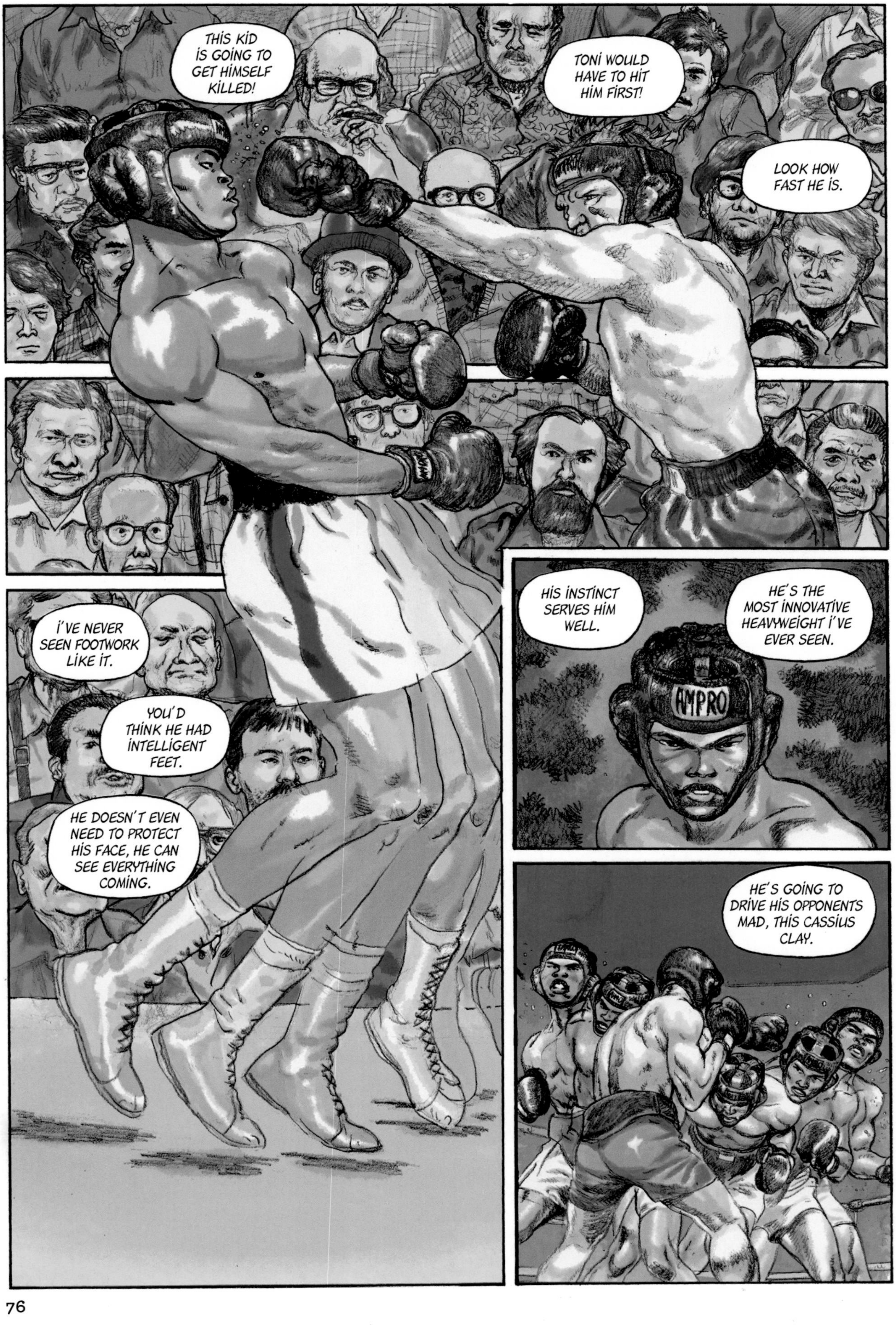
THIS KID IS GOING TO GET HIMSELF KILLED!
TONI WOULD HAVE TO HIT HIM FIRST!
LOOK HOW FAST HE IS.
HIS INSTINCT SERVES HIM WELL.
HE'S THE MOST INNOVATIVE HEAVYWEIGHT I'VE EVER SEEN.
I'VE NEVER SEEN FOOTWORK LIKE IT.
YOU'D THINK HE HAD INTELLIGENT FEET.
HE DOESN'T EVEN NEED TO PROTECT HIS FACE, HE CAN SEE EVERYTHING COMING.
AMPRO
HE'S GOING TO DRIVE HIS OPPONENTS MAD, THIS CASSIUS CLAY.

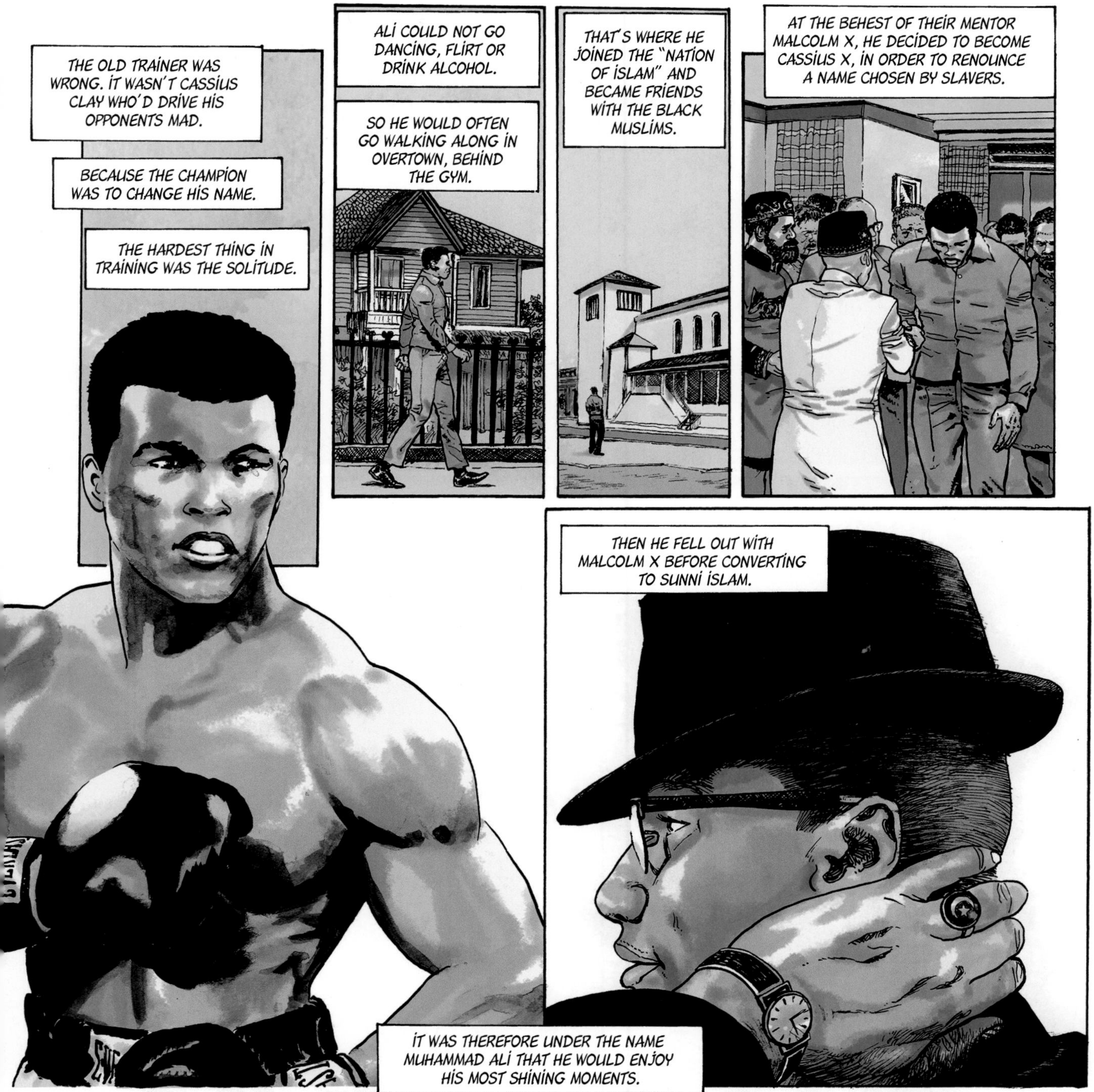
THE OLD TRAINER WAS WRONG. IT WASN'T CASSIUS CLAY WHO'D DRIVE HIS OPPONENTS MAD.
BECAUSE THE CHAMPION WAS TO CHANGE HIS NAME.
THE HARDEST THING IN TRAINING WAS THE SOLITUDE.
ALI COULD NOT GO DANCING, FLIRT OR DRINK ALCOHOL.
SO HE WOULD OFTEN GO WALKING ALONG IN OVERTOWN, BEHIND THE GYM.
THAT'S WHERE HE JOINED THE "NATION OF ISLAM" AND BECAME FRIENDS WITH THE BLACK MUSLIMS.
AT THE BEHEST OF THEIR MENTOR MALCOLM X, HE DECIDED TO BECOME CASSIUS X, IN ORDER TO RENOUNCE A NAME CHOSEN BY SLAVERS.
THEN HE FELL OUT WITH MALCOLM X BEFORE CONVERTING TO SUNNI ISLAM.
IT WAS THEREFORE UNDER THE NAME MUHAMMAD ALI THAT HE WOULD ENJOY HIS MOST SHINING MOMENTS.

MUHAMMAD ALI

IN SPORT,
FIGHTING AMONG OTHERS...

JIM ROBINSON.

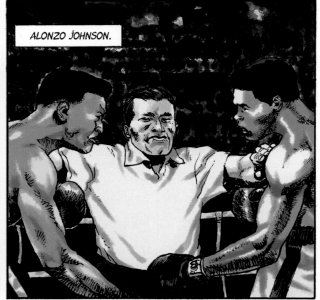

ALONZO JOHNSON.

WILLIE BESMANOFF.

CHARLEY POWELL.

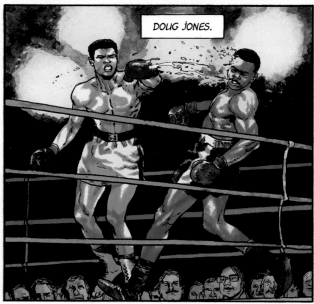

DOUG JONES.

SONNY LISTON,
THE FIRST TIME...

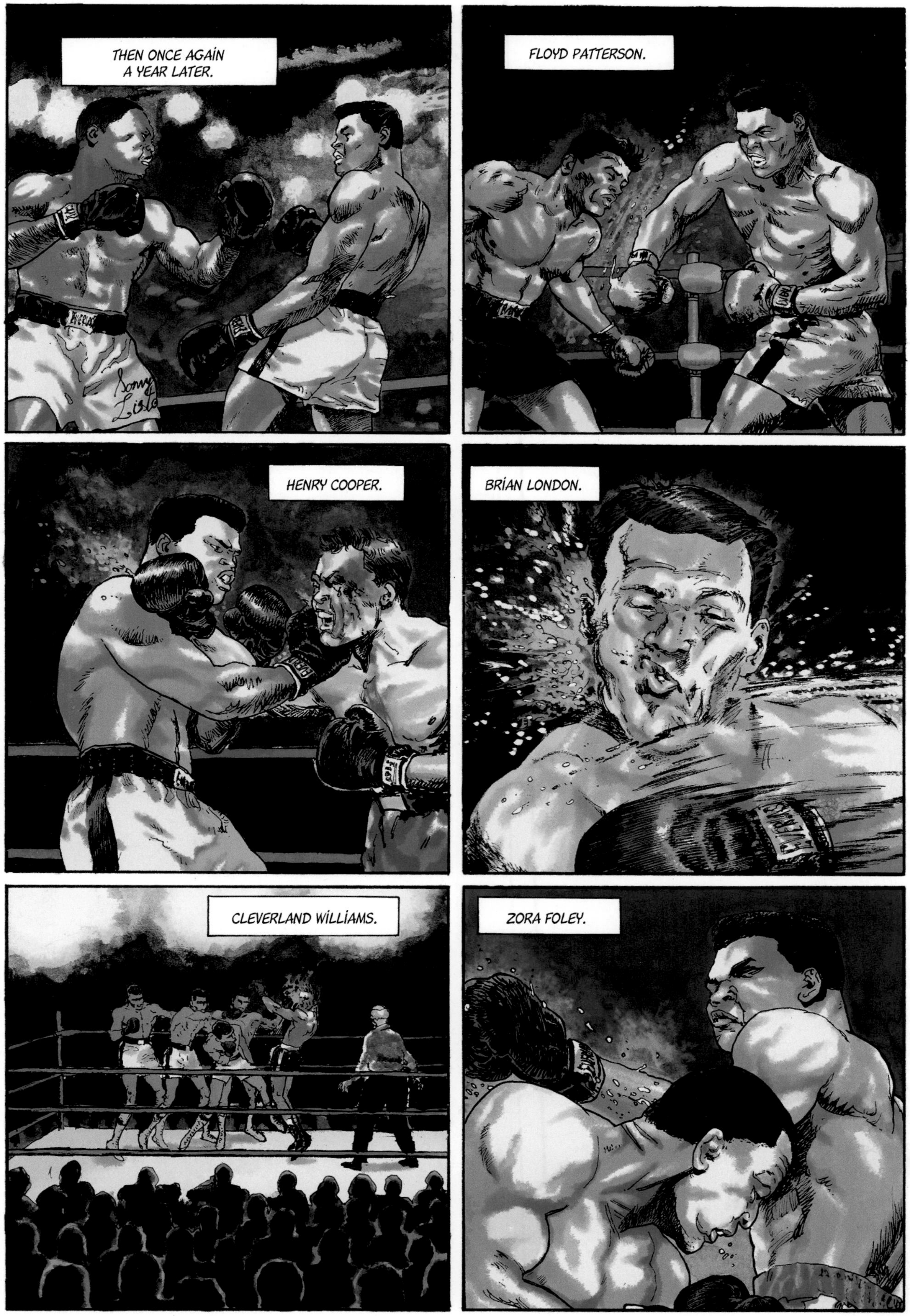
THEN ONCE AGAIN
A YEAR LATER.
FLOYD PATTERSON.
HENRY COOPER.
BRIAN LONDON.
CLEVERLAND WILLIAMS.
ZORA FOLEY.

BUT EQUALLY BECAUSE HIS ATTITUDE AND THE COMPANY HE KEPT STRONGLY DISPLEASED THE AUTHORITIES.

HE BECAME A CONSCIENTIOUS OBJECTOR, REFUSING TO FIGHT IN VIETNAM.

NO VIETNAMESE PERSON HAS EVER TREATED ME LIKE A NEGRO.

ON APRIL 28TH 1967, HE DID NOT SHOW UP TO THE RECRUITMENT CENTER HE'D BEEN DRAFTED TO.

HE WAS TAKEN TO COURT ON THE 8TH OF MAY AND SENTENCED ON JUNE 20TH TO A FINE OF 10,000 DOLLARS AND FIVE YEARS IN PRISON.

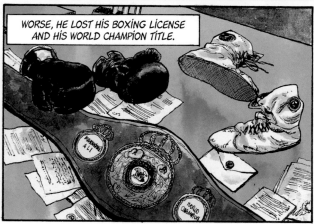

WORSE, HE LOST HIS BOXING LICENSE AND HIS WORLD CHAMPION TITLE.

UPON APPEAL, HE AVOIDED PRISON UNTIL 1971, WHEN THE SUPREME COURT TOOK ON THE CASE.

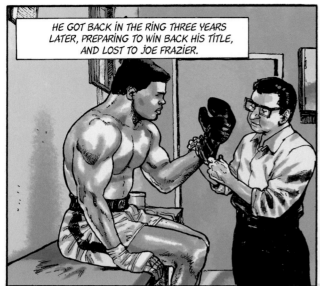

HE GOT BACK IN THE RING THREE YEARS LATER, PREPARING TO WIN BACK HIS TITLE, AND LOST TO JOE FRAZIER.

HE DEFEATED JERRY QUARRY BY K.O. IN THE THIRD ROUND.

THEN OSCAR BONAVENTURA BY TECHNICAL K.O. IN THE 15TH ROUND.

ON MARCH 10TH 1971, AT NEW YORK'S MADISON SQUARE GARDEN, "THE FIGHT OF THE CENTURY" TOOK PLACE.

THE MATCH LIVED UP TO ITS NAME...

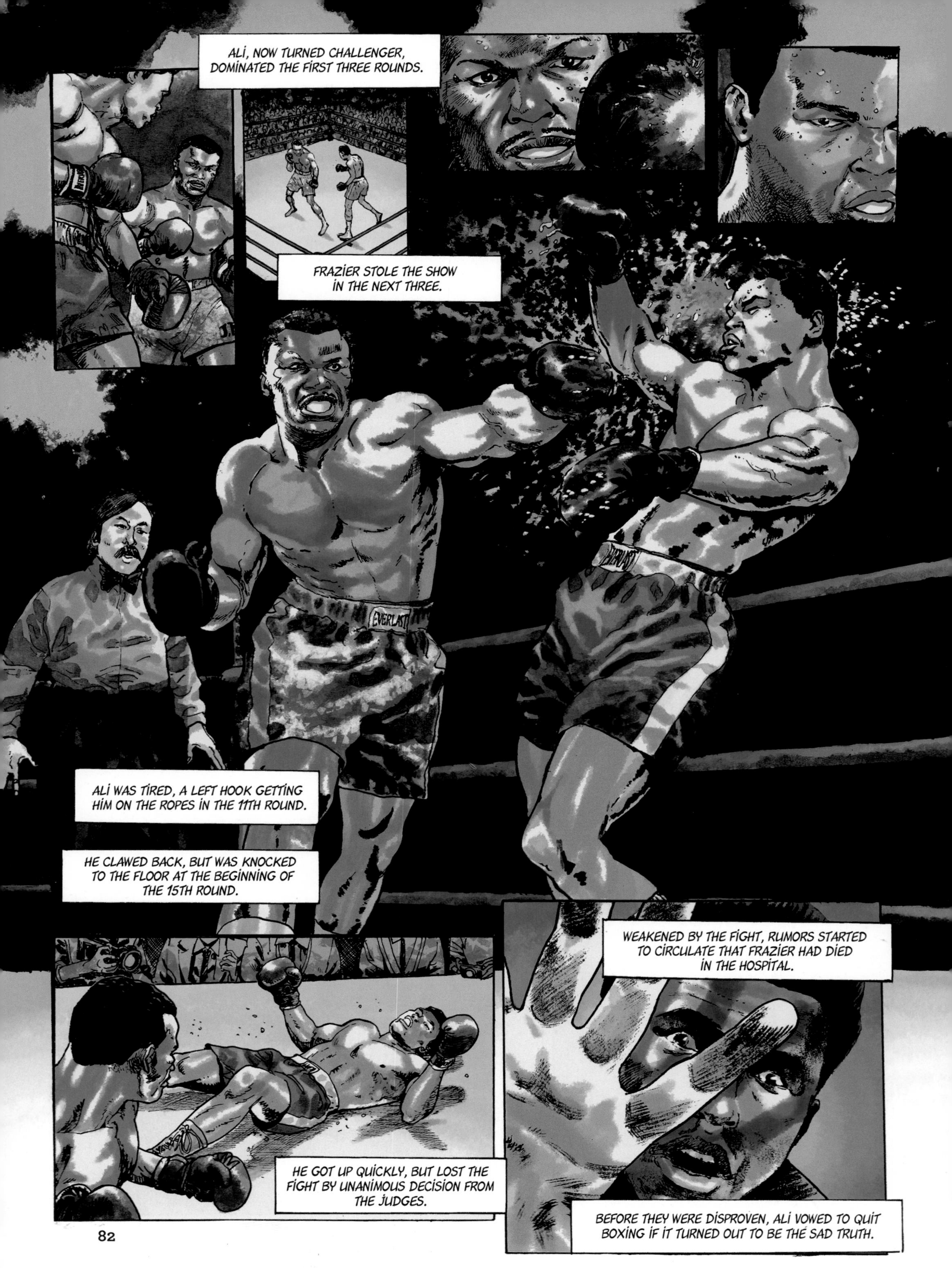
ALI, NOW TURNED CHALLENGER, DOMINATED THE FIRST THREE ROUNDS.
FRAZIER STOLE THE SHOW IN THE NEXT THREE.
EVERLAST
ALI WAS TIRED, A LEFT HOOK GETTING HIM ON THE ROPES IN THE 11TH ROUND.
HE CLAWED BACK, BUT WAS KNOCKED TO THE FLOOR AT THE BEGINNING OF THE 15TH ROUND.
HE GOT UP QUICKLY, BUT LOST THE FIGHT BY UNANIMOUS DECISION FROM THE JUDGES.
WEAKENED BY THE FIGHT, RUMORS STARTED TO CIRCULATE THAT FRAZIER HAD DIED IN THE HOSPITAL.
BEFORE THEY WERE DISPROVEN, ALI VOWED TO QUIT BOXING IF IT TURNED OUT TO BE THE SAD TRUTH.

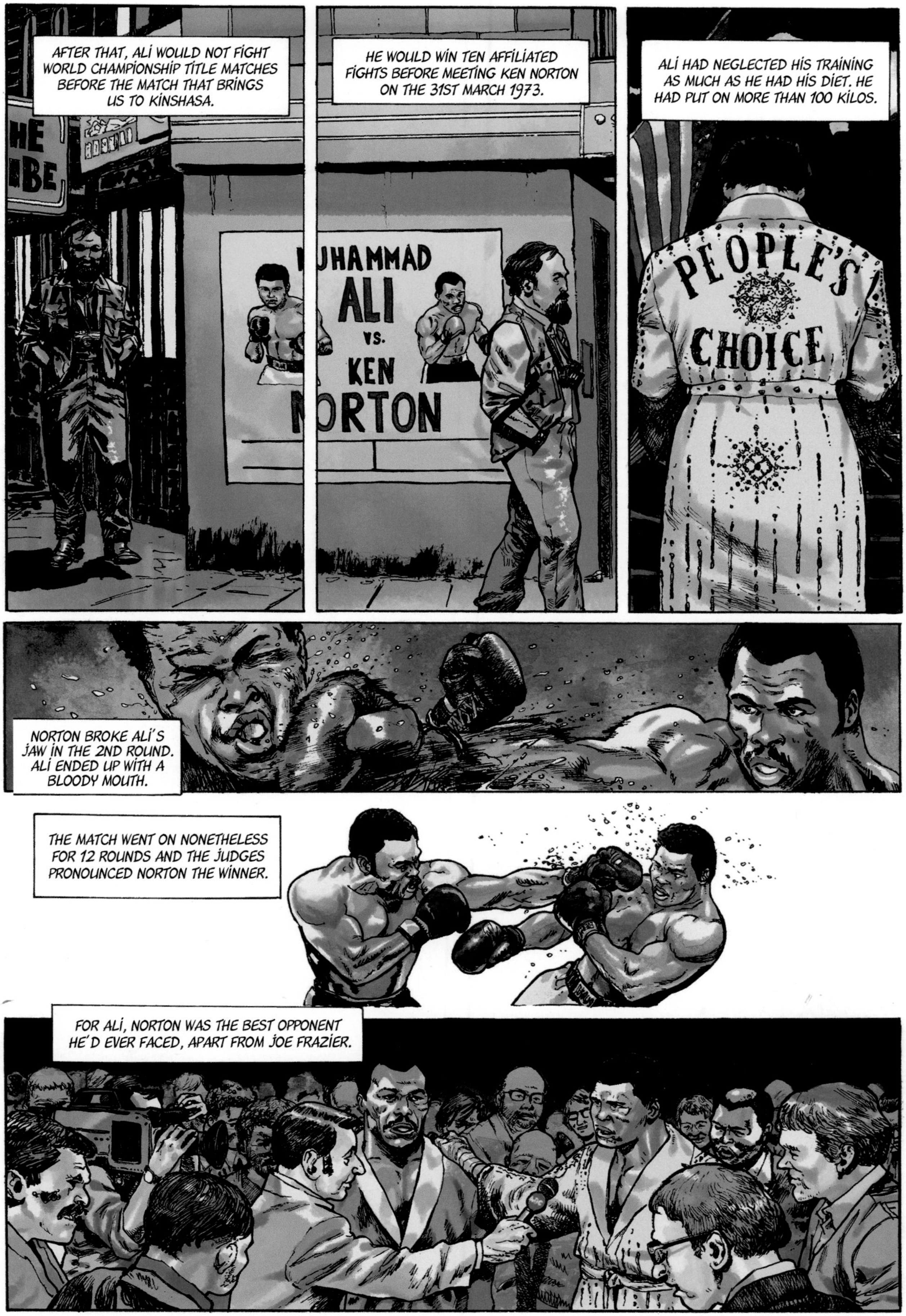

AFTER THAT, ALİ WOULD NOT FIGHT WORLD CHAMPIONSHIP TITLE MATCHES BEFORE THE MATCH THAT BRINGS US TO KINSHASA.
HE WOULD WIN TEN AFFILIATED FIGHTS BEFORE MEETING KEN NORTON ON THE 31ST MARCH 1973.
MUHAMMAD ALI VS. KEN NORTON
ALİ HAD NEGLECTED HIS TRAINING AS MUCH AS HE HAD HIS DIET. HE HAD PUT ON MORE THAN 100 KILOS.
PEOPLE'S CHOICE
NORTON BROKE ALİ'S JAW IN THE 2ND ROUND. ALİ ENDED UP WITH A BLOODY MOUTH.
THE MATCH WENT ON NONETHELESS FOR 12 ROUNDS AND THE JUDGES PRONOUNCED NORTON THE WINNER.
FOR ALİ, NORTON WAS THE BEST OPPONENT HE'D EVER FACED, APART FROM JOE FRAZIER.

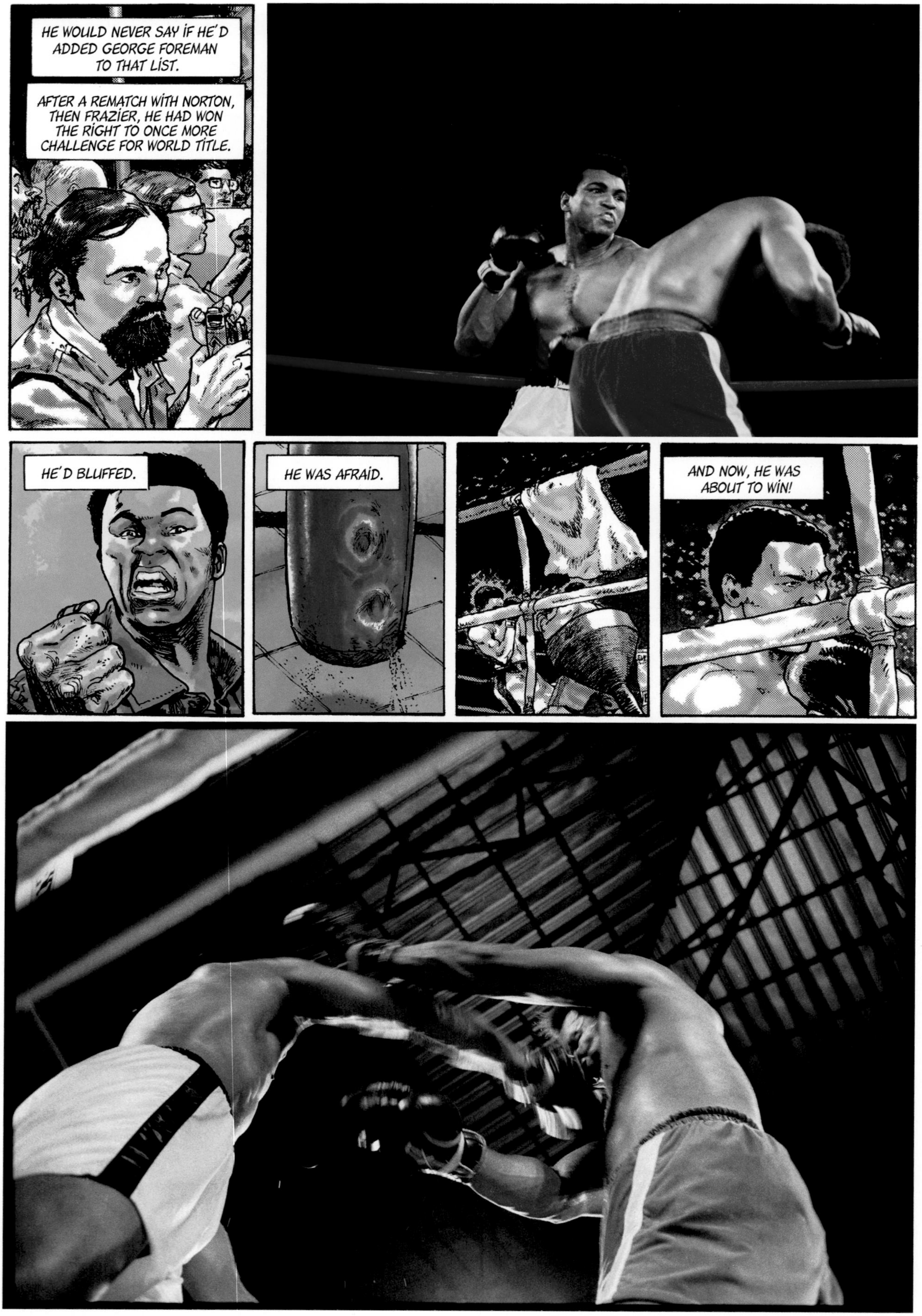
HE WOULD NEVER SAY IF HE'D ADDED GEORGE FOREMAN TO THAT LIST.
AFTER A REMATCH WITH NORTON, THEN FRAZIER, HE HAD WON THE RIGHT TO ONCE MORE CHALLENGE FOR WORLD TITLE.
HE'D BLUFFED.
HE WAS AFRAID.
AND NOW, HE WAS ABOUT TO WIN!

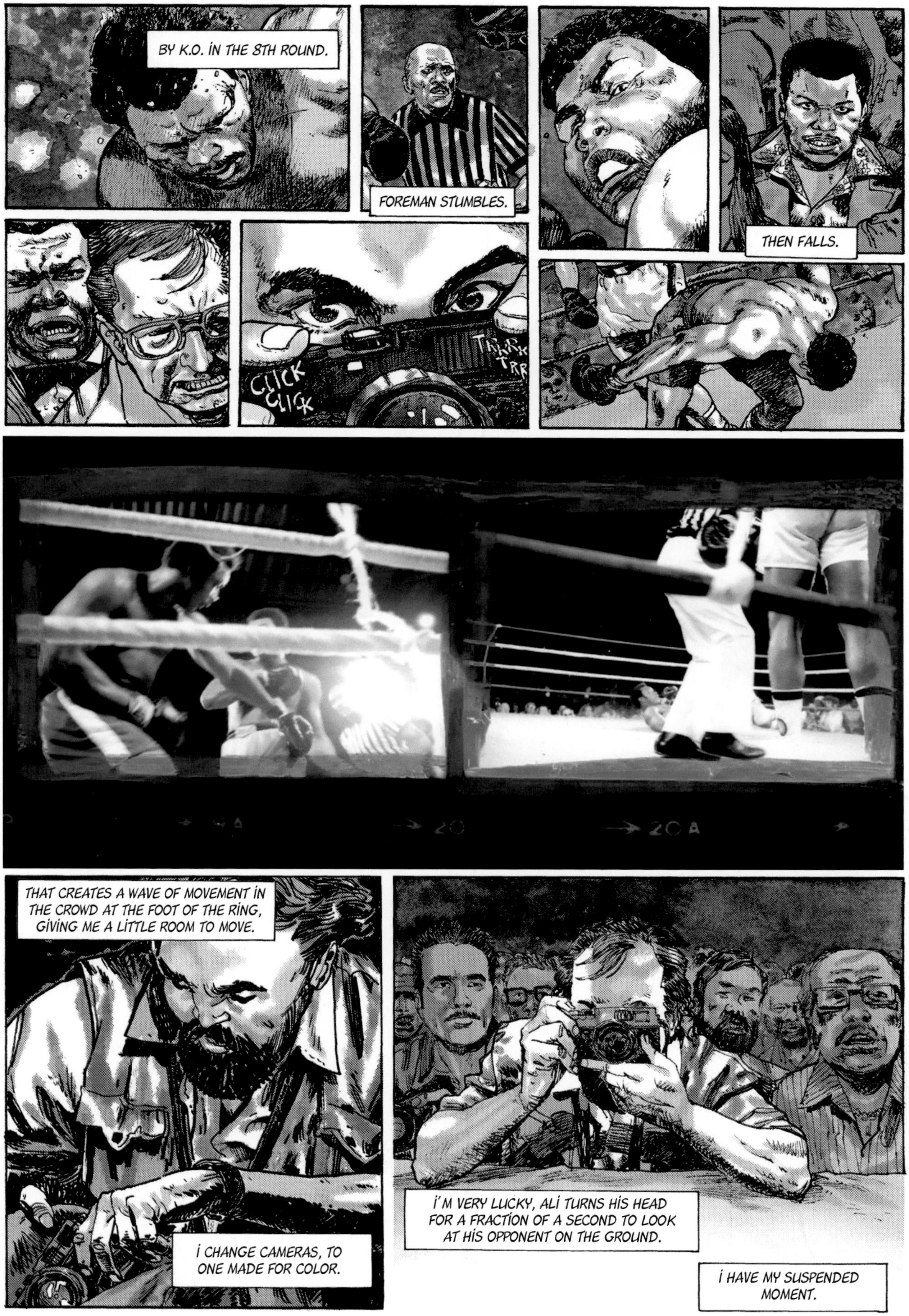
BY K.O. IN THE 8TH ROUND.
FOREMAN STUMBLES.
THEN FALLS.
TRRRK TRR
CLICK CLICK
20
20A
THAT CREATES A WAVE OF MOVEMENT IN THE CROWD AT THE FOOT OF THE RING, GIVING ME A LITTLE ROOM TO MOVE.
I CHANGE CAMERAS, TO ONE MADE FOR COLOR.
I'M VERY LUCKY, ALI TURNS HIS HEAD FOR A FRACTION OF A SECOND TO LOOK AT HIS OPPONENT ON THE GROUND.
I HAVE MY SUSPENDED MOMENT.

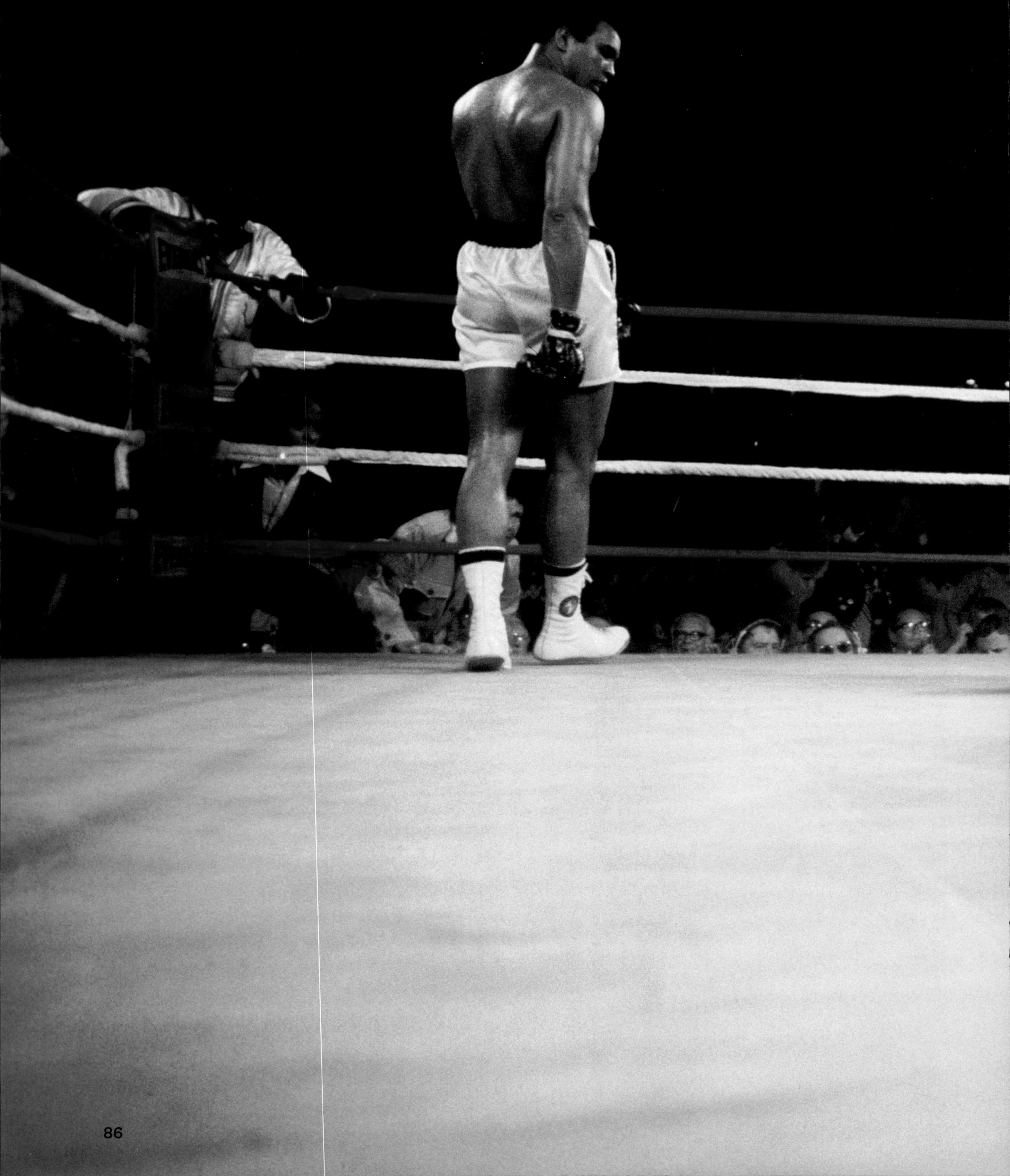

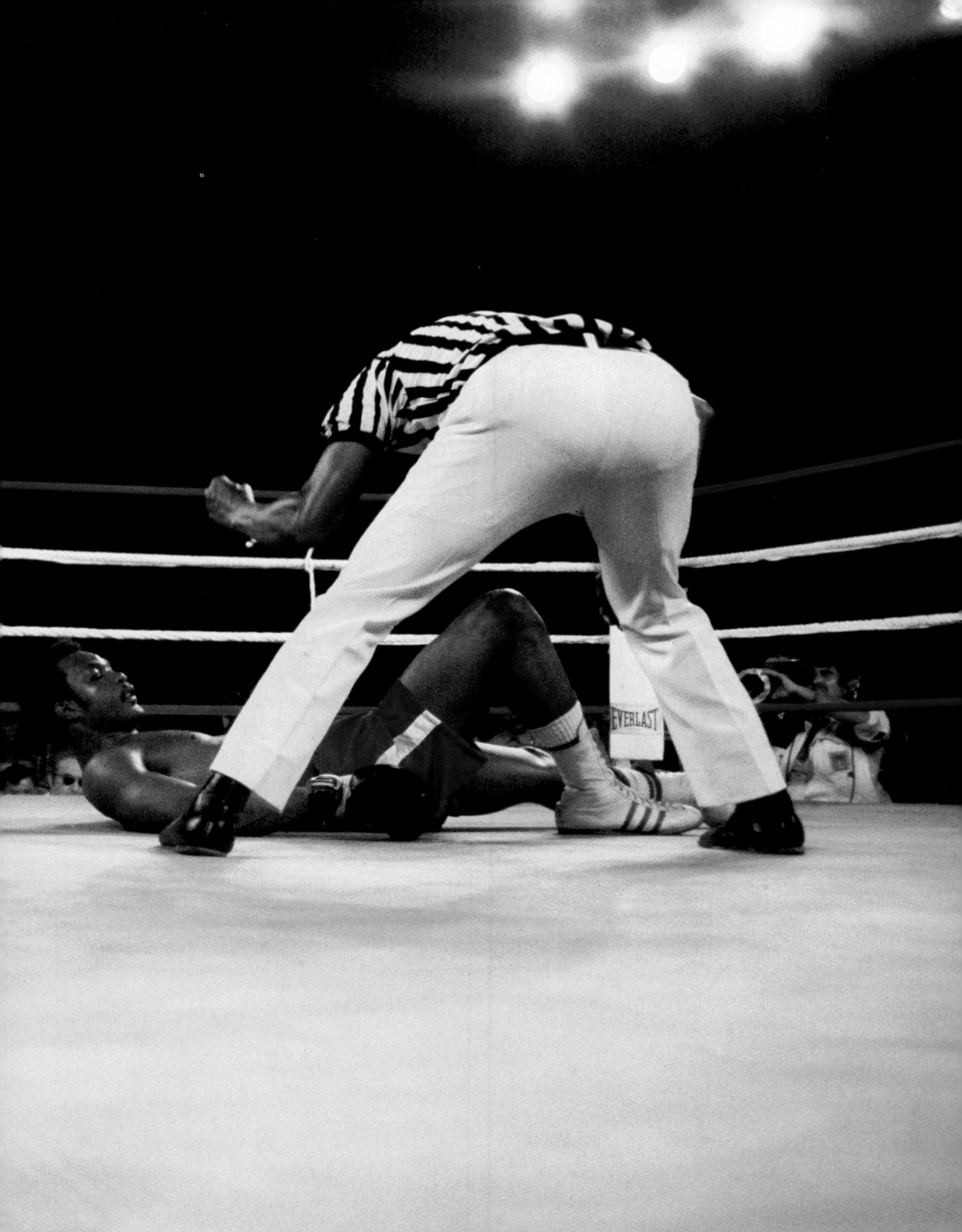
EVERLAST

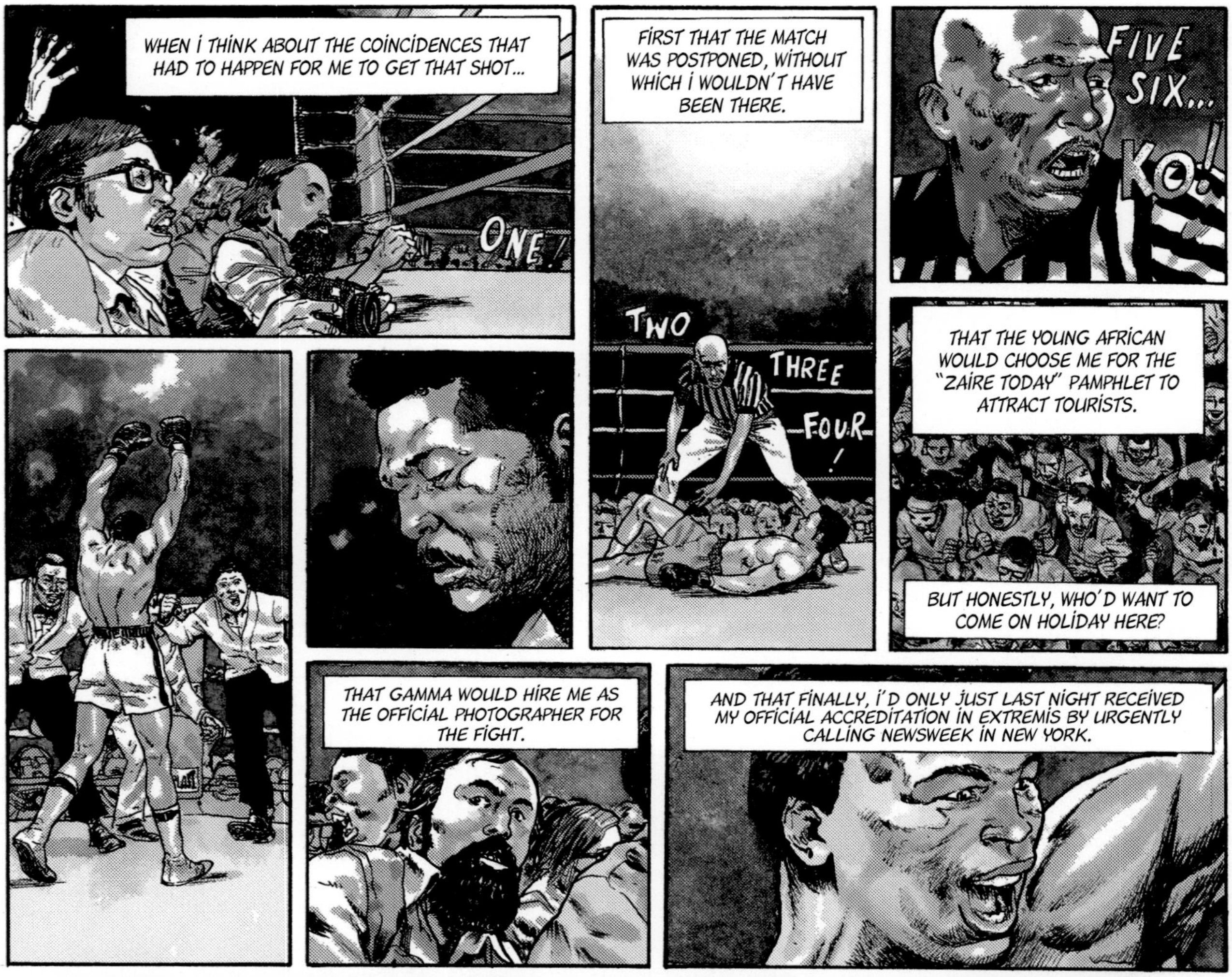
WHEN I THINK ABOUT THE COINCIDENCES THAT HAD TO HAPPEN FOR ME TO GET THAT SHOT...
ONE!
FIRST THAT THE MATCH WAS POSTPONED, WITHOUT WHICH I WOULDN'T HAVE BEEN THERE.
TWO
THREE
FOUR!
FIVE
SIX...
KO!
THAT THE YOUNG AFRICAN WOULD CHOOSE ME FOR THE "ZAIRE TODAY" PAMPHLET TO ATTRACT TOURISTS.
BUT HONESTLY, WHO'D WANT TO COME ON HOLIDAY HERE?
THAT GAMMA WOULD HIRE ME AS THE OFFICIAL PHOTOGRAPHER FOR THE FIGHT.
AND THAT FINALLY, I'D ONLY JUST LAST NIGHT RECEIVED MY OFFICIAL ACCREDITATION IN EXTREMIS BY URGENTLY CALLING NEWSWEEK IN NEW YORK.

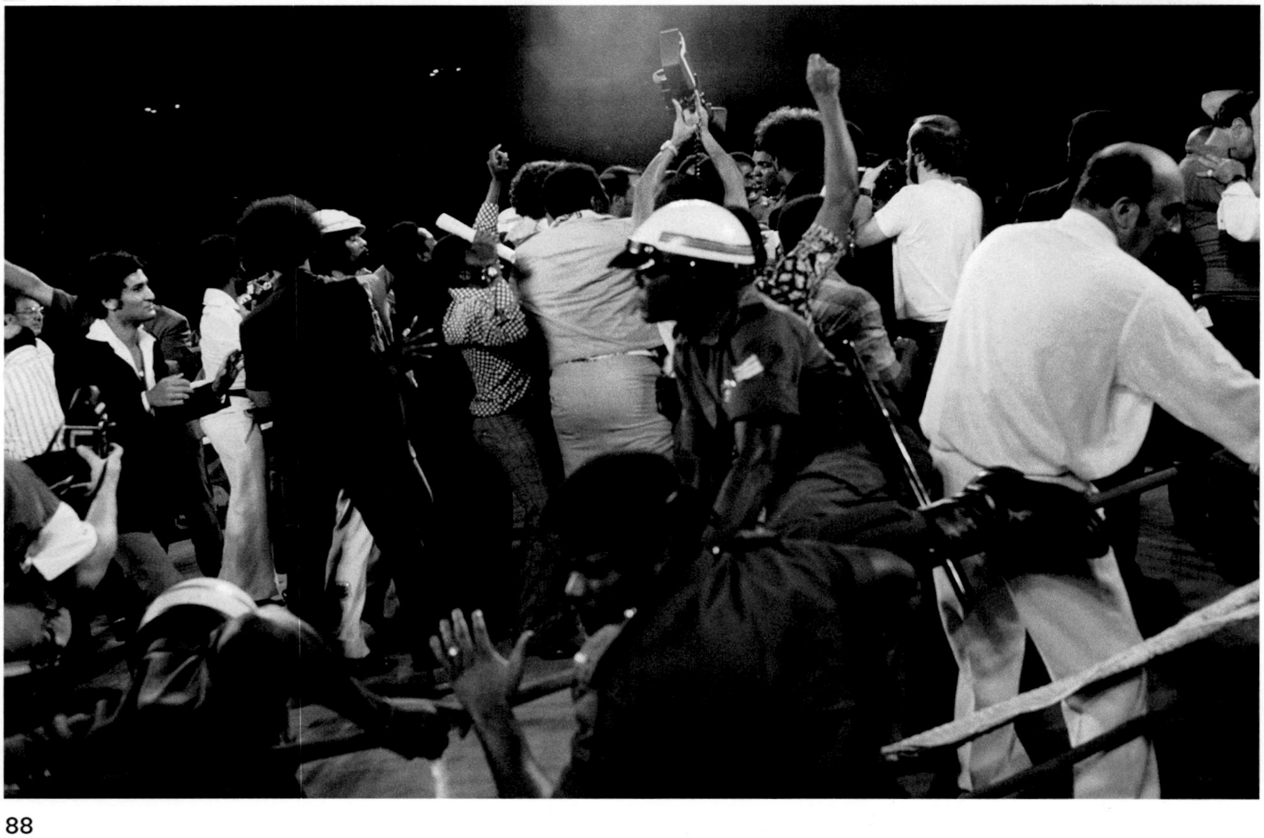

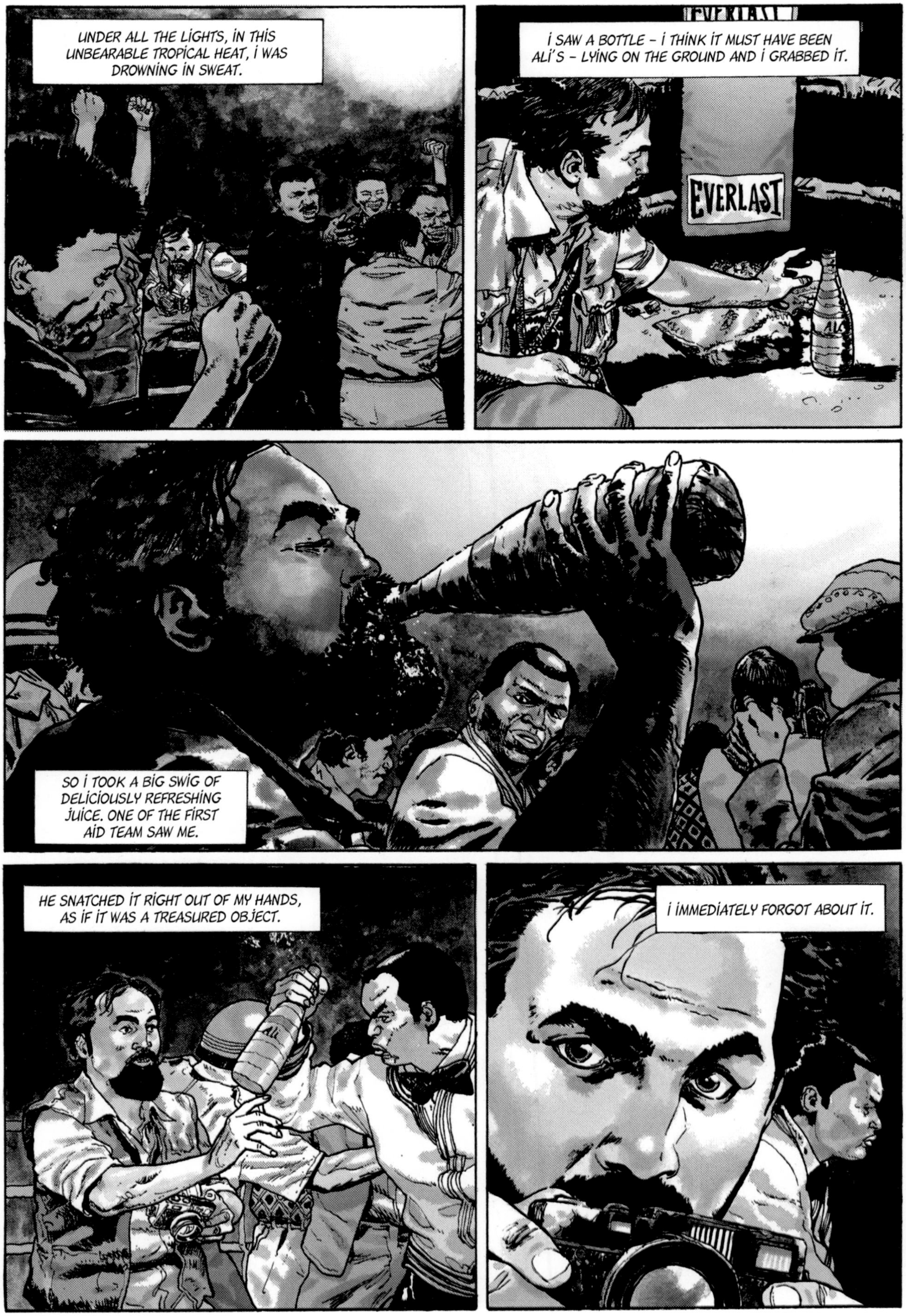
UNDER ALL THE LIGHTS, IN THIS UNBEARABLE TROPICAL HEAT, I WAS DROWNING IN SWEAT.
I SAW A BOTTLE – I THINK IT MUST HAVE BEEN ALI'S – LYING ON THE GROUND AND I GRABBED IT.
EVERLAST
SO I TOOK A BIG SWIG OF DELICIOUSLY REFRESHING JUICE. ONE OF THE FIRST AID TEAM SAW ME.
HE SNATCHED IT RIGHT OUT OF MY HANDS, AS IF IT WAS A TREASURED OBJECT.
I IMMEDIATELY FORGOT ABOUT IT.

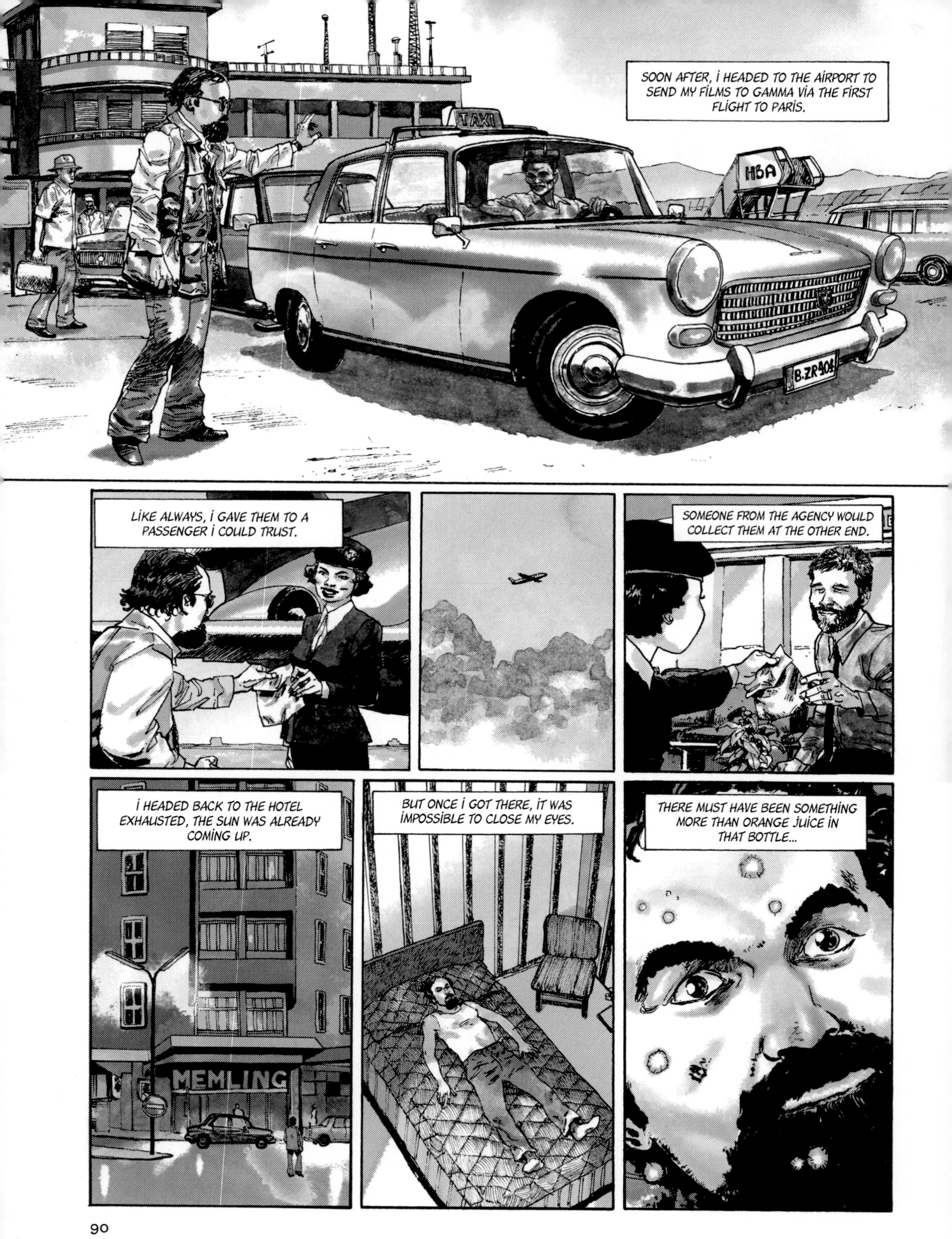
SOON AFTER, I HEADED TO THE AIRPORT TO SEND MY FILMS TO GAMMA VIA THE FIRST FLIGHT TO PARIS.
TAXI
HBA
LIKE ALWAYS, I GAVE THEM TO A PASSENGER I COULD TRUST.
SOMEONE FROM THE AGENCY WOULD COLLECT THEM AT THE OTHER END.
I HEADED BACK TO THE HOTEL EXHAUSTED, THE SUN WAS ALREADY COMING UP.
MEMLING
BUT ONCE I GOT THERE, IT WAS IMPOSSIBLE TO CLOSE MY EYES.
THERE MUST HAVE BEEN SOMETHING MORE THAN ORANGE JUICE IN THAT BOTTLE...

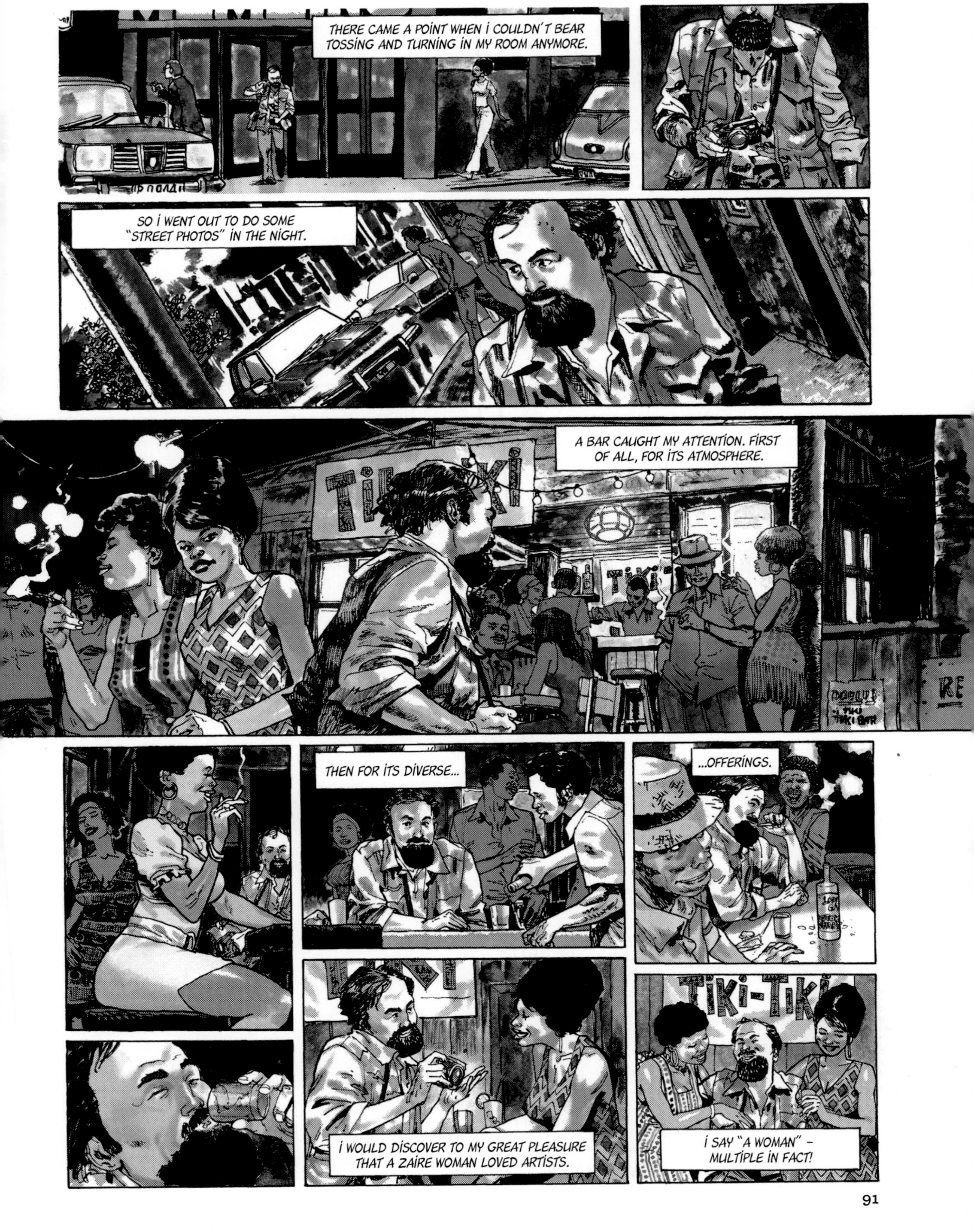

THERE CAME A POINT WHEN I COULDN'T BEAR TOSSING AND TURNING IN MY ROOM ANYMORE.
SO I WENT OUT TO DO SOME "STREET PHOTOS" IN THE NIGHT.
A BAR CAUGHT MY ATTENTION. FIRST OF ALL, FOR ITS ATMOSPHERE.
TIKI
TIKI
THEN FOR ITS DIVERSE...
...OFFERINGS.
I WOULD DISCOVER TO MY GREAT PLEASURE THAT A ZAIRE WOMAN LOVED ARTISTS.
TIKI-TIKI
I SAY "A WOMAN" – MULTIPLE IN FACT!

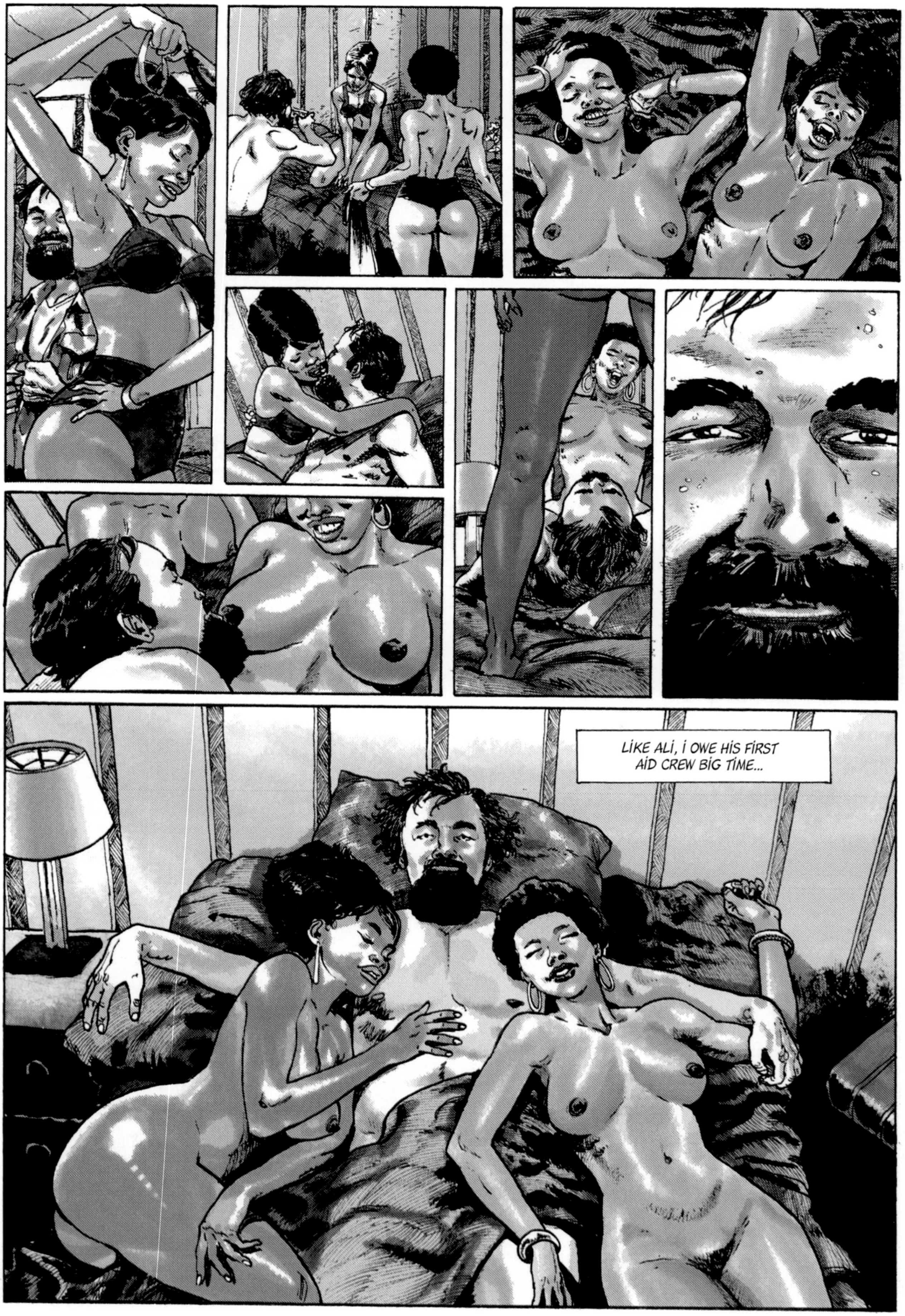
LIKE ALI, I OWE HIS FIRST AID CREW BIG TIME...

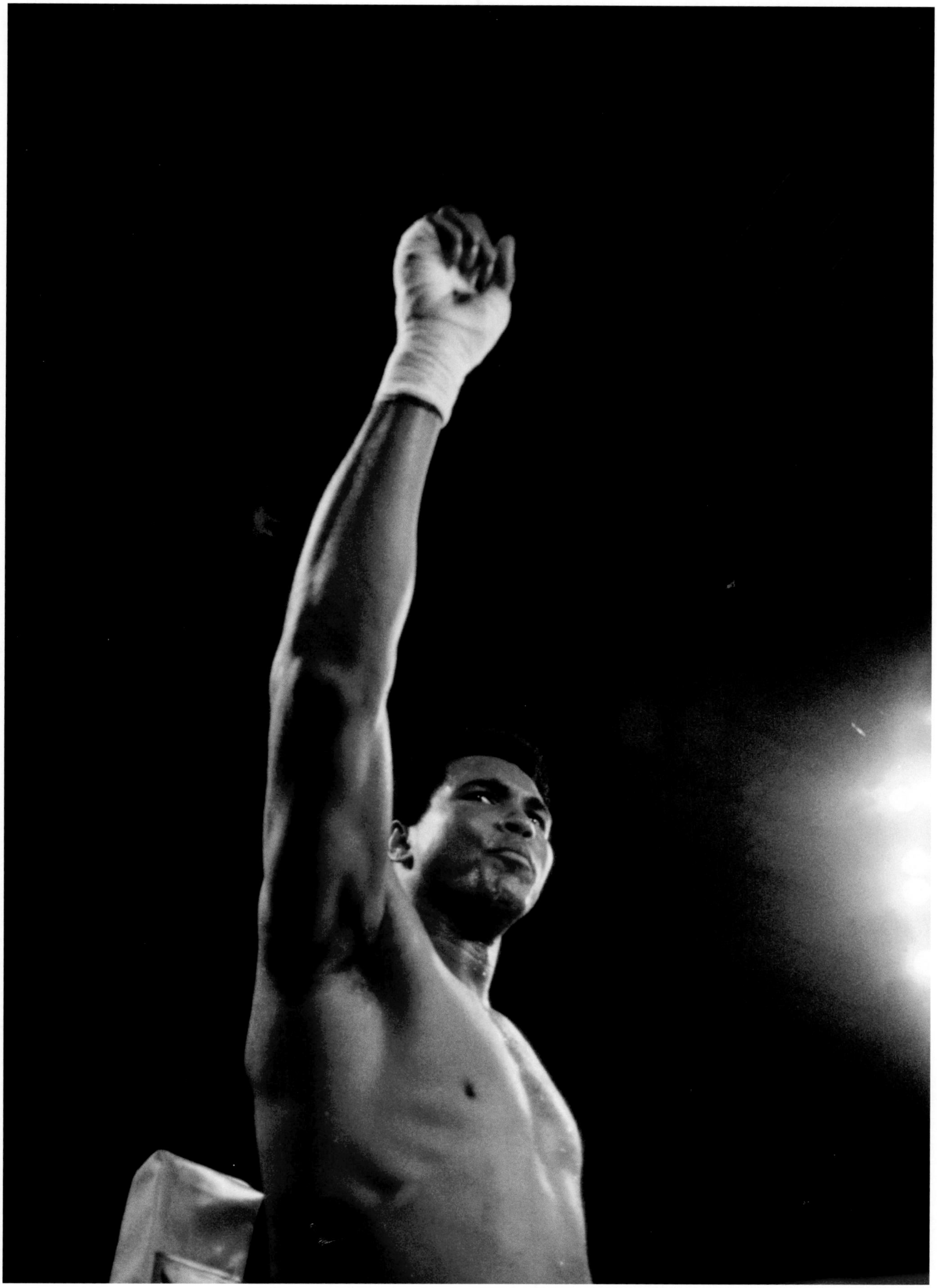

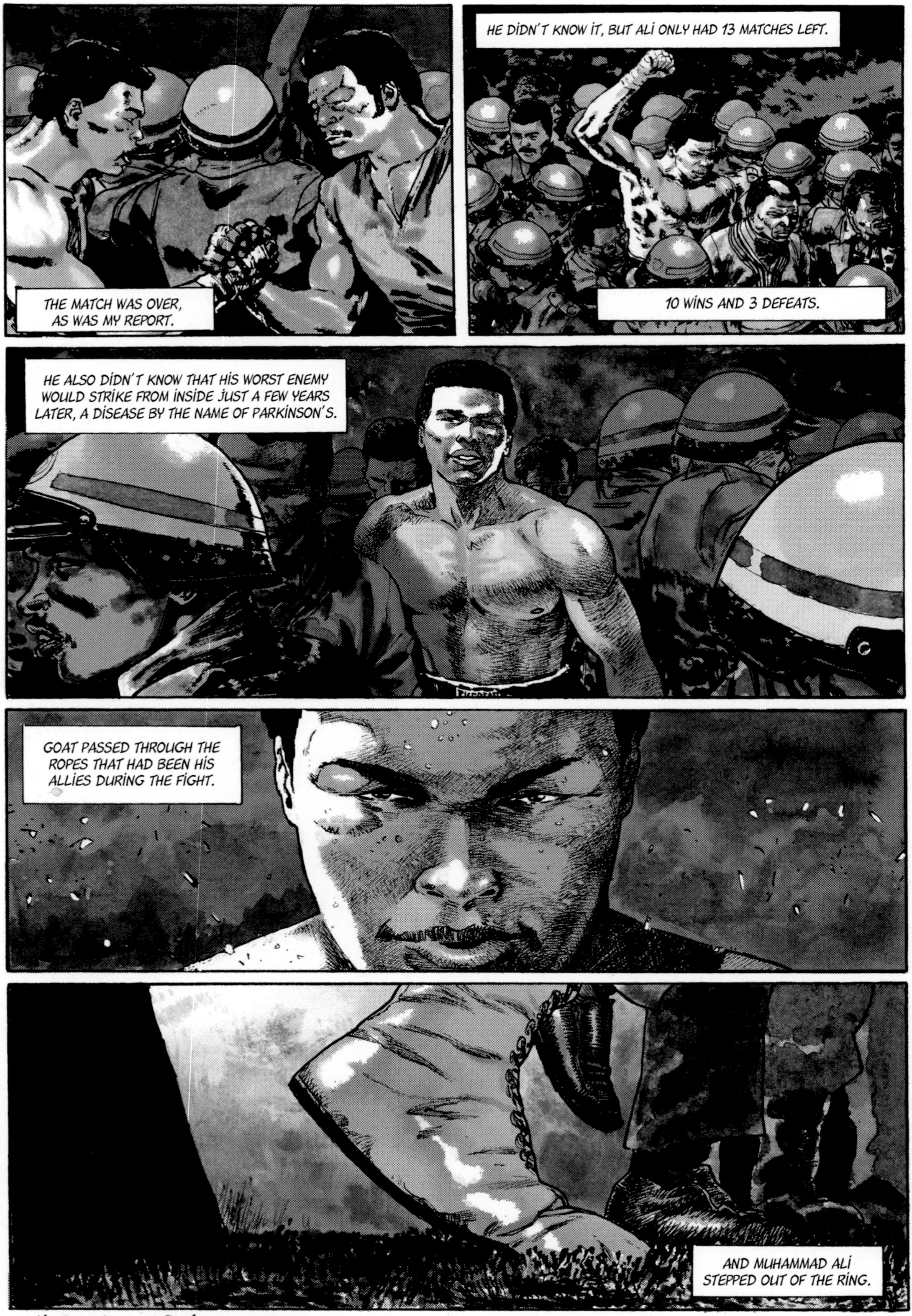
THE MATCH WAS OVER, AS WAS MY REPORT.
HE DIDN'T KNOW IT, BUT ALI ONLY HAD 13 MATCHES LEFT.
10 WINS AND 3 DEFEATS.
HE ALSO DIDN'T KNOW THAT HIS WORST ENEMY WOULD STRIKE FROM INSIDE JUST A FEW YEARS LATER, A DISEASE BY THE NAME OF PARKINSON'S.
GOAT PASSED THROUGH THE ROPES THAT HAD BEEN HIS ALLIES DURING THE FIGHT.
AND MUHAMMAD ALI STEPPED OUT OF THE RING.

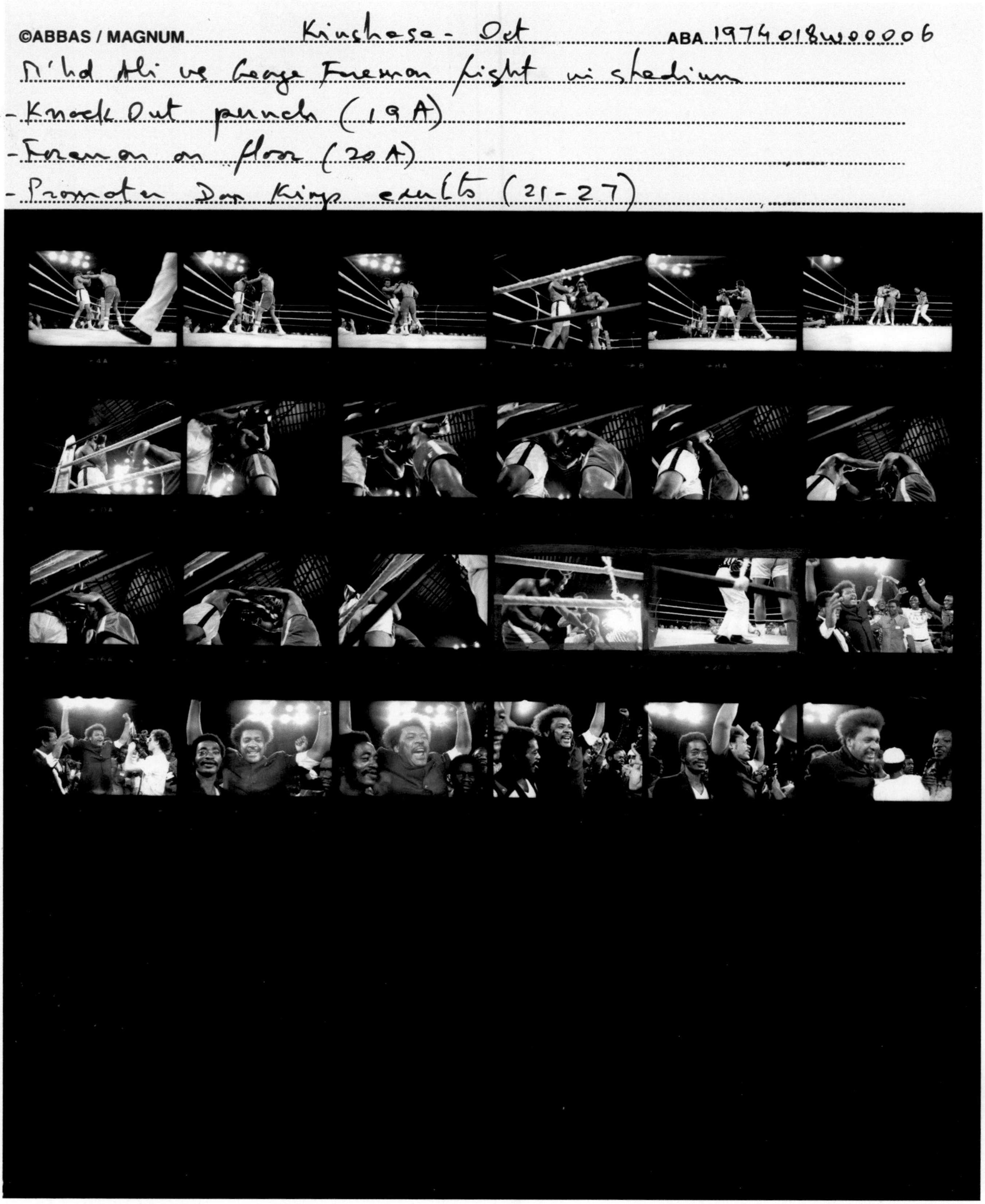
©ABBAS / MAGNUM
Kinshasa - Oct
ABA 1974018W00006
M'hd Ali vs George Foreman fight in stadium
- Knock Out punch (19A)
- Foreman on floor (20A)
- Promoter Don King exults (21-27)

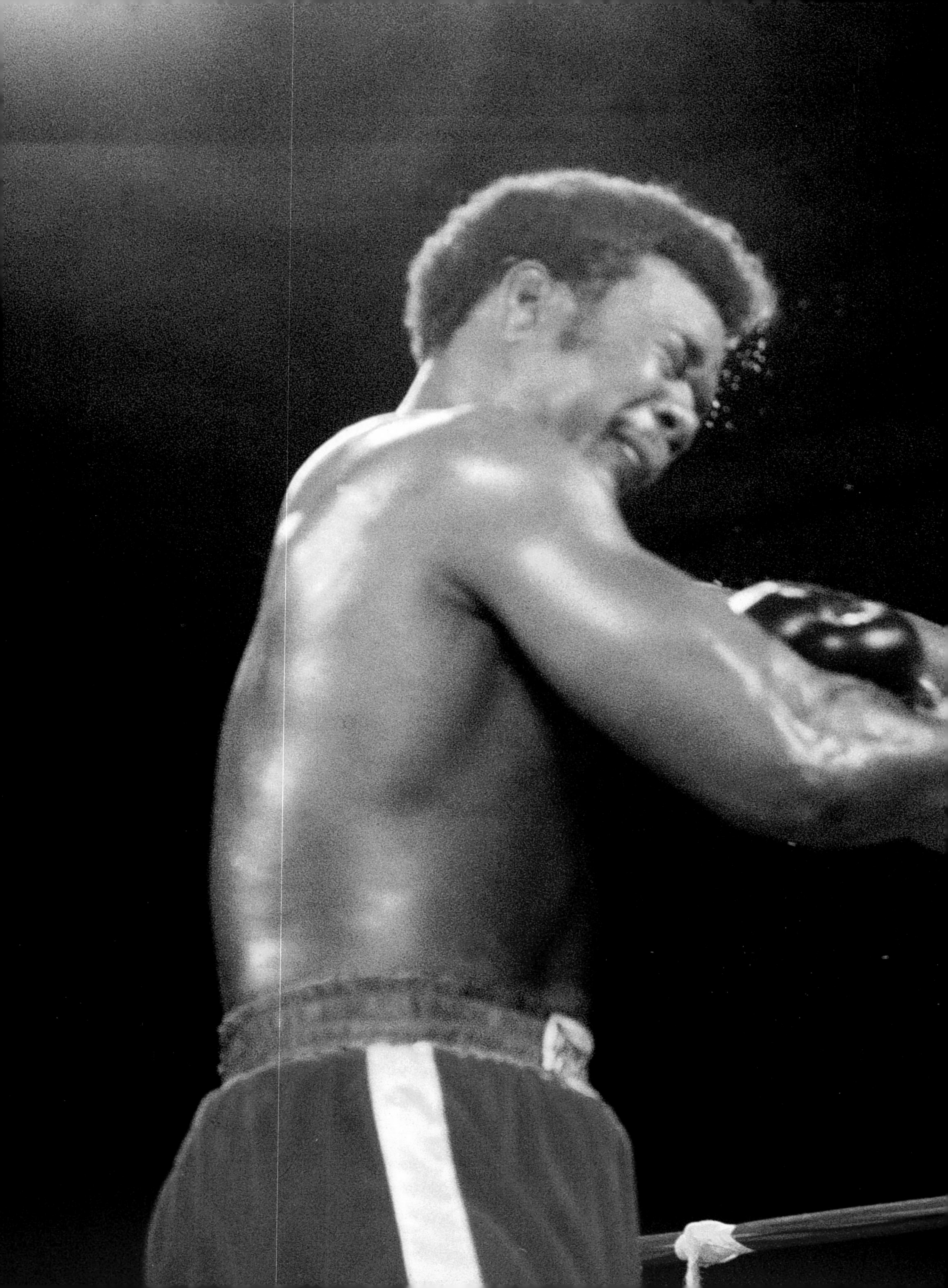

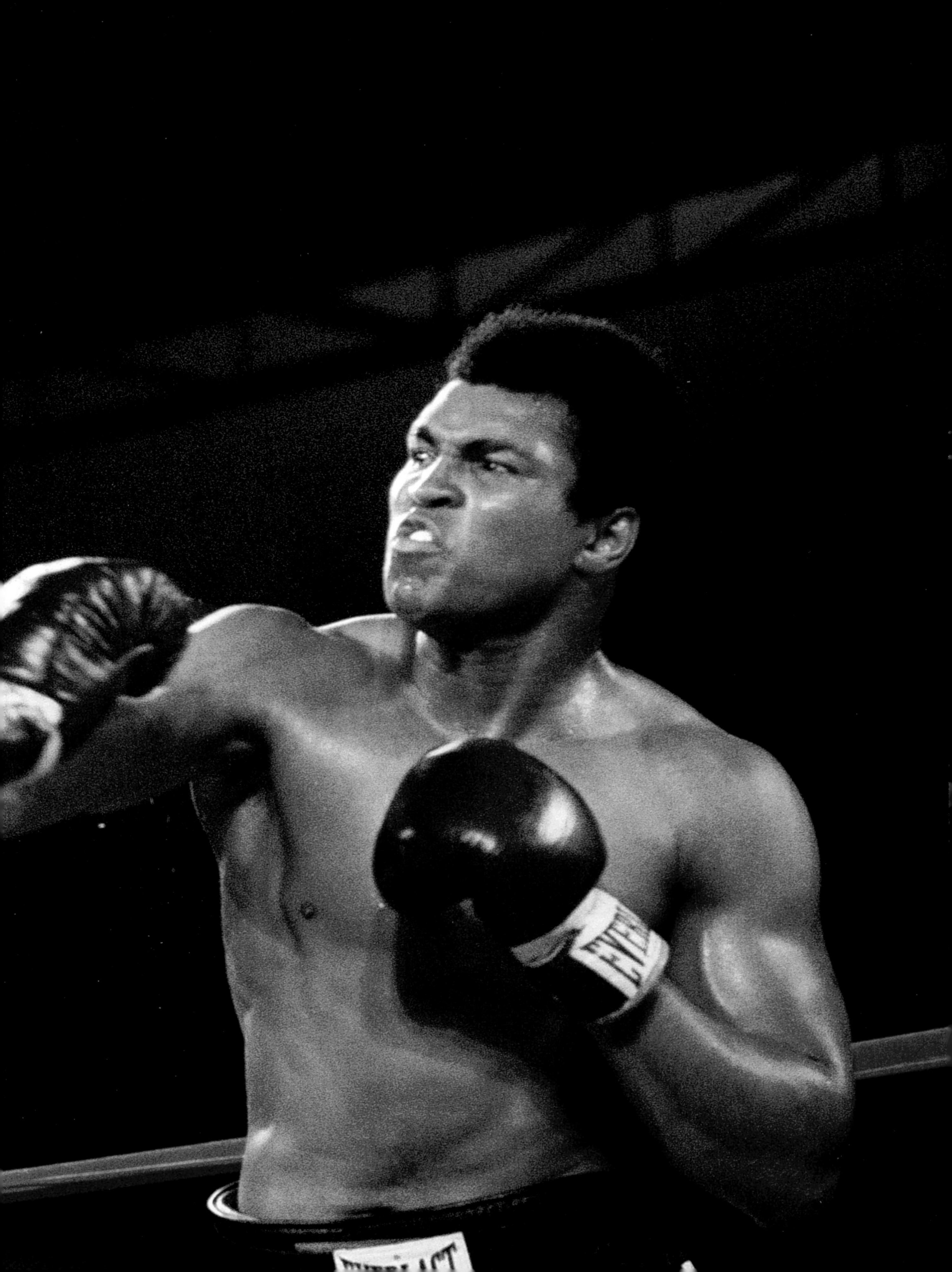

THE STORY OF THE STORY

Every story contains other stories mixed in.

Some more than others. That's the case for the one we tell in this book. It's seen many twists and turns along the way – some of which could have spelled the end for it – before falling into your hands.

In opposition to the narration of our tale, let's start at the beginning.

One night, while flicking through piles of photography books on the carpet, I asked myself if, being a fan of comics, wouldn't it be cool to tell the story of photographers' lives through comic panels.

And the easiest thing would be to go through an agency rather than to contact them individually. I chose the oldest and most famous: Magnum Photos.

I found a contact address on their website and wrote to them.

I went to sleep and got back to my daily business the next day, believing that there was no chance my email would amount to anything.

Five days later, to my great surprise, I got a reply. It wasn't particularly long, but I called Mr Saccomani, who showed great interest. We arranged to meet.

The next Thursday at 11:30, I found myself standing in front of the agency of most of my favorite photographers. I asked Séverine Tréfouel, my collaborator, to accompany me.

I rang the bell, and Josef Koudelka welcomed us in. He was very likeable, offering us cakes before retiring to the first room on the right. We sat on the huge couches encircling the waiting room, after perusing the striking shots displayed on the walls: those of Jerôme Sessini, who we later learned had dreamed of becoming a comic creator.

Clément Saccomani arrived and the discussion went extremely well. We decided to launch the project between us before talking to publishers.

At its heart: we should never redraw a photo as it stood, to reframe it, and to never put a speech balloon or text over it. That would kill the image.

At the same time, we asked artist friends if they could create an illustration using a Magnum photo as a point of inspiration, to represent the photographer in the middle of taking it.

Benoît Blary, Fred Boot, Julien Bouhier, Dominique Driller, Kim Hyunjin, Kim Jung-Gi, Étienne Le Roux, Olivier Martin, Nicolas Nemiri, Gaelle Hersent, Roberto Ricci, Benoît Springer and Terreur Graphics answered the call. May they be blessed for all eternity.

Jean David Morvan

Magnum Photos in Comic Form?

To: Clément Saccomani

Dear Sir,
I am writing to you because I am a comics professional, as well an amateur photography fan.
To quickly introduce myself, my name is Jean-David Morvan. I've been a writer for over twenty years, and have written some 200 comic albums, primarily on the Spirou and Fantasio series, for which I wrote books 47 to 50. My bestselling series Sillage is translated into more than 15 languages and has reached volume 15.
Please find below the link to my Wikipedia page, not to big myself up (that would be ridiculous!), but to show you that I am indeed a professional, and write to you in a serious manner.
https://en.wikipedia.org/wiki/Jean-David_Morvan
First of all, I hope I am not disturbing you, and that it is indeed yourself who might be able to have a reply to such a request... If not, please excuse the mistake. If this is the case, I would be very grateful if you could be so kind as to point me in the right direction of who to contact.
Let me get to the heart of this email:
I would like to create a comic, with the publisher to be decided later, a collection that would recount the lives of Magnum photographers and would revolve around one of their famous photos.
A biography if you will, told through striking images.
And there you have it, it's a fairly simple concept that you may have already been offered, but it seems to me a thrilling project. I would be remiss if I didn't discuss it with you.
With many thanks for your attention, and best regards,
Jean David Morvan.

Clément Saccomani

Re: Magnum Photos in Comic Form?

To: Jean David Morvan

Hello,
Thank you for your email.
It's an ambitious project, and I think we should meet soon.
Are you available next week? What about Thursday morning?

Looking forward to your reply,
CS

MAGNUM
Comic Project

Concept

Magnum Comics offer the chance to experience the story of a photographer, through drawn images. And thus, of the report for which they worked. And as a further result, of the photographer's life.

This "decisive moment" is only the visible tip of the iceberg. This project reveals – finally – those invisible aspects.

Structure

Each report will be tackled in 8 pages of drawn comic. We could create several stories about the same photographer.

The advantage of telling the reports through short stories allows us to recruit the best international comic artists of the European scene to participate. If their schedule is too busy for a full album, they could make time for 8 pages for an exceptional project such as our own.

In this way, we would have the advantage of having the best comic artists illustrating the best photographers.

Furthermore, it makes it possible to work with authors living in the country the report is about, in order to raise the credibility of the project. This will help the publication of the books in different countries.

Preliminary list

I've created a preliminary list of photographers and their report, to which I've attached – as a general idea for now – some artists.

These are people who I currently have easy access to.

Once the project has been launched, with your authorization to print, it's clear that the prestigious nature of the project will allow me to convince more prestigious artists. It's also important to have a few for the launch who will get people talking.

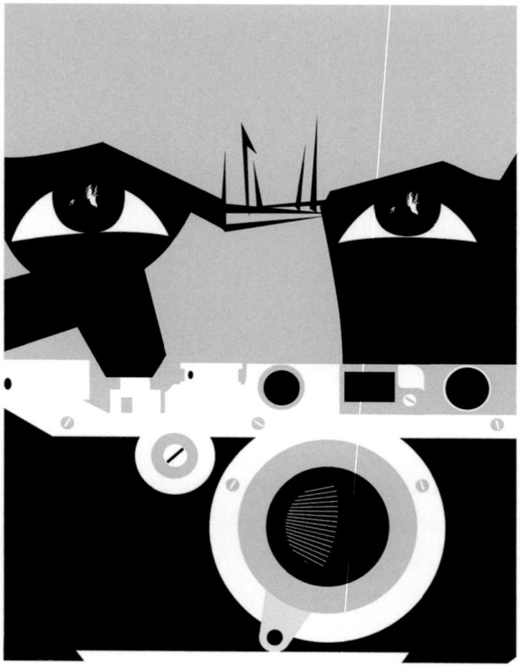

Chim

Fred Boot

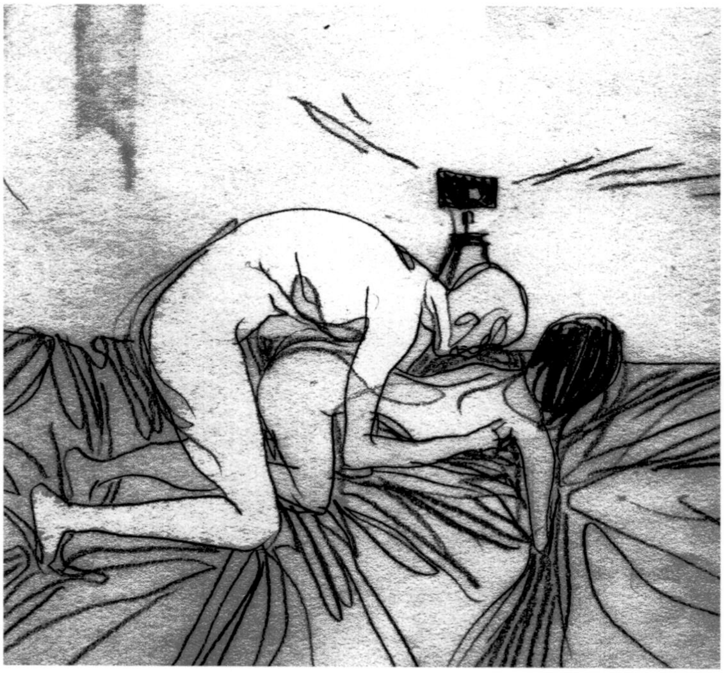

Antoine D'Agata

Nicolas Nemiri

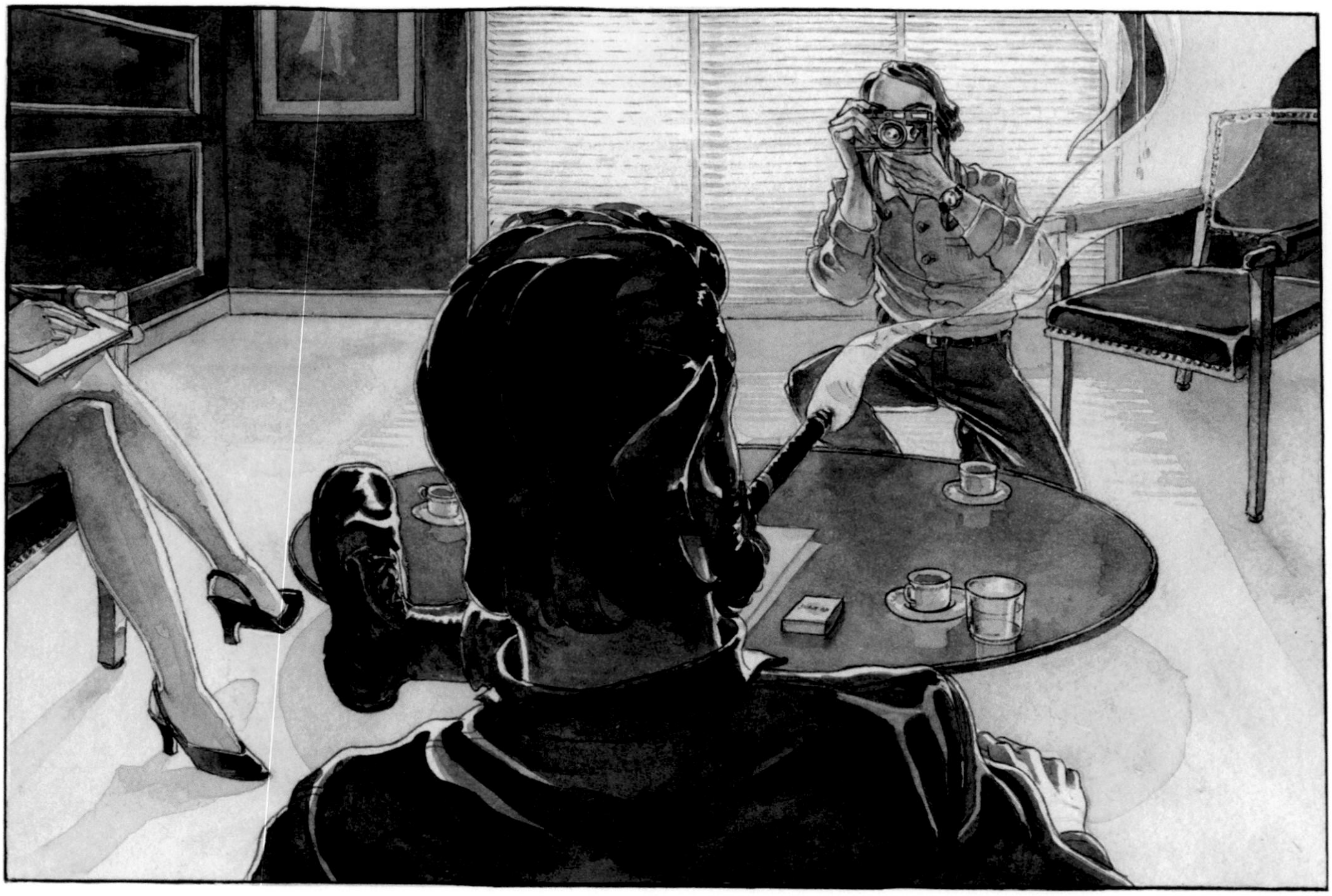

René Burri

Benoît Blary

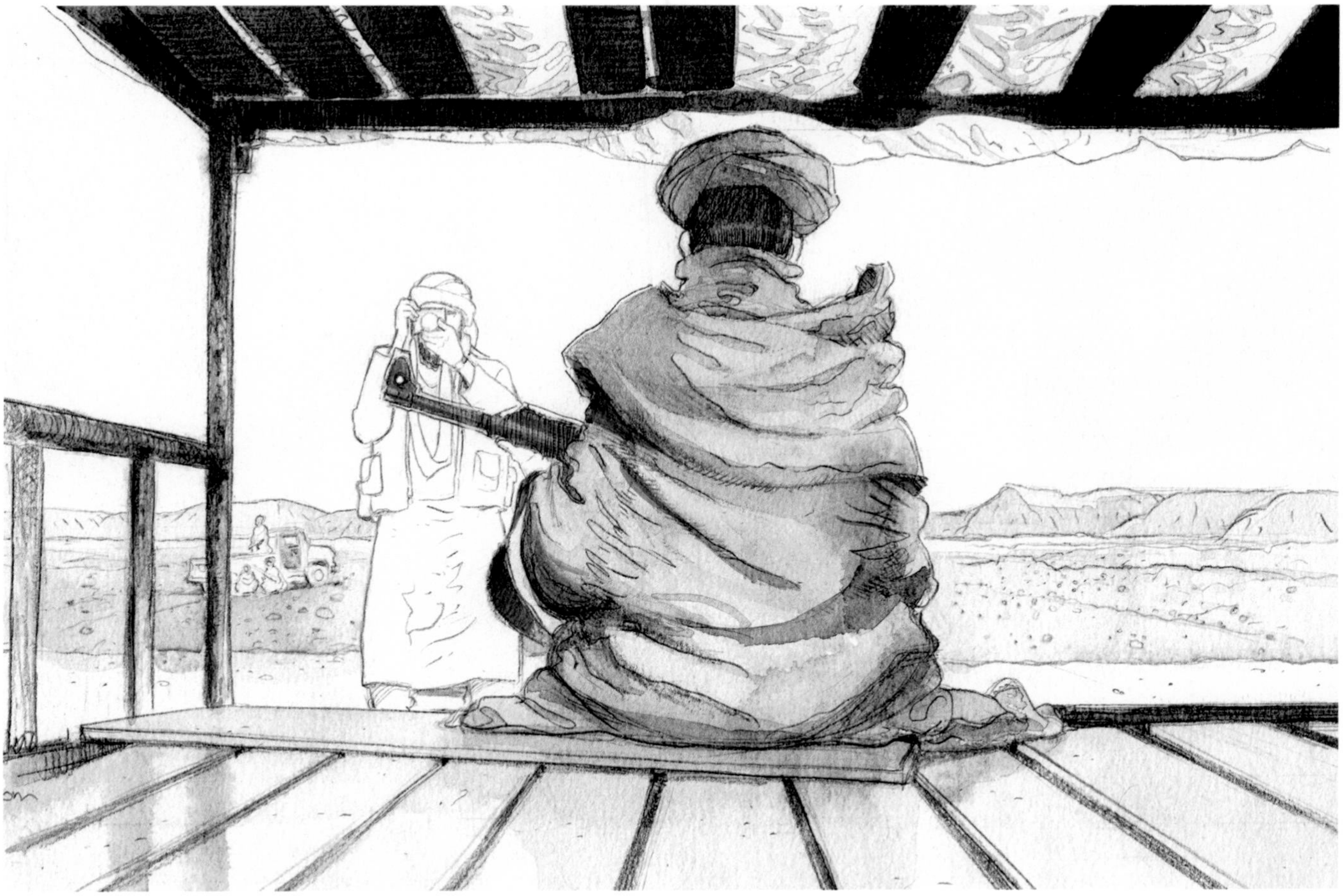

Abbas

Olivier Martin

(Artists demonstrate their perspective on photographers capturing their iconic moments.)

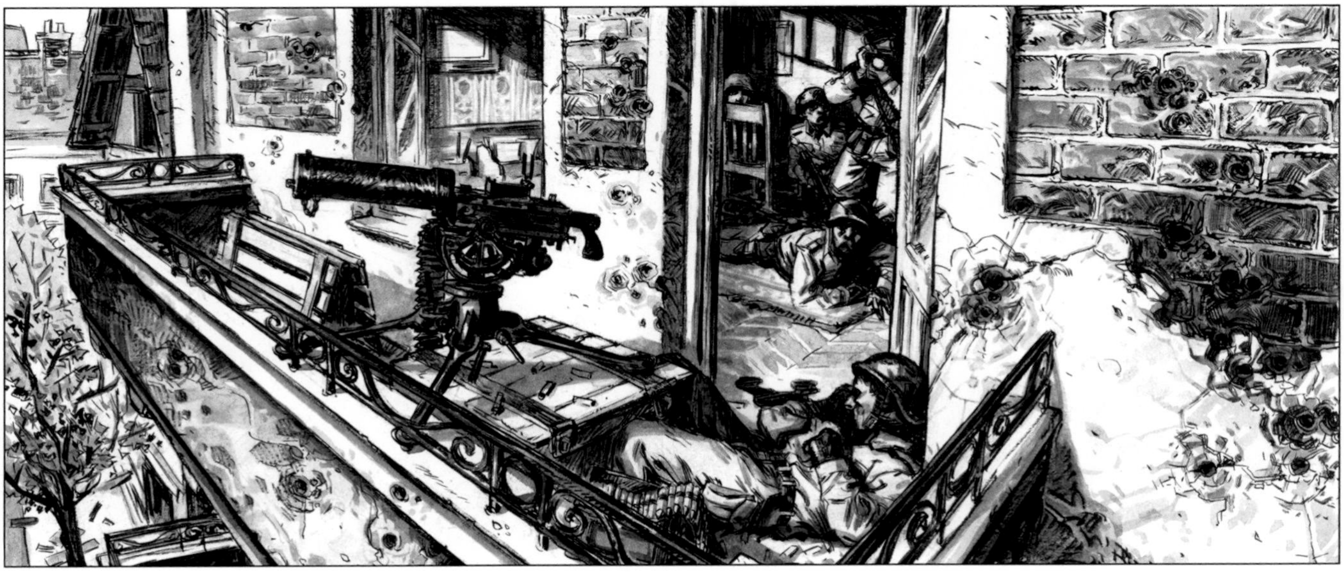

Robert Capa

Roberto Ricci

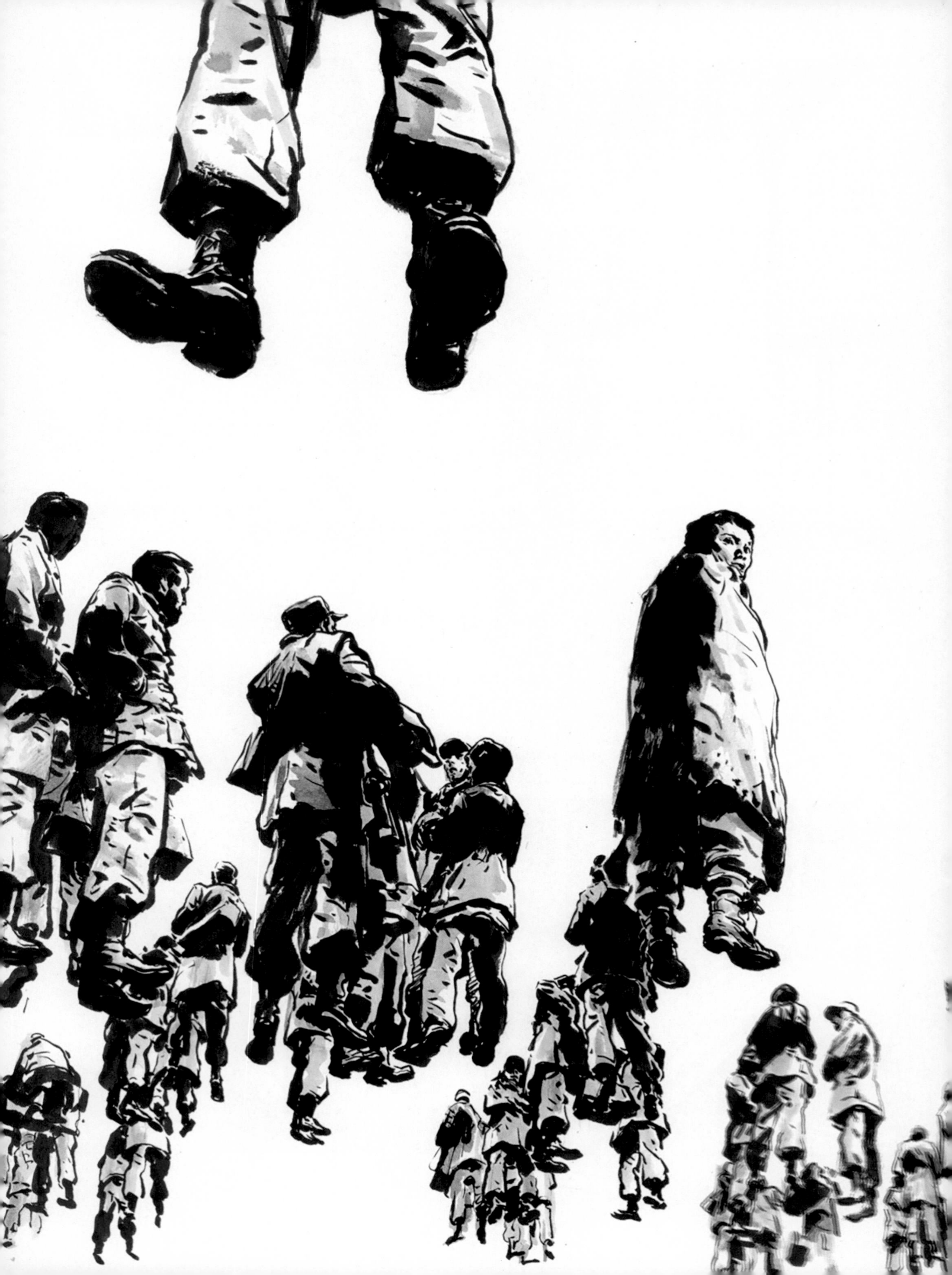

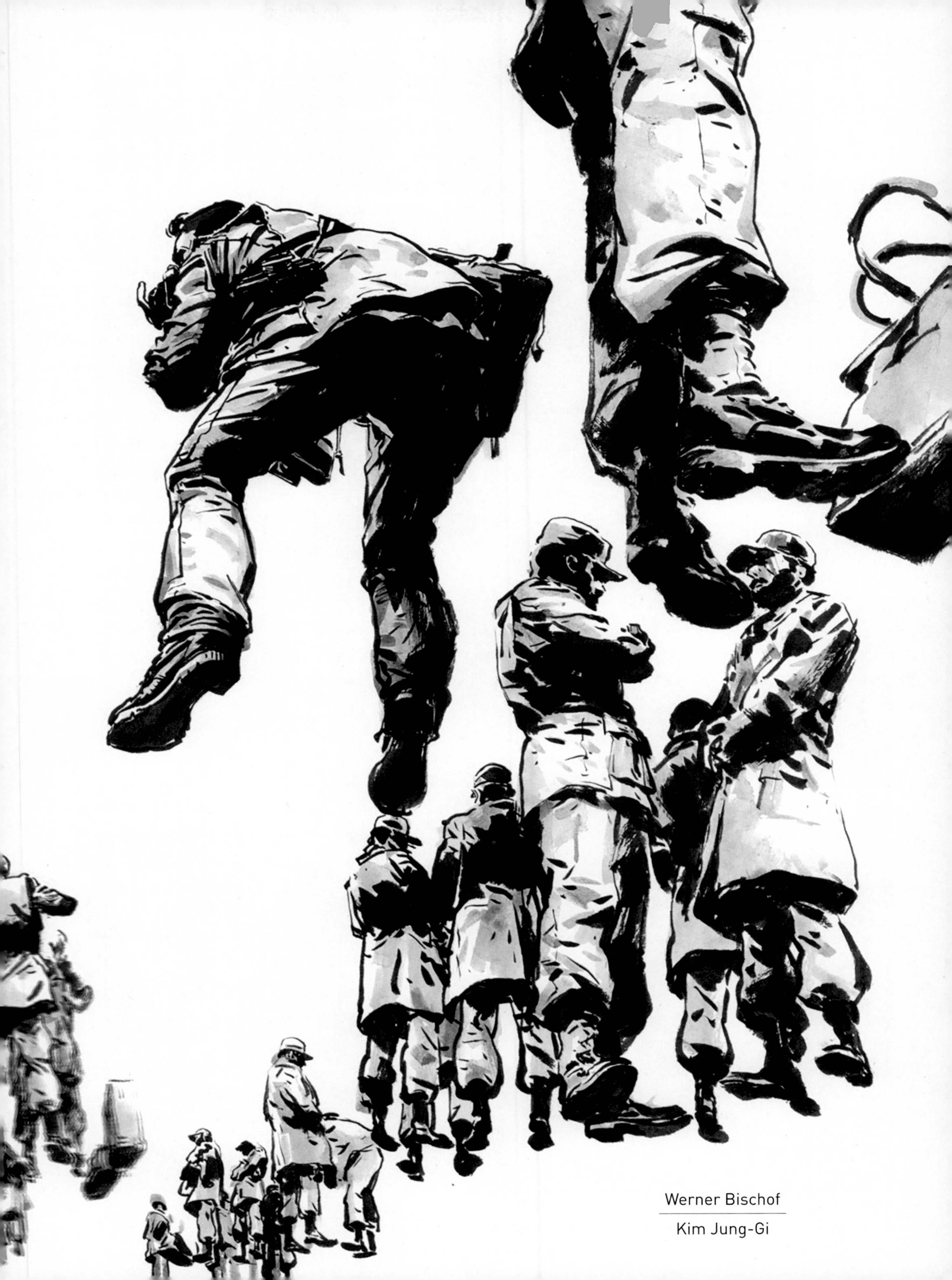

Werner Bischof

Kim Jung-Gi

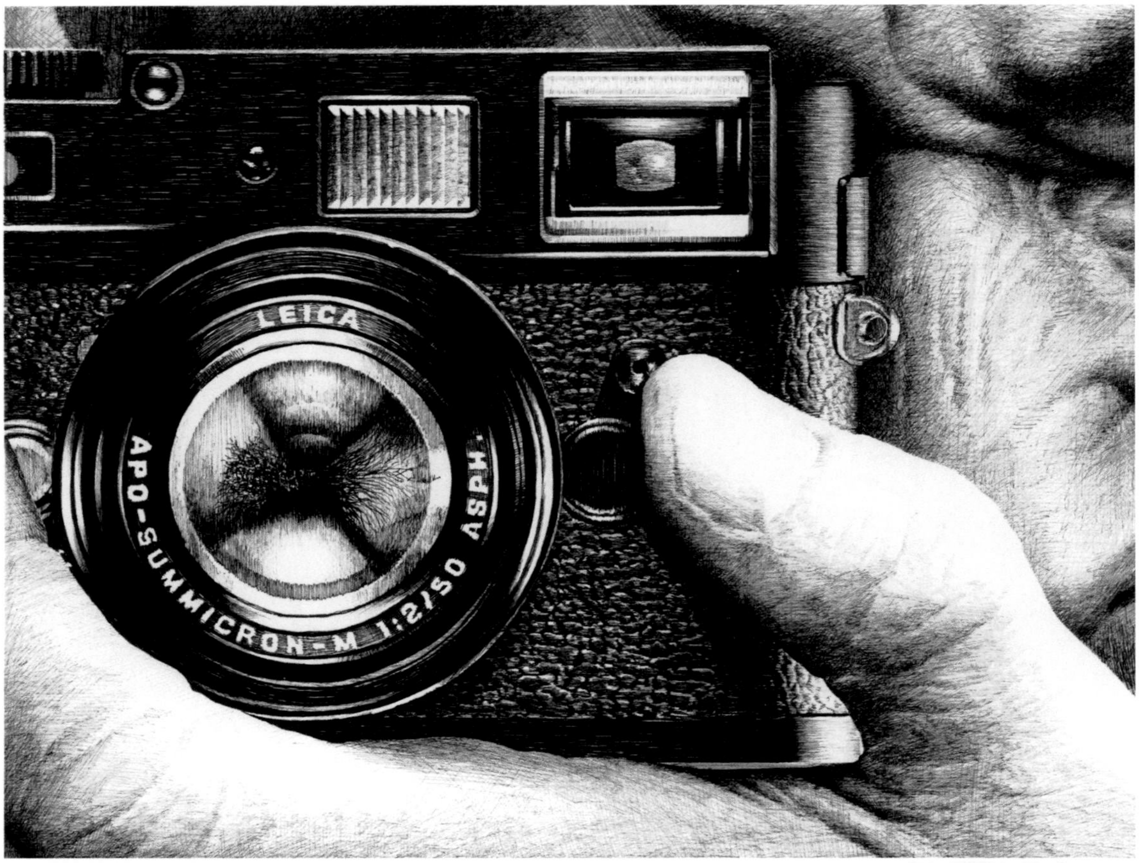
LEICA
APO-SUMMICRON-M 1:2/50 ASPH.

Jacob Aue Sobol

HyunJin Kim

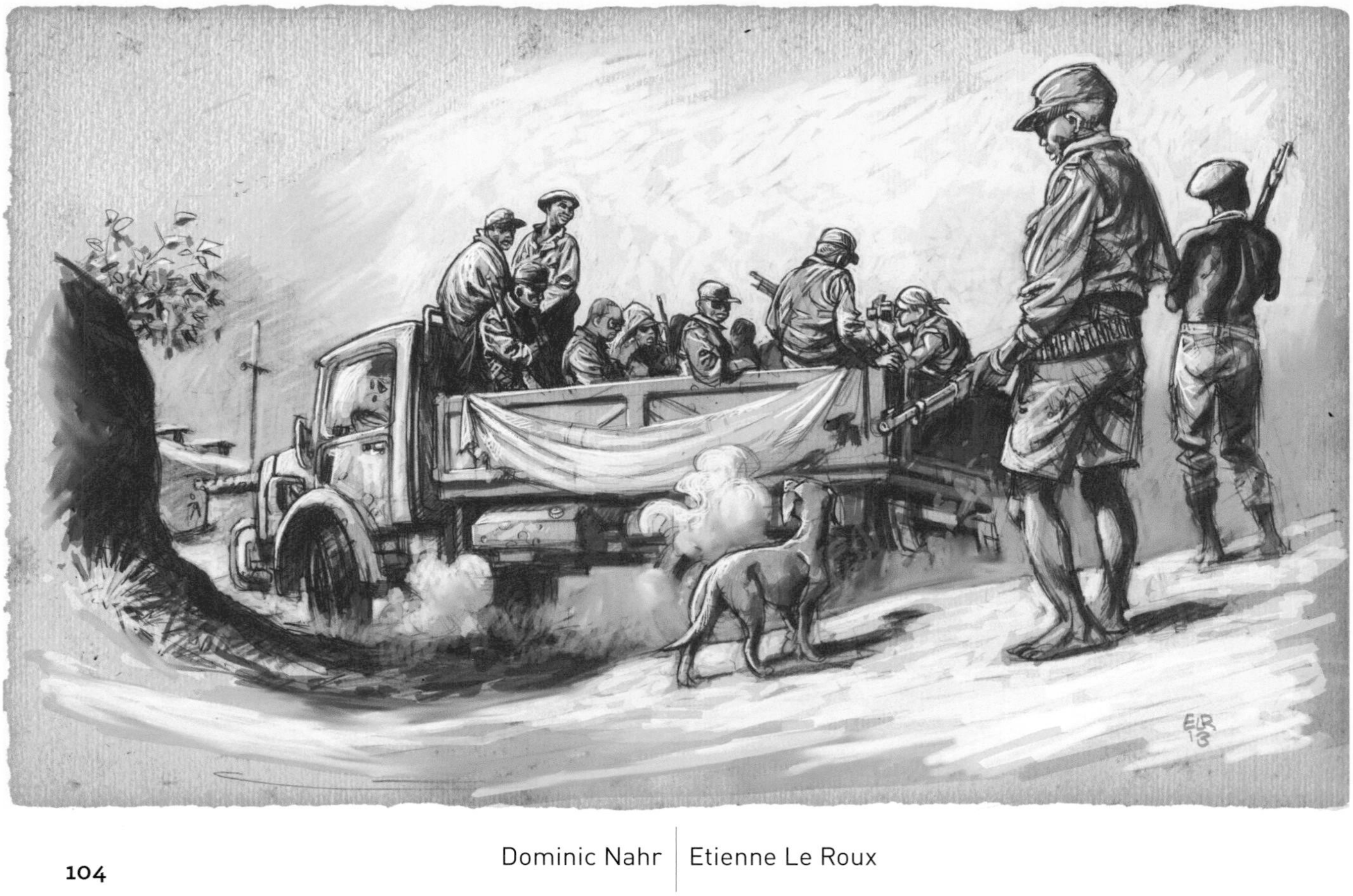

Dominic Nahr | Etienne Le Roux

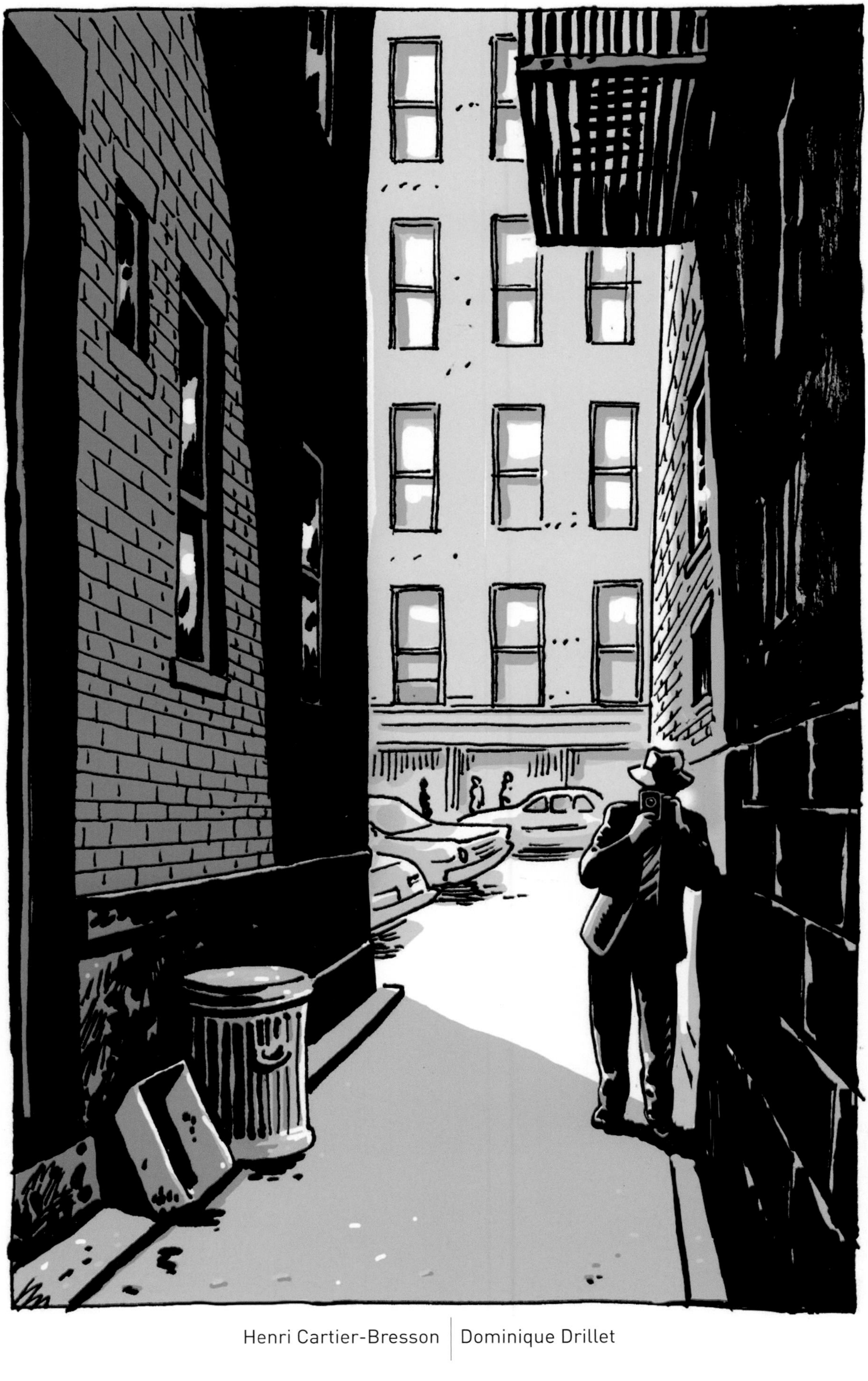

Henri Cartier-Bresson | Dominique Drillet

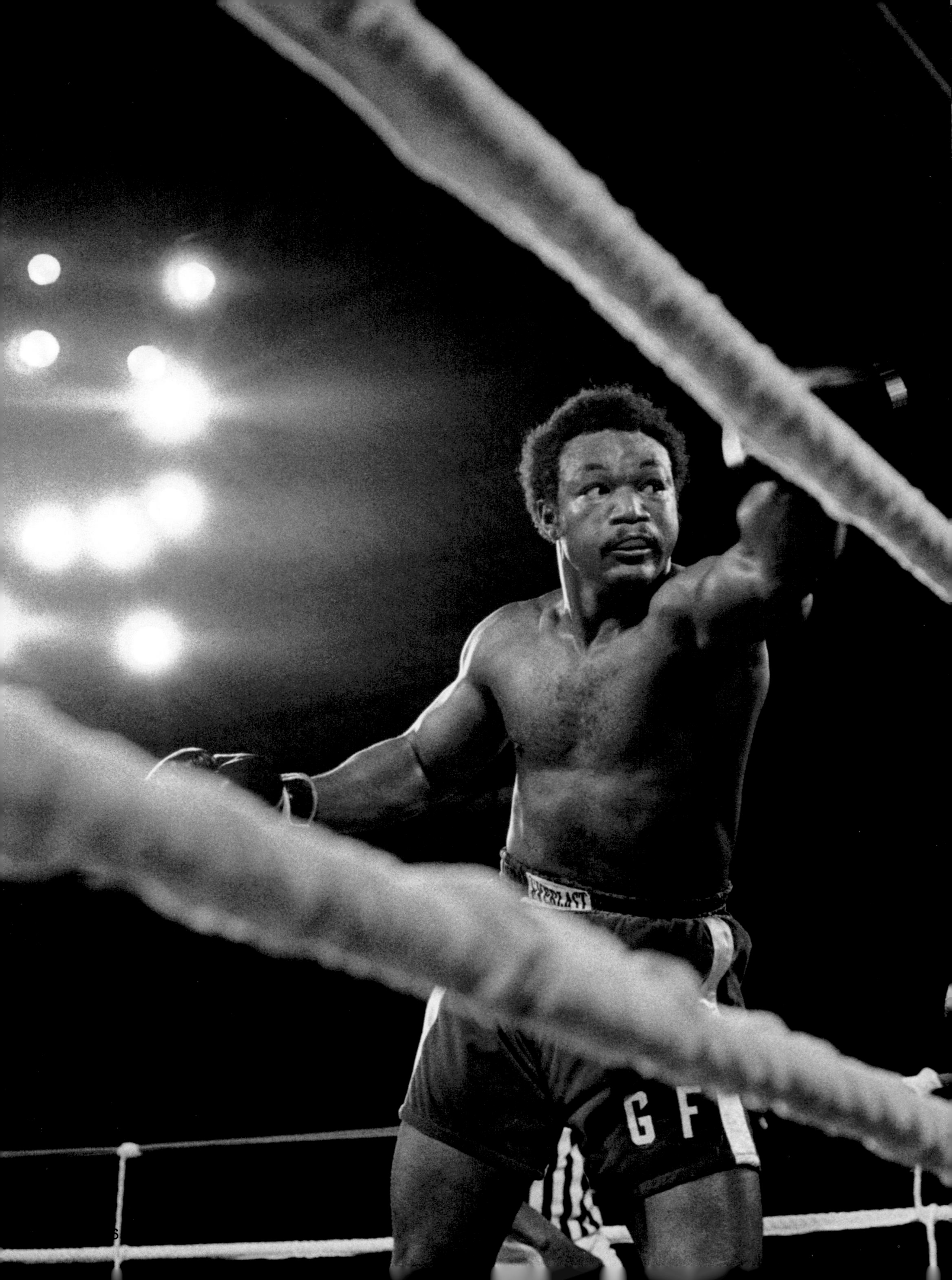

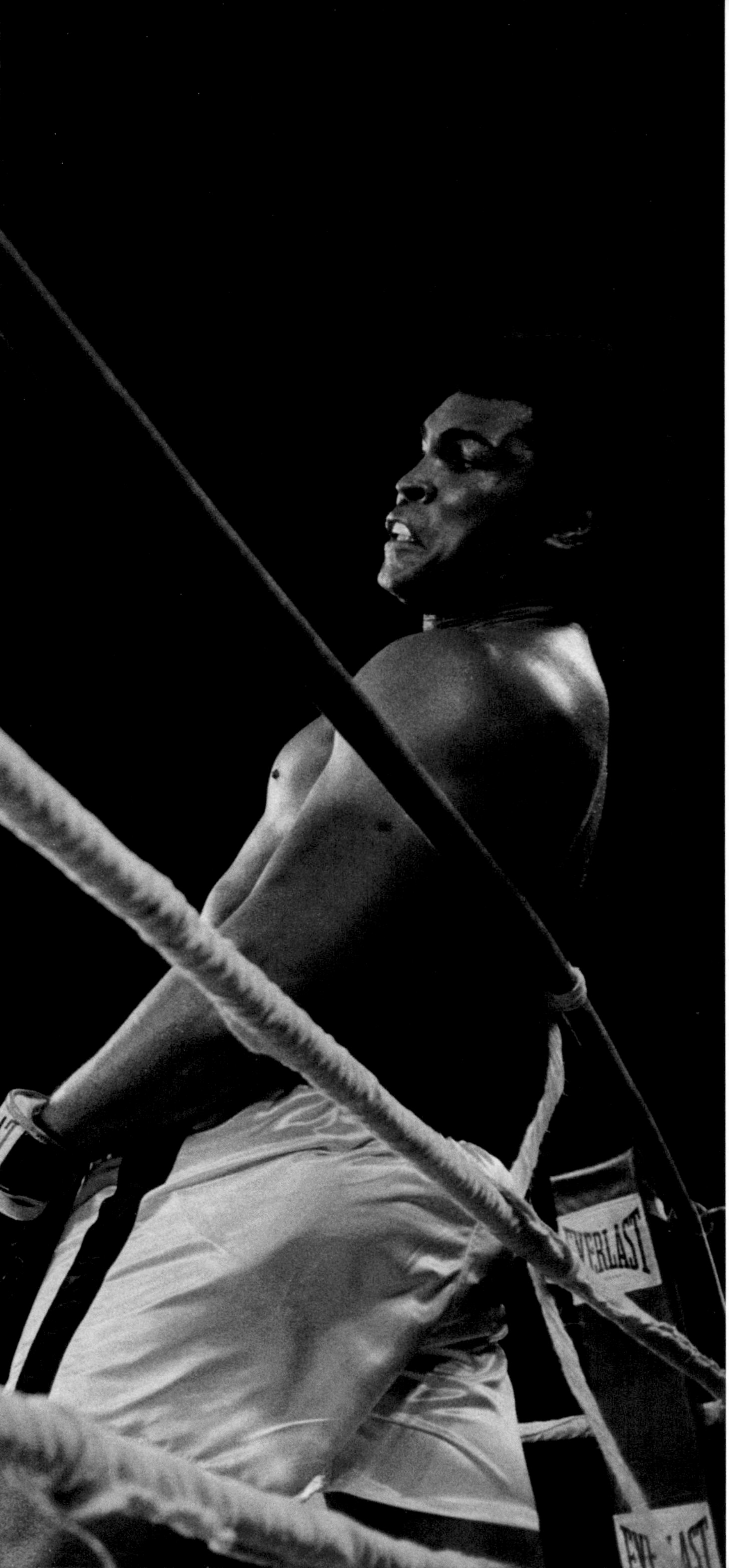
EVERLAST

With this first concept in hand, I spoke to my mentor, Jean-Claude Camano. He came to see us at Magnum, and made us think deeper about it, just as an advisor (as he couldn't publish these types of stories in his *Tchô!* Collection).

A few days later, I was invited to lunch with Chritian Lerolle who was organizing the jury for the Angouleme festival's school competition in Reims. Thierry "The Boss" Tinlot, former editor-in-chief of *Spirou* and *Fluide Glacial*, was there. We ate lunch sitting face to face. He asked me what I was working on right now, and I brought up the project, to which he immediately replied that he wanted to publish it. Score!

He spoke about it to José-Louis Bocquet and Sergio Honorez, both huge photography fans, and fitted us into *Aire Libre*, the prestigious collection with *Dupuis*.

Over the course of a meeting, we chose emblematic photos and the subjects they evoked. A list was established. As we were coming up to the 70th anniversary of the D-day landing, it seemed completely logical to pay homage to Robert Capa, the founder of this mythical agency.

We needed a great, speedy artist.

On our way back to the station, Séverine and I bumped into Dominique Bertail. We exchanged a few jokes and went on our way. While we were walking, Séverin voiced the thought I was already having in my head. Dominique would be perfect to draw our Capa!

I sent him a text message and we agreed to meet to discuss the project.

Incredibly, he agreed.

He stayed six months... we had a real drive for work.

We headed to New York, to the ICP (International Center of Photography) building, which held the rights to Capa's work.

We were lucky enough to get to see the original film in the archives for the Magnificent Eleven.

They told me to steer clear of Bob's autobiography – as he had the tendency to tell a legend rather than the historic truth – and they gave me a list of books to work from.

I wrote and wrote.

Dominique drew like a madman, the pages were sublime, and he finished them all ahead of time.

We held the launch at Magnum Photos in Paris.

The book, in English, was presented to Barack Obama, Queen Elizabeth II, Vladimir Putin and François Hollande on the day of the Omaha Beach commemoration. A huge moment for us all.

Thierry Tinlot had to leave the Magnum ship, with Louis-Antoine Dujardin taking over the captaincy.

I was already in the process of writing the next book about Henri Cartier-Bresson and his experience in the POW camps. The Foundation supported us at every step, giving us access to personal anecdotes and rare documents. Even better, I was lucky enough to be able to work on this book with my friend Sylvan Savoia, who I'd met in the Tenth Grade (age 15), as artist.

Then, well... The commemoration of the 15th anniversary of September 11th was upon us. Several Magnum photographers had been on the scene, each telling what unfolded in their own unique way. Steve McCurry had just returned from a trip. He ran in the opposite direction to the crowd, towards danger, from Washington Square Park to where he lived on Wall Street, in order to document the events.

Louis-Antoine and myself met up with him at the Paris Photo event on November 13th 2015, just before he headed to Stade de France to watch the France-Germany game. We all now know the details of that tragic night of terrorist attacks. Here is the beginning of our text exchanges:

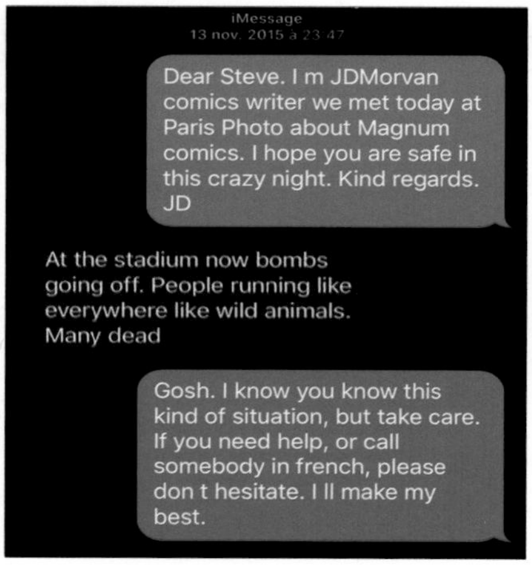
iMessage
13 nov. 2015 à 23:47
Dear Steve. I m JDMorvan comics writer we met today at Paris Photo about Magnum comics. I hope you are safe in this crazy night. Kind regards. JD
At the stadium now bombs going off. People running like everywhere like wild animals. Many dead
Gosh. I know you know this kind of situation, but take care. If you need help, or call somebody in french, please don t hesitate. I ll make my best.

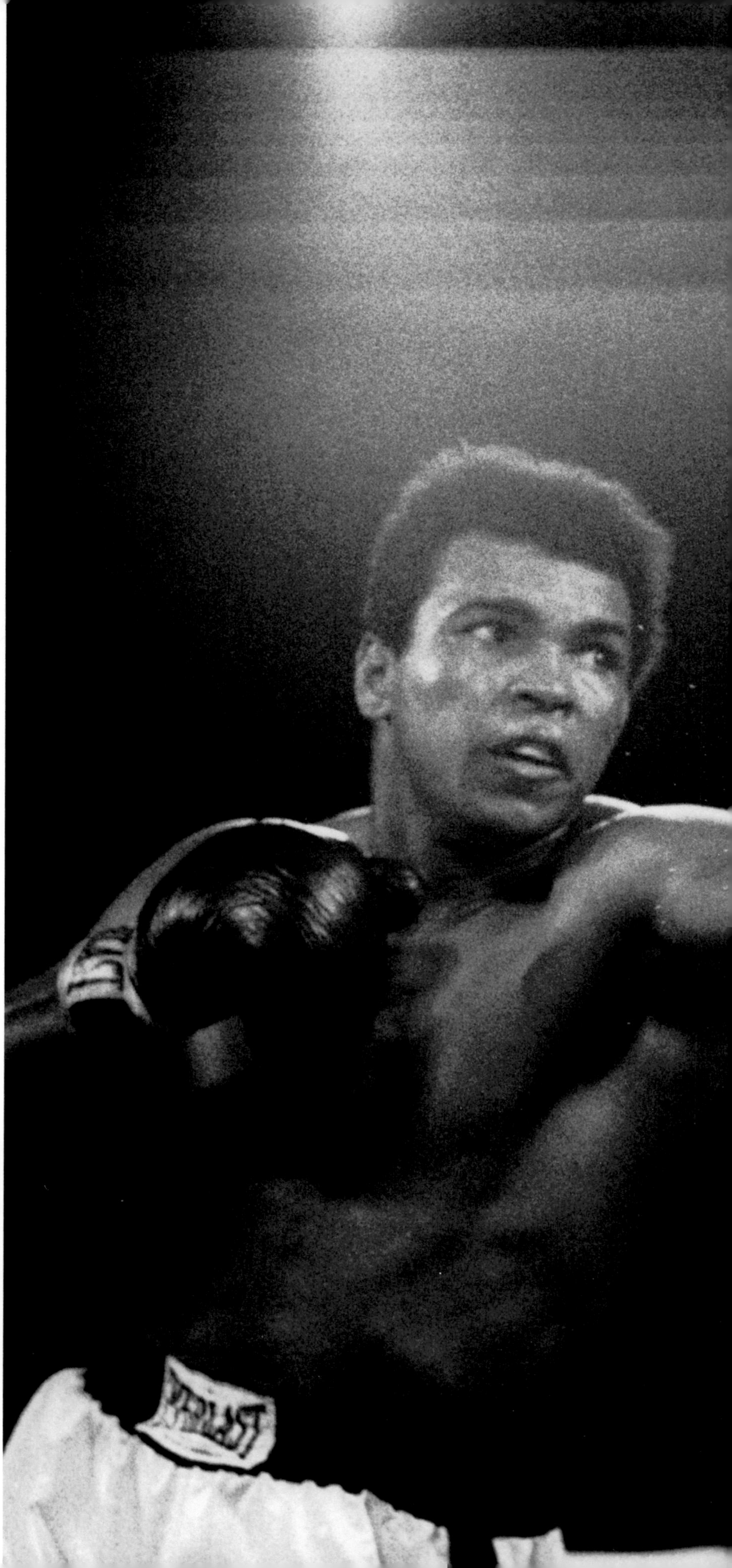
EVERLAST

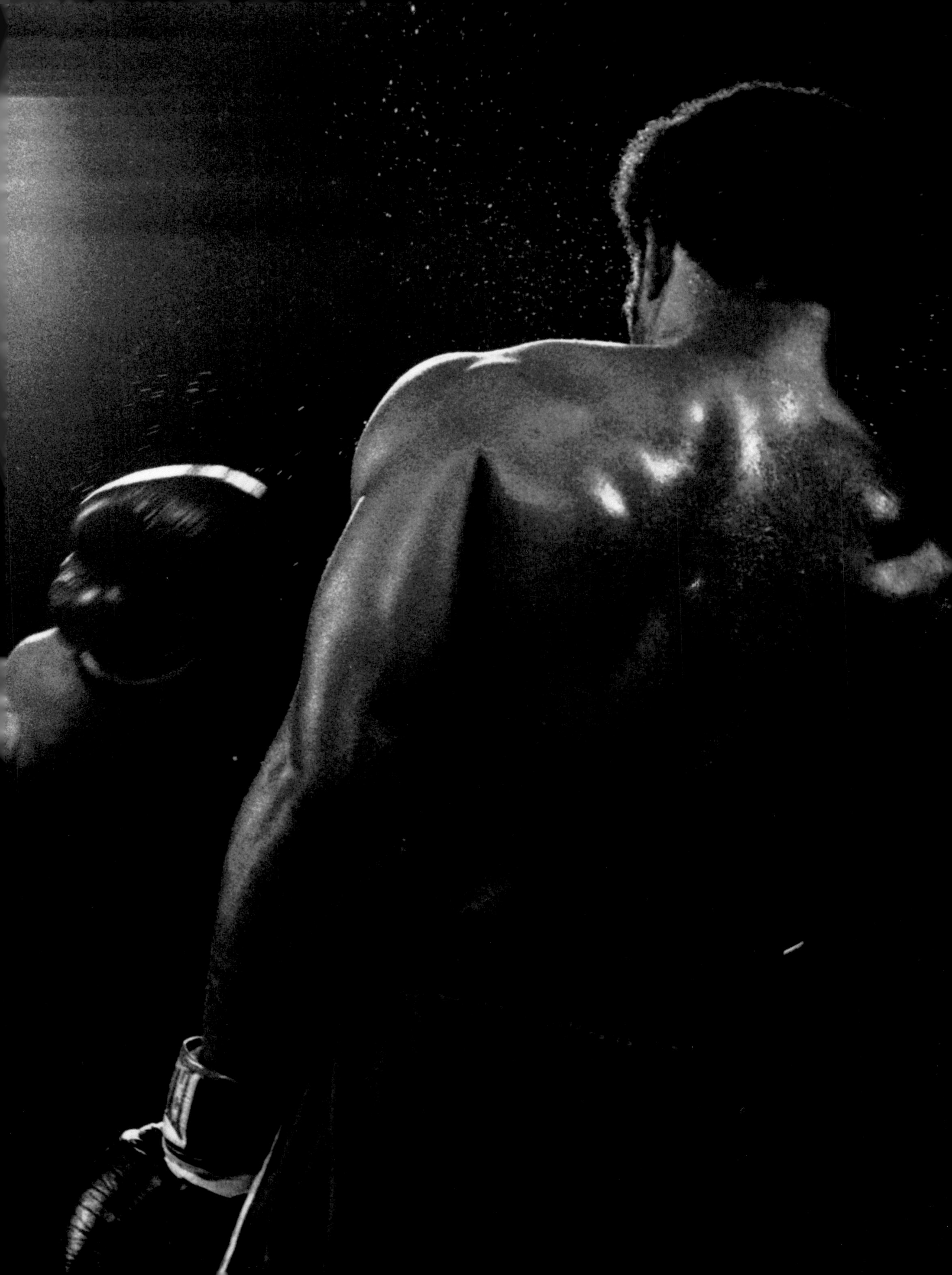

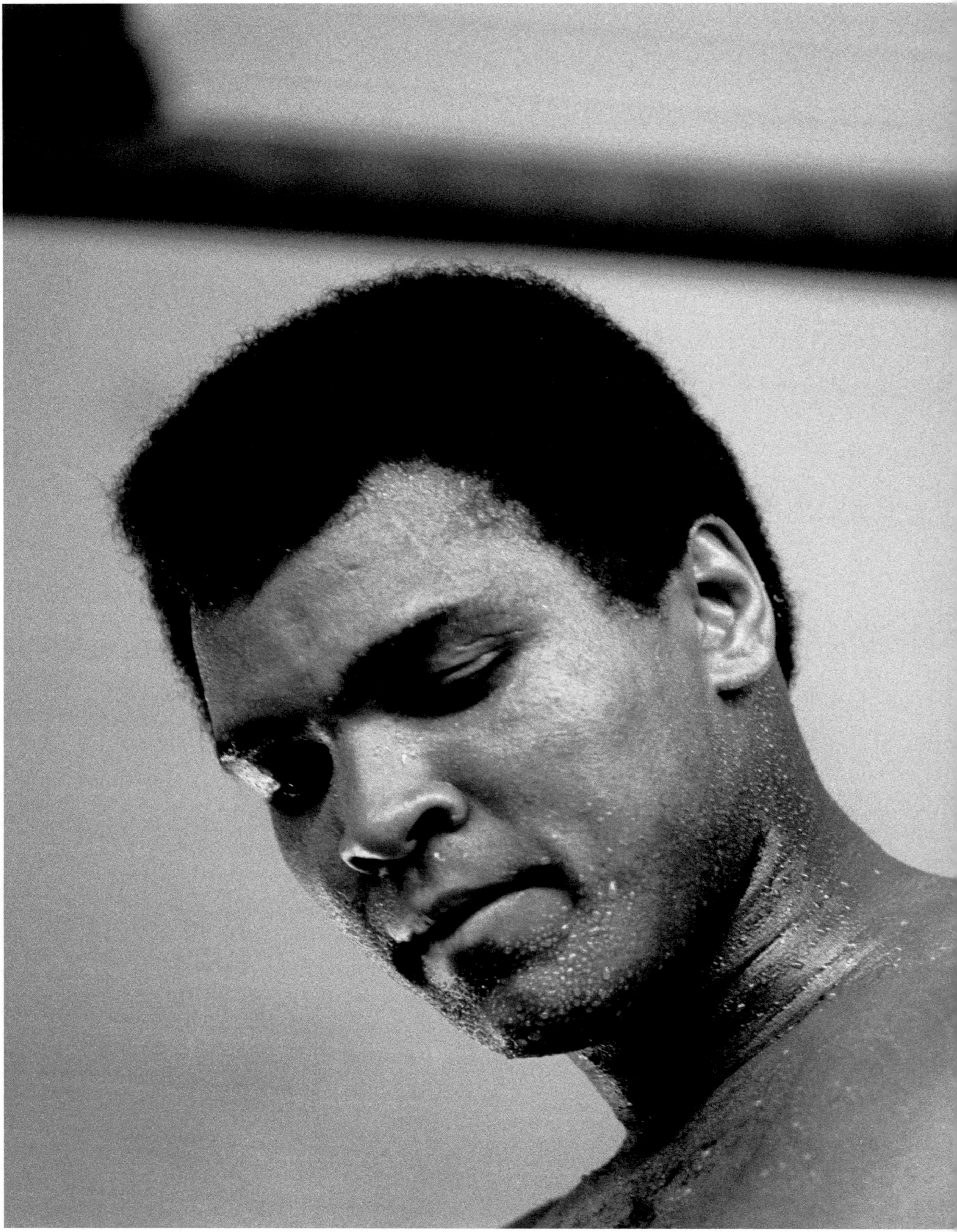

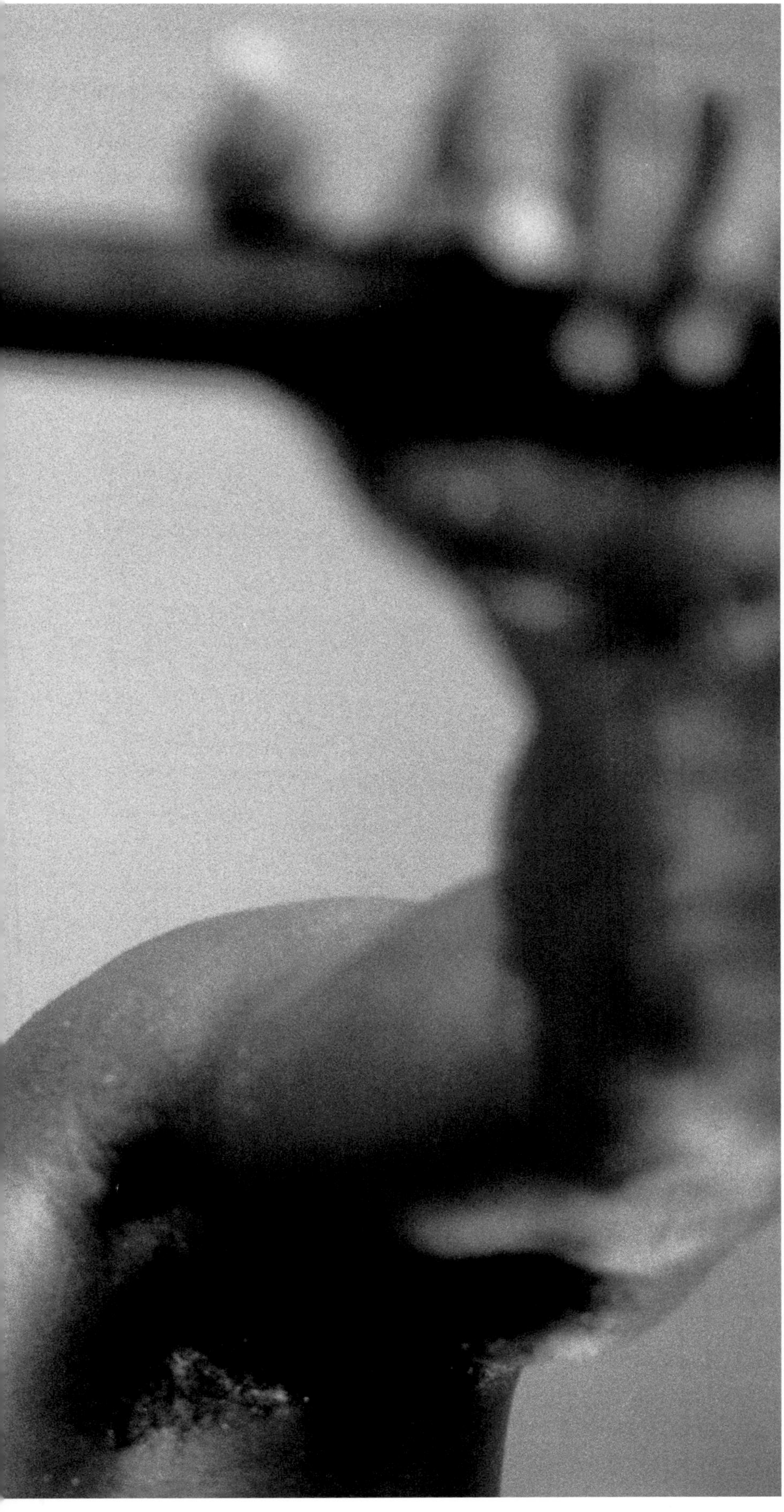

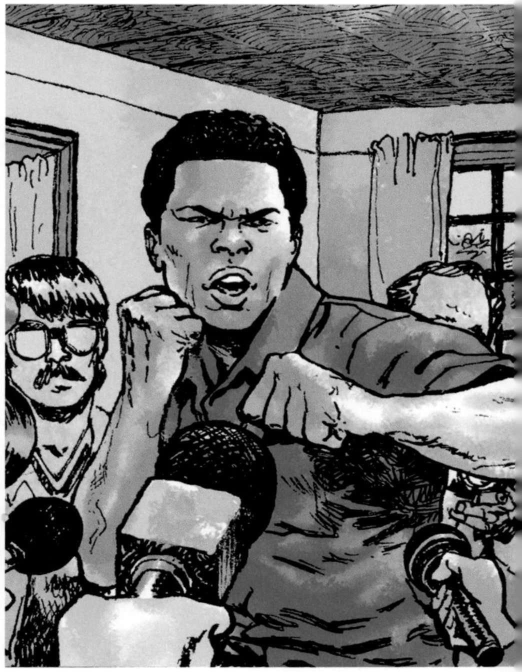

A few days later, Kim Jung-Gi accepted the job of drawing the book. I needed him for the grandiose side of the events. We started the comic in his workshop in Seoul, and finished it in my living room-cum-studio.

This book was notable, because it was the first time we'd integrated the photos into the narration in the collection, all while keeping our core concept in focus.

For the first time too, we dared to try color, encouraged by Walter's talent. But we took it in more a conceptual direction, so that Steve's color photos were surrounded by drawn strip in color while his black and whites would have a monochrome art style.

And then came the Abbas/Ali project.

We had our concept from the start.

I wrote the album in one go.

We met Horacio Altuna in Barcelona. Louis-Antoine and I were already fans of his work. He accepted the job and we didn't look back.

I met him again a few weeks later at the Crack Bang Boom festival in Rosario, Argentina. He had a few completed original pages, but said he was exhausted.

We prayed it would pass.

It was only then that I met Abbas for the first time, after having sent him the script and the first finished pages by Altuna.

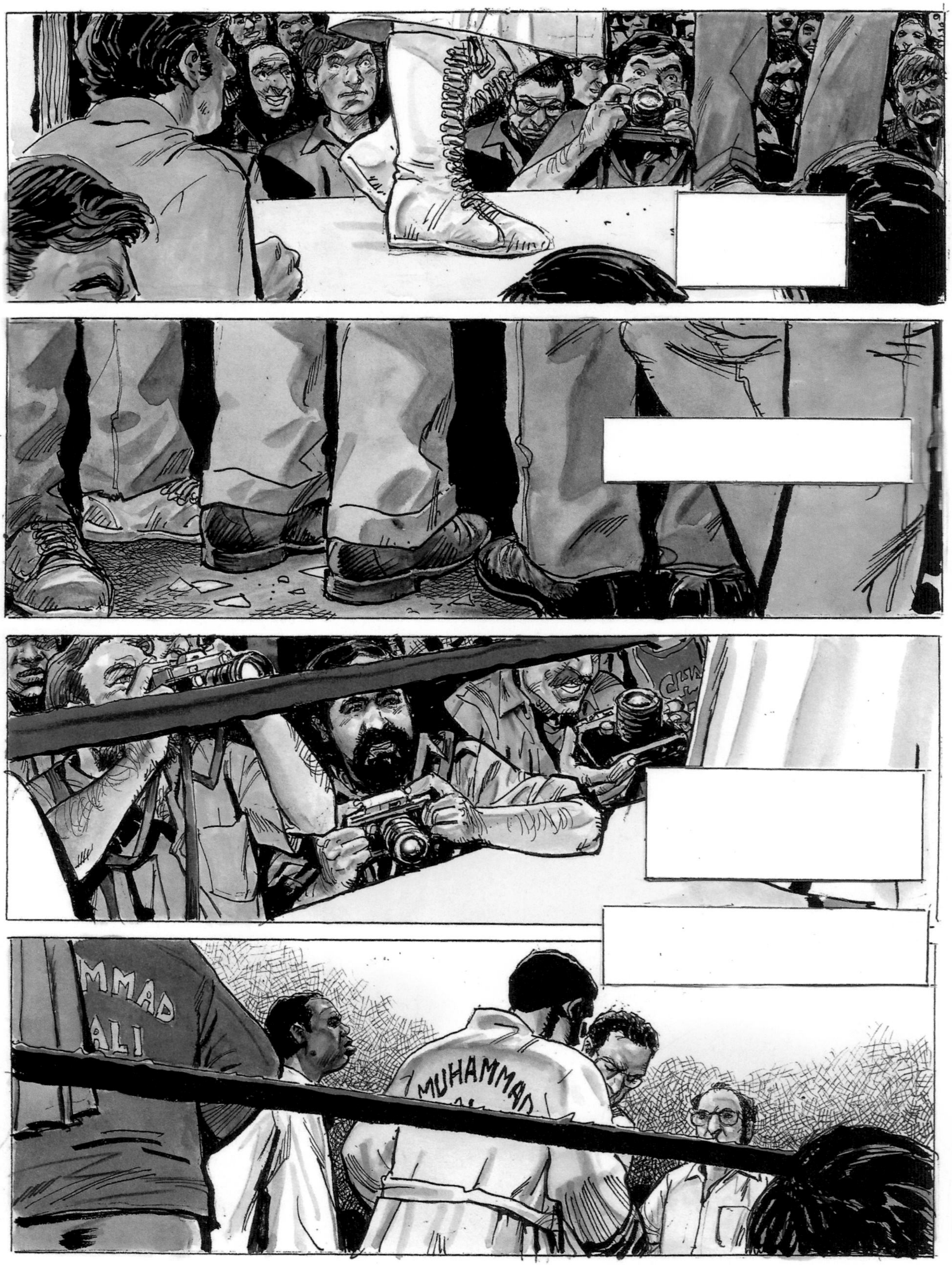
MMAD
ALI
MUHAMMAD

The following pages are by Horacio Altuna

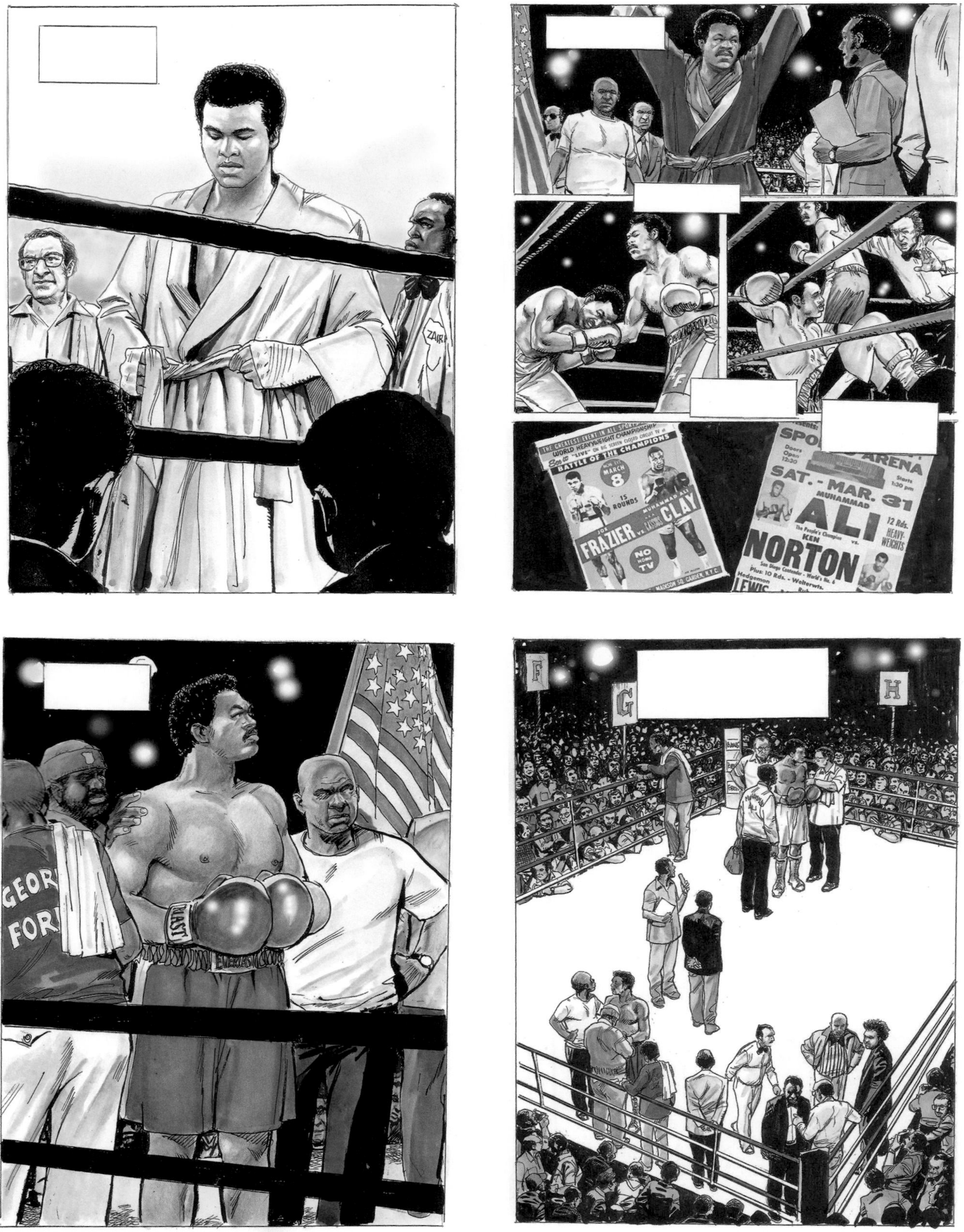
ZAIRE
BATTLE OF THE CHAMPIONS
WORLD HEAVYWEIGHT CHAMPIONSHIP
MARCH 8
15 ROUNDS
FRAZIER
CLAY
NO HOME TV
SAT. - MAR. 31
MUHAMMAD
ALI
12 Rds.
HEAVY-WEIGHTS
The People's Champion vs.
KEN
NORTON
ARENA
LEWIS
GEORGE FORE
EVERLAST
F
G
H

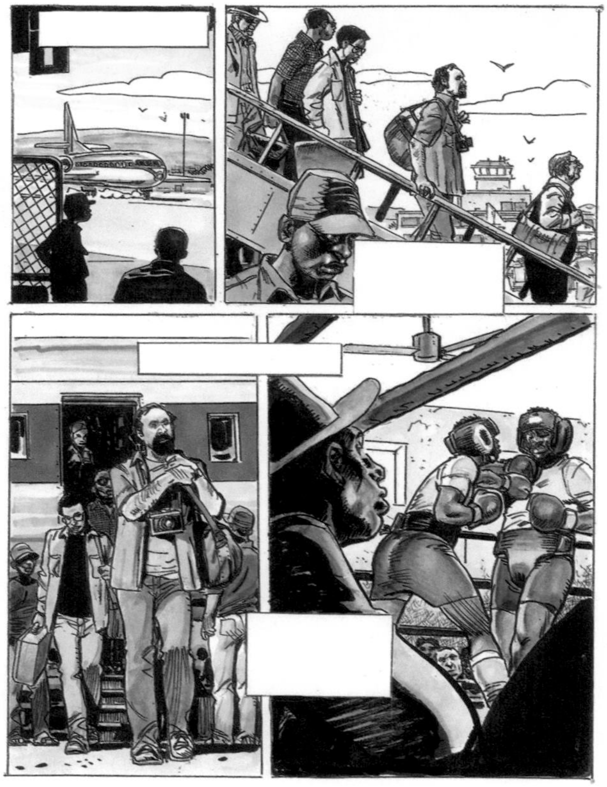

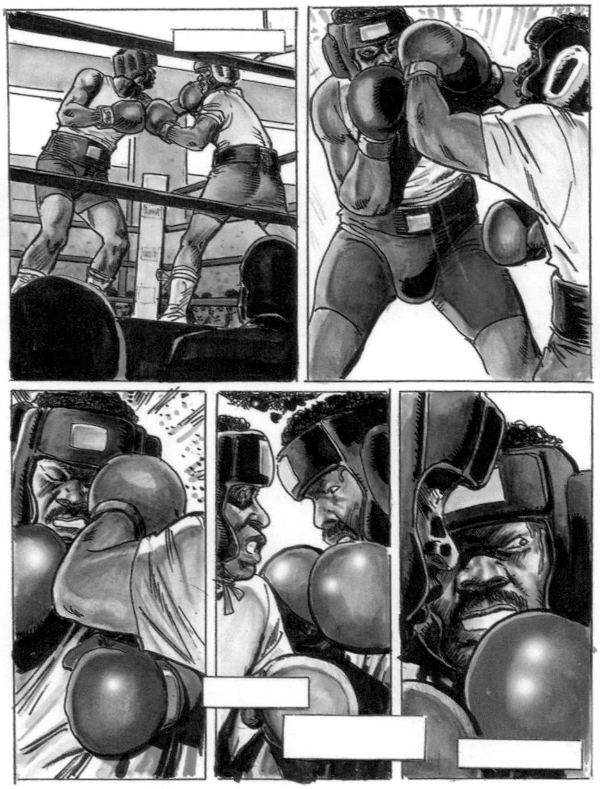

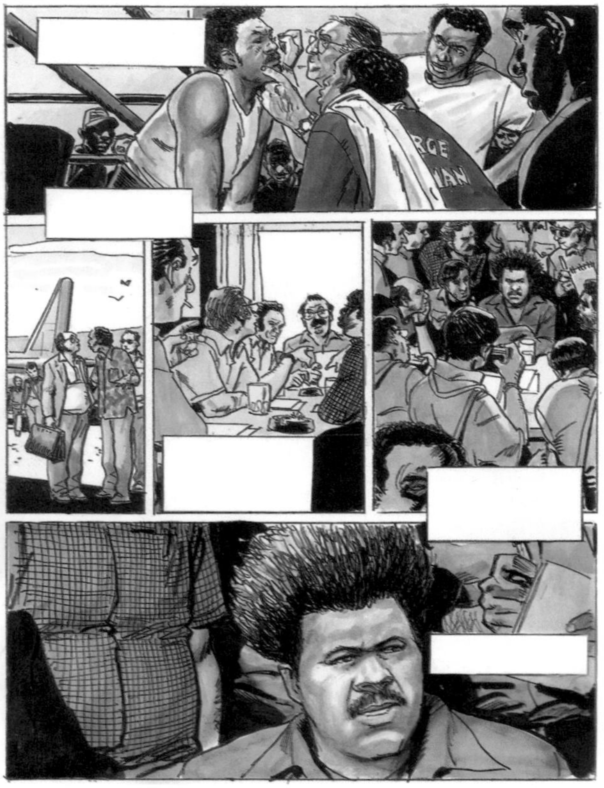

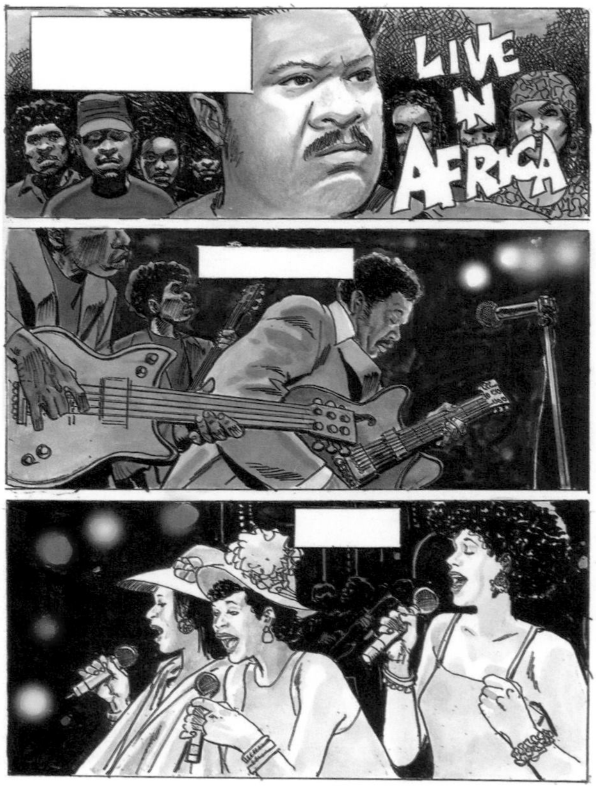
LIVE IN AFRICA

Thistledown
PARK

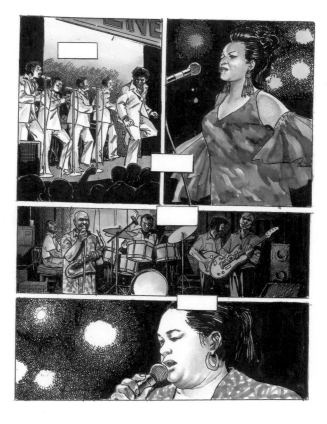

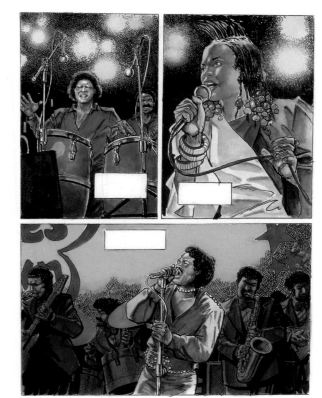

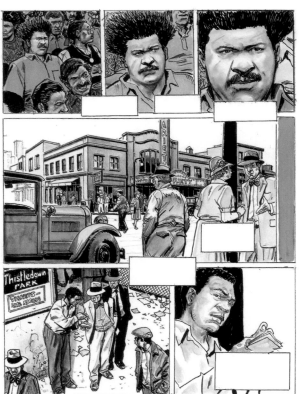

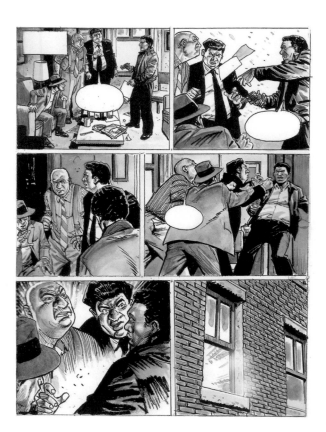

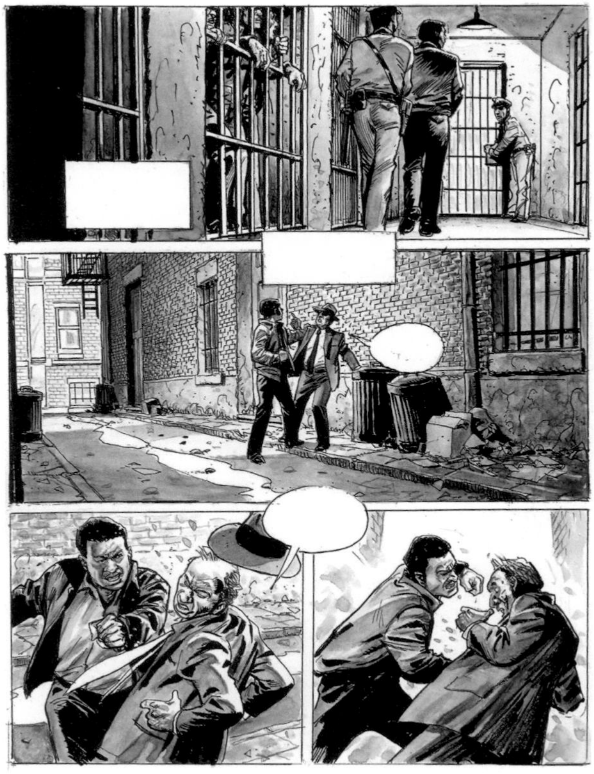

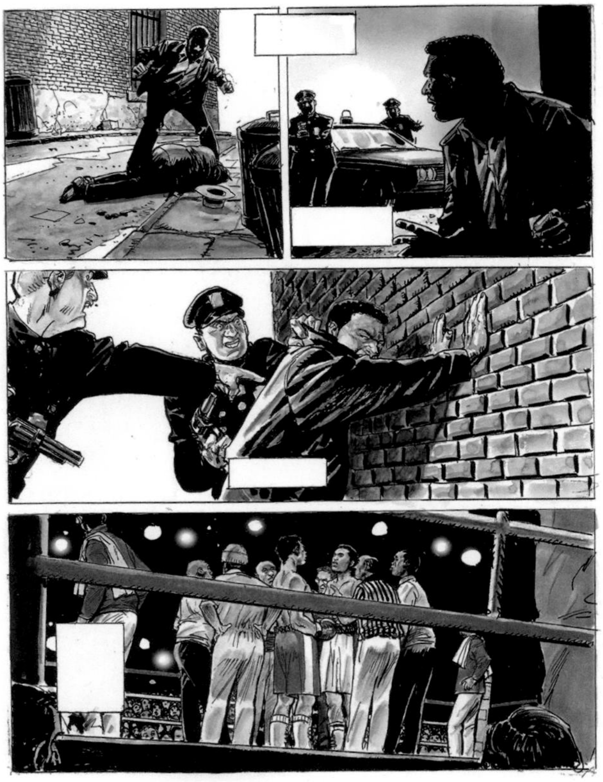

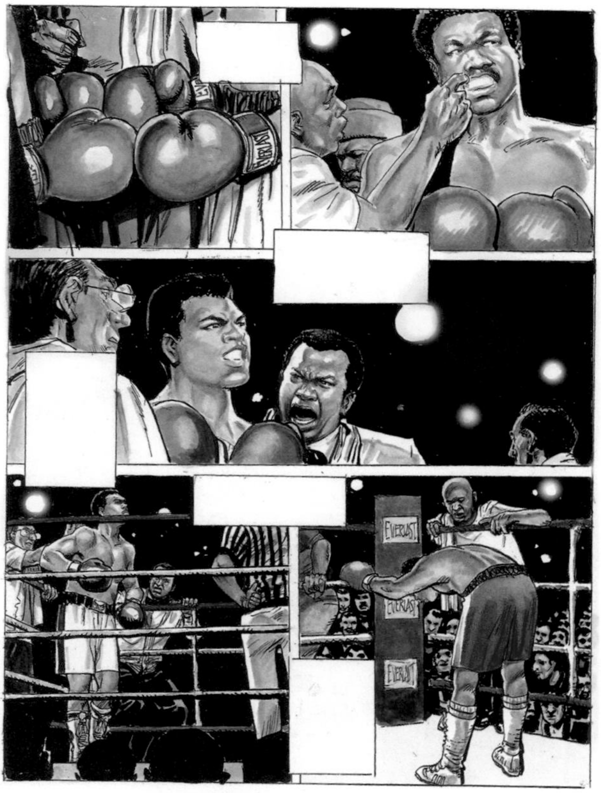
EVERLAST

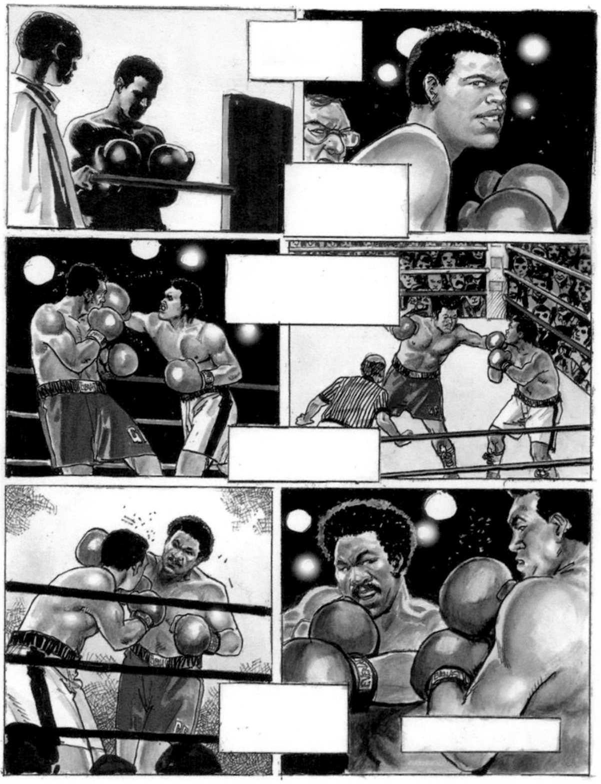

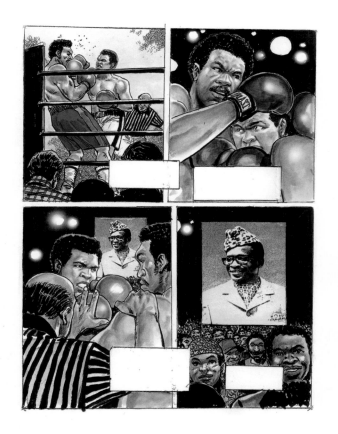

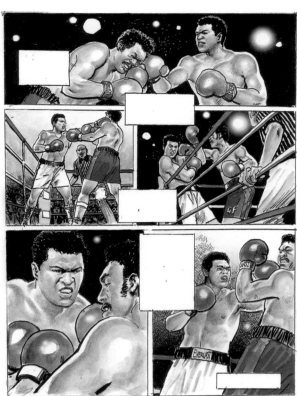

Born in 1941 in Argentina, Horacio Altuna is a major player in the South American comics scene. His collaboration was a major asset to this project, but after completing the first twenty pages, the artist decided to pull out of the project for personal reasons.

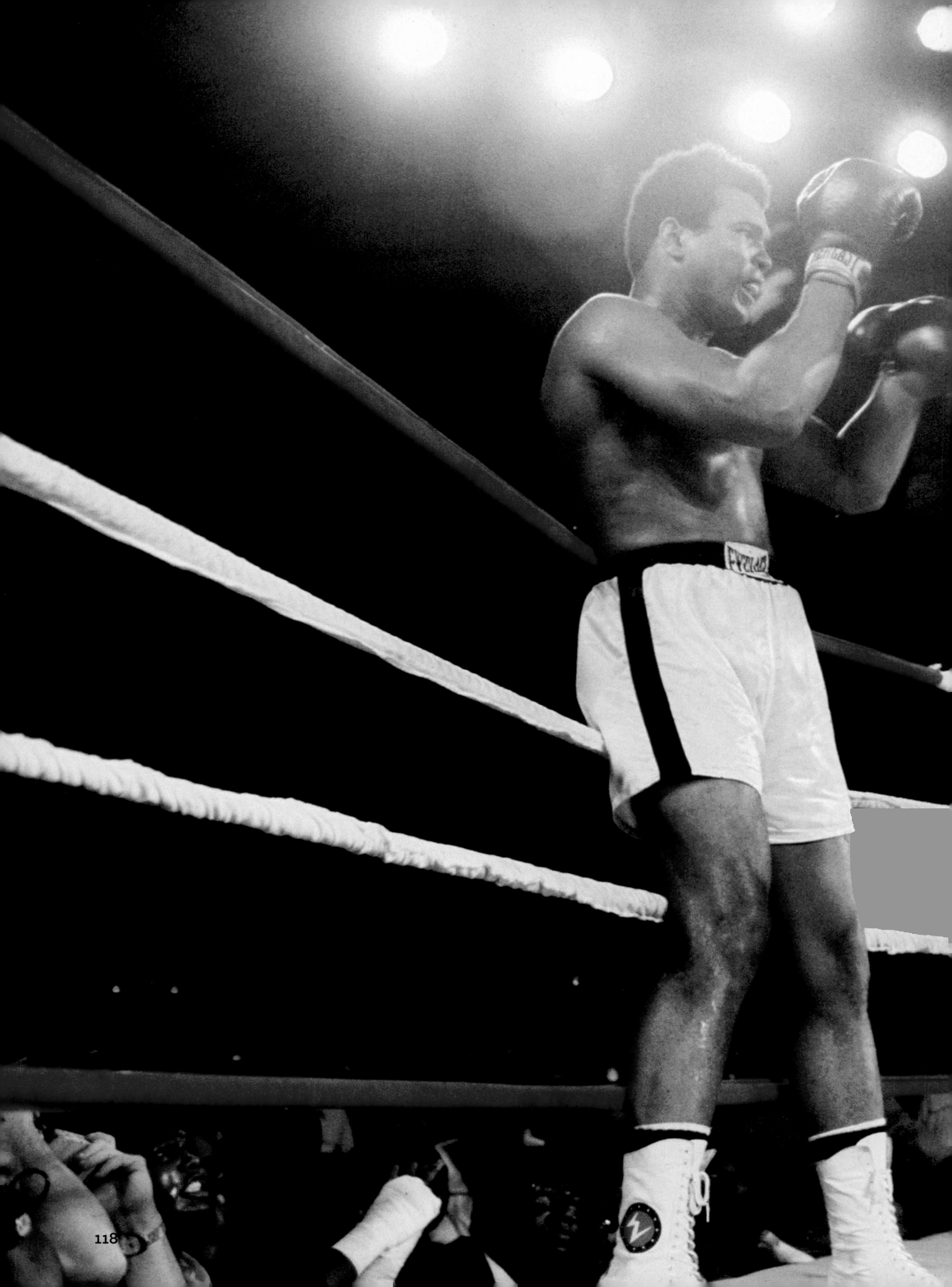

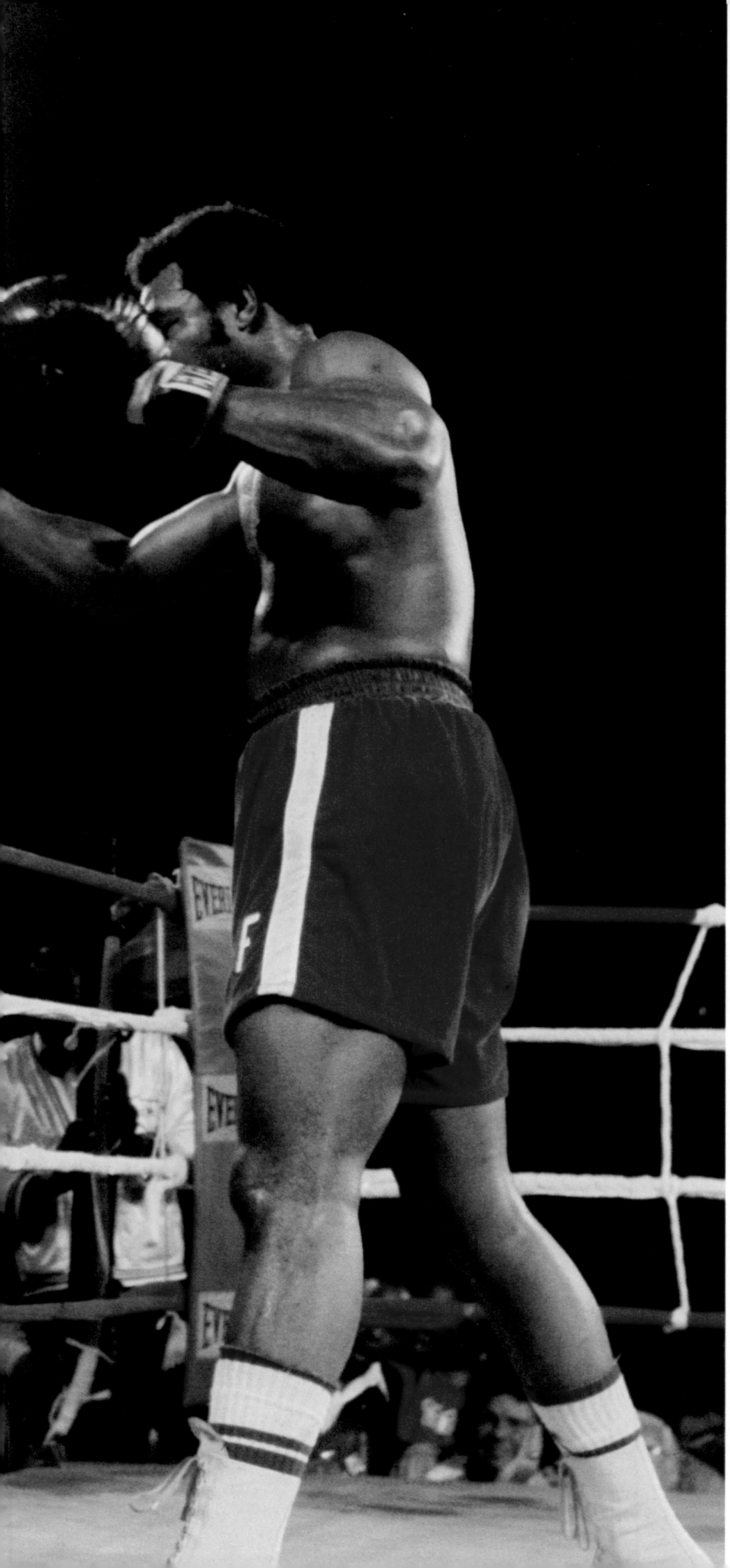

I hadn't received any reply from Abbas, except an invitation to come to the office for a meeting to discuss the project.

Abbas was the director of the Magnum Foundation at the time, and that meant that he was the one who'd given the green light for this comic project in the first place.

It wasn't until much later that we proposed to create this work about him and his report on The Rumble in the Jungle.

For the meeting, I got off the metro at La Fourche and walked a few blocks before arriving at Magnum. I had already been there on several occasions, to conceptualize the collection of which this book belongs to.

I arrived in front of the chalk-striped front door. I rang, the door opened, and Séverine and I went over the threshold.

We walked in front of the glass staircase, about which Henri Cartier-Bresson had said (at least what Magnum legend says he said, and we know from Capa that if the legend is better than reality, that's what you print): "We can't put an elevator here. If the photographers don't have the strength to tackle one flight of stairs – even a spiral one – they have no business being in a photography agency."

We sat ourselves down on the couches between a screen showing a Jérôme Sessini exhibition and the heavy industrial door that opened into the empty meeting room.

Abbas showed up.

He seemed a bit surly.

I wondered if the start of this meeting could turn into a rock n'roll fiasco.

And I was reminded of the first call we'd had with him at Séverine's place, after I'd sent him some questions via email...

JEAN-DAVID MORVAN – Hello?

ABBAS – Hello.

JD – Can you hear me?

A – Yes I can hear you very well.

JD – Ok, great, I can hear you well too. How are you?

A – Ok.

JD – Great, good.

A – So this is about the book then?

JD – Yes that's right, for the book about Ali. I just needed a couple of extra pieces of information about you, if you would be so kind. You're the hero of the story after all.

A – The "hero," come now let's not exaggerate. I wasn't the one boxing. Ah... so you're the one writing the script then?

JD – Exactly, yes!

A – Alright, I'll get back to your email. Right, so do you know why I say "I was born a photographer?"

JD – No.

A – Exactly so I don't have to reply to the questions you're asking me.

JD – Ah right, I did wonder, I wondered if it was something like that. Like...

A – Yes, it's that, because I believe that everything is in the art.

JD – Yes.

A - Photographers who talk about their childhoods, their mothers and fathers, that really rubs me the wrong way. So I try not to bore the people who look at my photos, because everything is already there.

JD – I completely understand that, but all the same, for the comic I need just a few little flashes, little things that you want to say, nothing forced.

A – So something like "Where were you born?". Alright, let's say that I was born in Iran. But it was Algeria that made me a journalist... at the start I did both, at first, I wrote and took pictures and then realized I got more pleasure out of clicking the button on a camera than forming sentences. That's why when I make a book I always have some text, a sort of travel diary you see, so I keep the control over it.

Back to our meeting. He sat down and began his attack.

A - I thought this was supposed to be a comic about me, and I don't see myself very much in the pages.

I found this beginning of the conversation fantastic, because at least there was no beating around the bush. Now we could speak frankly.

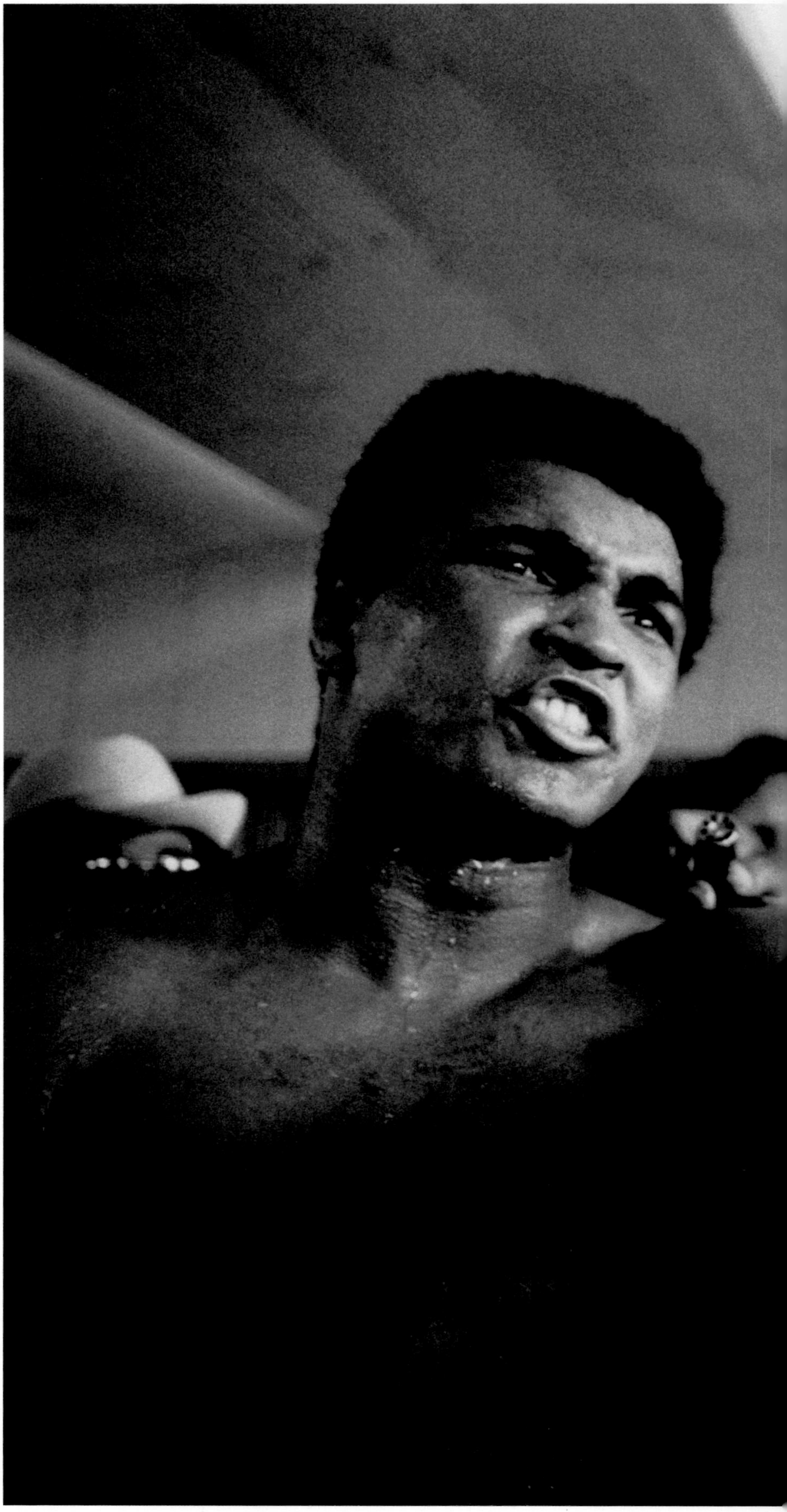

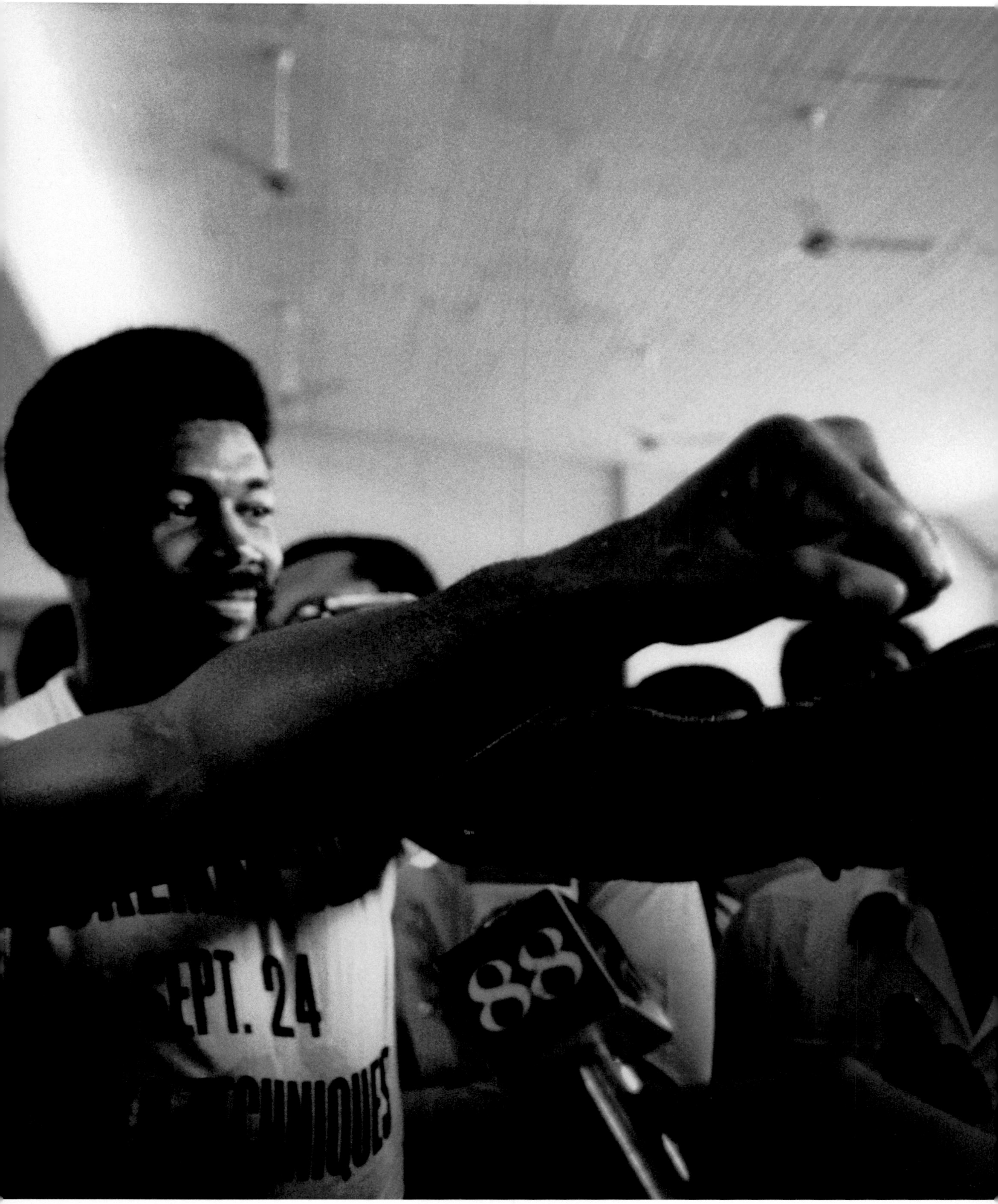
EPT. 24
88

I took a deep breath to speak with some fresh air. I knew I had to let this wave just pass.

JD – Dear Mr. Abbas, if that's what you think then you haven't read the script, because you're the one who's talking from beginning to end. You're the main driving force of the story, through which the reader relives the match from the inside.

And besides, you're the only character we see in full body shot on page 1.

He looked at the pages on the table for a few minutes.

Nobody broke the silence until he spoke again.

A – Hmmm, that's true. But... I don't think you've drawn me very well.

This one I should have expected. Everyone knows that a drawing of a real person which looks too much like reality can upset the subject.

But in this case, I knew there was nothing really behind it. What he wanted was to test me. In the same way that guys will insult each other in a bar, get into a fight, and end up as the best of buds before the night is over.

JD – Well Horacio is a great artist. But I can ask him to make some tweaks. What is it you don't like? Are you too small? Too fat? Not handsome enough?

A – No that's not it. And plus, he can't draw women very well either.

JD – You know, Horacio has drawn a strip for Playboy every month for years, so the readers must have felt for a long time that he draws women well...

A – Is he Black?

JD – Uh no. He's Argentinian.

A – He draws Black people very well, I'll give you that. The faces and attitudes.

JD – Yes, he's a great artist you know. Very well known. For his field, he's on your level.

A – Really?

JD – Yes, an artist admired by all the artists in the world. Not really well known by the public, but better than that. Infinite respect from the profession. Besides, he's about your age. Your careers have been pretty similar, really.

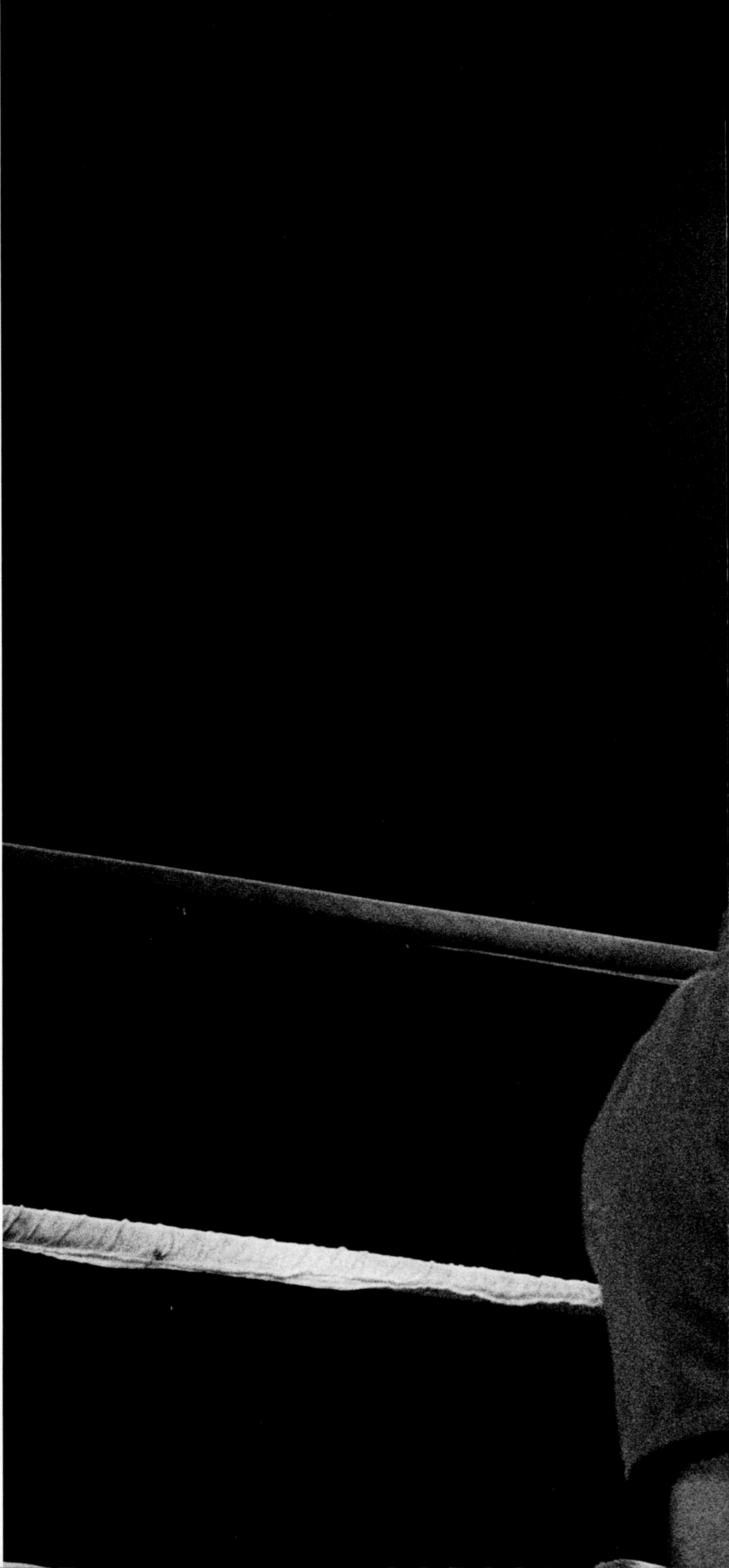

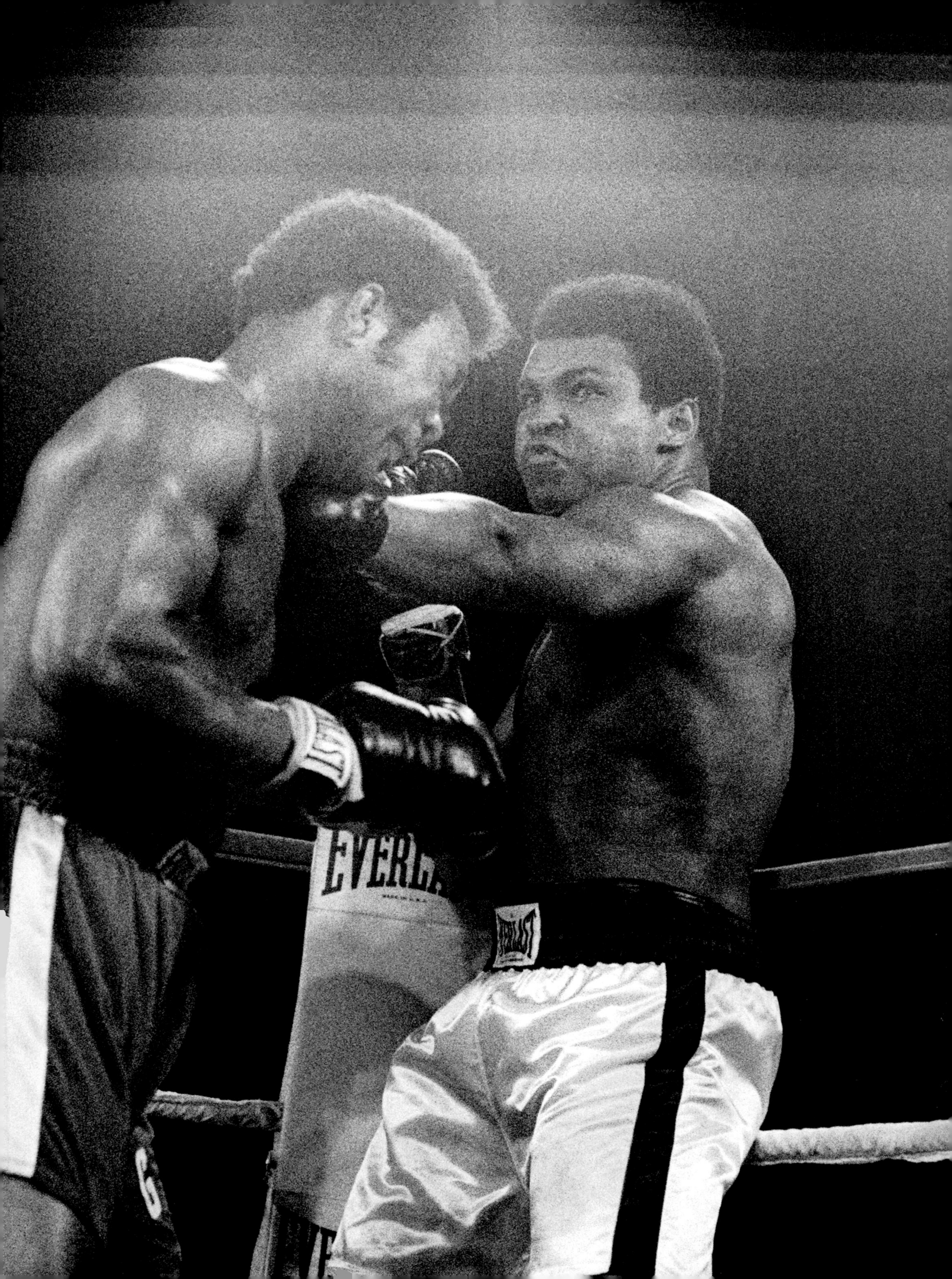
EVERLA

A – It's true that his Black women are superb. I think he'll be perfect for our comic because... there's a little anecdote I've never told, and we could put it into the story.

JD – Ah well I'll take even the tiniest anecdote.

A – Well alright then. The Zaire women are very beautiful and I'm convinced they love artists. One night, I couldn't sleep, so I went out to take some photos with my camera...

I won't add any more, you've already read what happened next.

The meeting ended cordially with good humor and laughter.

The hand shake was warm and friendly.

I came out of Magnum with two things I didn't have before:

1. A tasty anecdote that I promised would be in the book.

2. And more importantly, I had the feel for my main character, as I had seen his way of handling an argument... which is often the reflection of how we handle life.

Abbas was not only with me, but he was also now inside my head.

I could from then on write him without betraying him.

But the bad news was soon to come. Horacio Altuna would make no more pages. He had to give up the project.

The loss was felt heavily, and it was only when another Argentinian artist, Rafael Ortiz, came to live in France that our hope was reignited.

Later, we all lunched together with Abbas, finding him diminished by illness. Everything was calm however. I knew that he could be fierce, he knew that I could respond without flinching. We didn't need to do that anymore. We had won each other over.

He remained enthusiastic about the project, which he couldn't wait to read.

Alas, he would never get the chance.

I treasure this memory of him in the sun, with us taking a photo in front of Magnum. And of our editor José-Louis Bocquet saying as we left:

"My friends, today is a great day. We just took a photo with Abbas!"

It's true. And for me too, as I had the chance to take the photo...

From left to right: Naima Kaddour, Abbas, José-Louis Bocquet, Séverine Tréfouel, Rafael Ortiz.

This book was released two years after Abbas' death.

The book is of course dedicated to him, as without him, none of this would have been possible.

He was part of the comic project from the very start.

There's always a story at the heart of every story...

Thank you, Mr Attar.

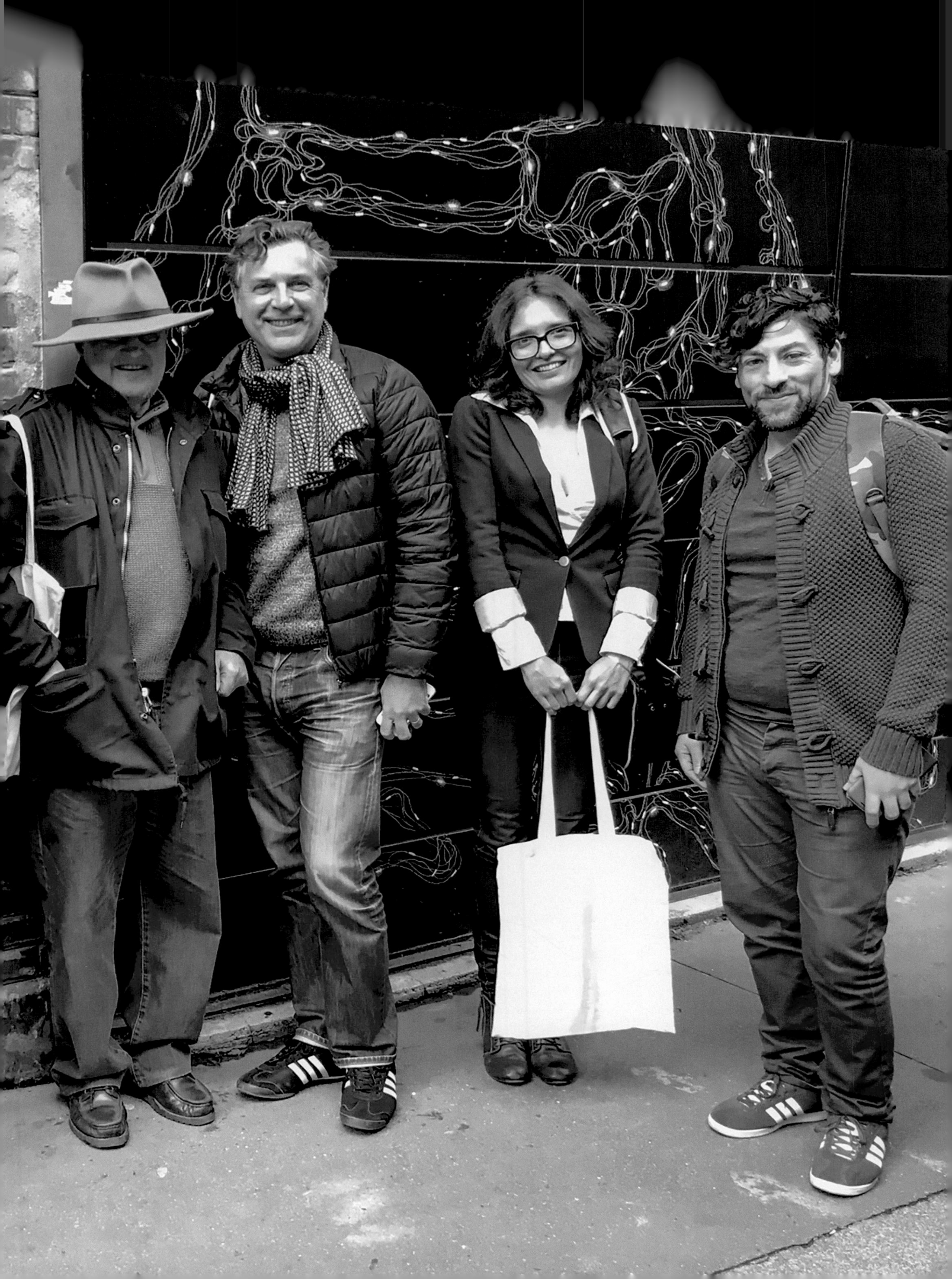

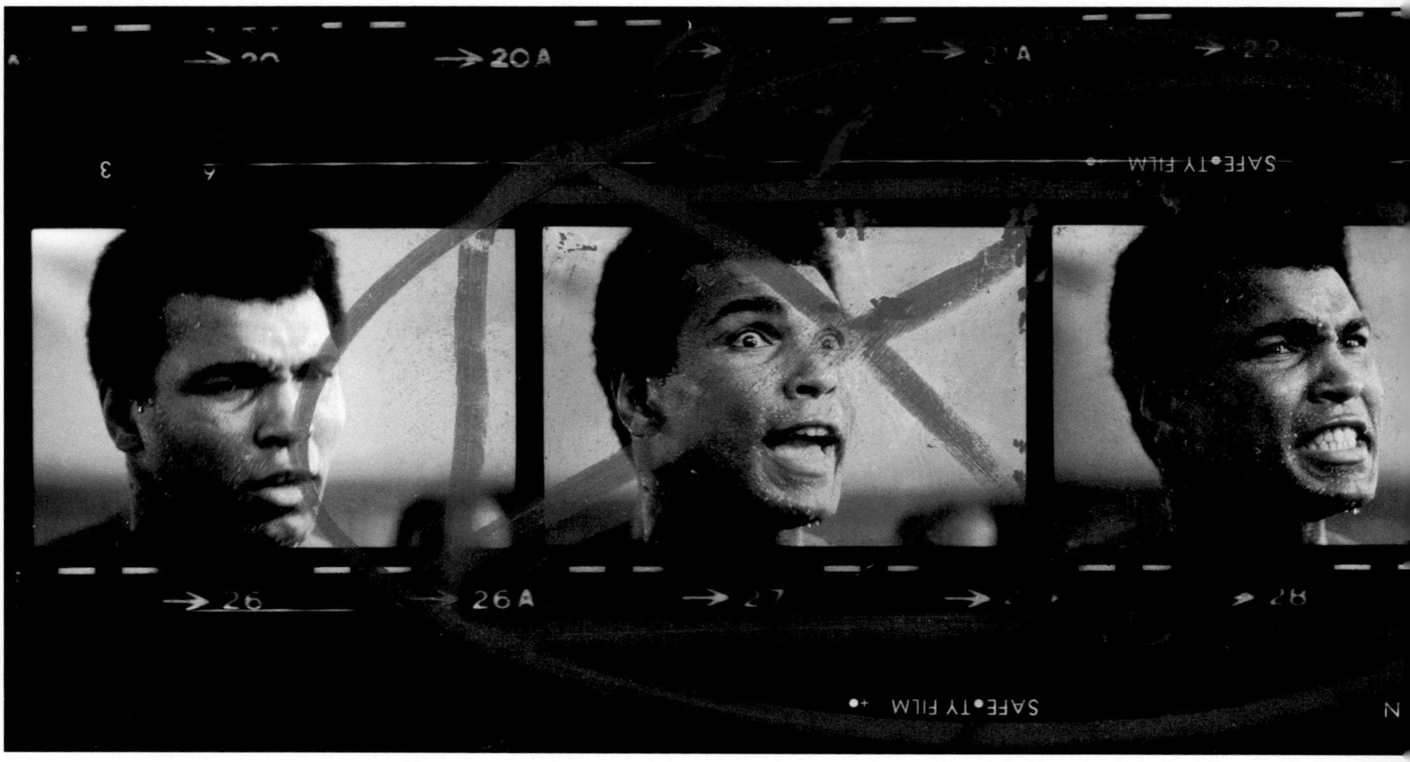
→ 20A
SAFE•TY FILM
26A
SAFE•TY FILM

MUHAMMAD ALI – TIMELINE

JANUARY 17th 1942 Birth of Cassius Marcellus Clay, later Muhammad Ali.

1954 Begins boxing through Joe Martin, a police officer and trainer. According to legend, Clay began to box to take revenge for his stolen bike.

1955-1960 As a high school student, he fights 136 matches without defeat and claims numerous amateur regional and national titles.

1959 Amateur champion at the National Golden Gloves in the light heavyweight category.

1960 Amateur champion at the National Golden Gloves in the heavyweight category. He takes the gold medal for the light heavyweights at the summer 1960 Olympic games in Rome. He goes professional, under the tutelage of Angelo Dundee and quickly becomes known for his unorthodox style. He becomes known as the "Louisville Lip".

OCTOBER 29th 1960 Now professional boxer, wins his first pro fight on points against Tunney Hunsaker. Clay leaves for Florida with his trainer Angelo Dundee. The 19-year-old young gold medalist takes several victories and even goes as far as completing an exhibition against the ex-World Champion, Ingemar Johansson.

NOVEMBER 15th 1962 Spectacular success against Archie Moore in four rounds. Clay had predicted that he would finish his opponent by the fourth round.

1963 Elected boxer of the year. He converts to Islam and joins the Black Muslims cause. First shot at the World Champion title. He scrapes a difficult win on points against Doug Jones. Then, in what will end up as the fight of the year, he makes a name for himself when the referee stops the fight against Henry Cooper due to Cooper's injury in the fifth round. In the previous round, Cooper had knocked down Clay for the first time in his career.

As boxer of the year, it was natural that Clay became enemy of World Champion Sonny Liston. Despite 19 victories of which 15 were a KO and no defeats, it seemed unlikely that the boxer from Louisville would manage to beat a boxer thought to be invincible.

FEBRUARY 25th 1964 Fight against Sonny Liston in Miami. Victory in six rounds

FEBRUARY 6th 1967 Ali reclaims the WBA title in a reunification match against Ernie Terrell. Ali re-wins the title easily, but doesn't manage to break Terrell, who endures 15 rounds with his guard up.

MARCH 6th 1967 He KOs Zora Folley, a puncher deemed dangerous for the champion.

APRIL 28th 1967 Symbolically refuses to show up to the army recruitment center where he'd been drafted.

MAY 8th 1967 Appears in court.

JUNE 15th 1967 His legal problems relating to his refusal to join the American army prevent him from competing in any World Championship fights. He is only permitted to have exhibitions. He is publicly vilified for his stance as a conscientious objector to Vietnam for ideological reasons. He proclaimed that he "had nothing against the Vietnam people" and that "no Vietnam person ever treated me like a Negro." He is not yet incarcerated, but is deposed of his title and boxing license.

JUNE 20th 1967 Condemned to a fine of 10,000 dollars and to 5 years in prison, as well as the loss of his title and license.

Ali appealed, and would not go to prison, but would have financial problems until the case was resolved by the Supreme Court in 1971.

He would not fight again for four years.

1969 He participates in the "Super Fight," a virtual fight against Rocky Marciano.

1970 Ali officially renounces his title, permitting Joe Frazier, rising star in the weight category, to reunify the two federation titles at the expense of Jimmy Ellis. Ali wins his case when the American Supreme Court recognizes his right to refuse military service. He reclaims his license and puts his boxing gloves back on.

OCTOBER 26th 1970 Ali makes his great return against the white hopeful Jerry Quarry, who he beats in 3 rounds in Atlanta.

DECEMBER 7th 1970 Triumphs over the Argentinian Oscar Bonavena in New York in 15 rounds for the North American Boxing Federation's North American Champion title.

MARCH 8th 1971 Defeat. Ali takes on Joe Frazier in Madison Square Garden, New York. He took the risk against a high-level boxer after three years absent from the ring. Well hyped and mediatized, this fight has been qualified as "the fight of the

against the most powerful puncher of the age (1.84m for 99kg). The quality of Clay's feints and combinations made him fighter of the year once more.

At age 22, he rejoins the Nation of Islam and adopts the name Cassius X (the X in reference to the rejection of his slave name in absence of his real original African name, a common practice within the organization). Malcolm X was the only Muslim to support him before his fight against Liston (Malcolm had furthermore attended the first fight). Elijah Muhammed, the leader of the Nation of Islam, baptizes him "Muhammad Ali". Ali travels to Egypt, where he is welcomed by President Gamal Abdel Nasser as the Ambassador of the Black community of the United States.

MAY 25th 1965 The rematch against Liston would be particularly controversial. Less than two minutes into round one after a missed jab, Liston is countered by Ali's right hook and falls to the ground. Liston stays down too long. The referee was too busy trying to get a gesticulating Ali into his corner. The fight got going again for a few minutes before the referee, having been informed of his mistake by the timekeeper, stopped the fight (Liston had been down for more than ten seconds). He proclaimed Ali the victor. The public booed both boxers. The press decried the match as a fix, and accused Liston of throwing the fight.

NOVEMBER 22nd 1965 Victory. In Las Vegas, Ali beats ex-champion Floyd Patterson who had previously suffered a serious setback against Sonny Liston (losing in the first round twice). Ali kept his title through 12 rounds, and sent the challenger to the floor several times.

MARCH 1966 Though traditionally the World Champion fights two matches a year, Ali would take on five in 1966. He beats Canadian George Chuvalo in Toronto on points.

MAY 1966 He again fights Henry Cooper, the boxer who'd knocked him down, and turns the tables with a KO in London.

AUGUST 6th 1966 Still in the same city, he defeats Brian London in 3 rounds.

SEPTEMBER 10th 1966 Beats the German champion Karl Mildenberger in Frankfurt, and ends the year with a KO against Cleveland Williams in Houston.

The World Boxing Association, who didn't appreciate Ali's political stances, uses the pretext of the illegality of his fight against Liston to take away his belt, without his accord, and name Ernie Terrell World Champion. The title was divided between two men for the first time as Ali nonetheless remained uncontested champion for the World Boxing Council.

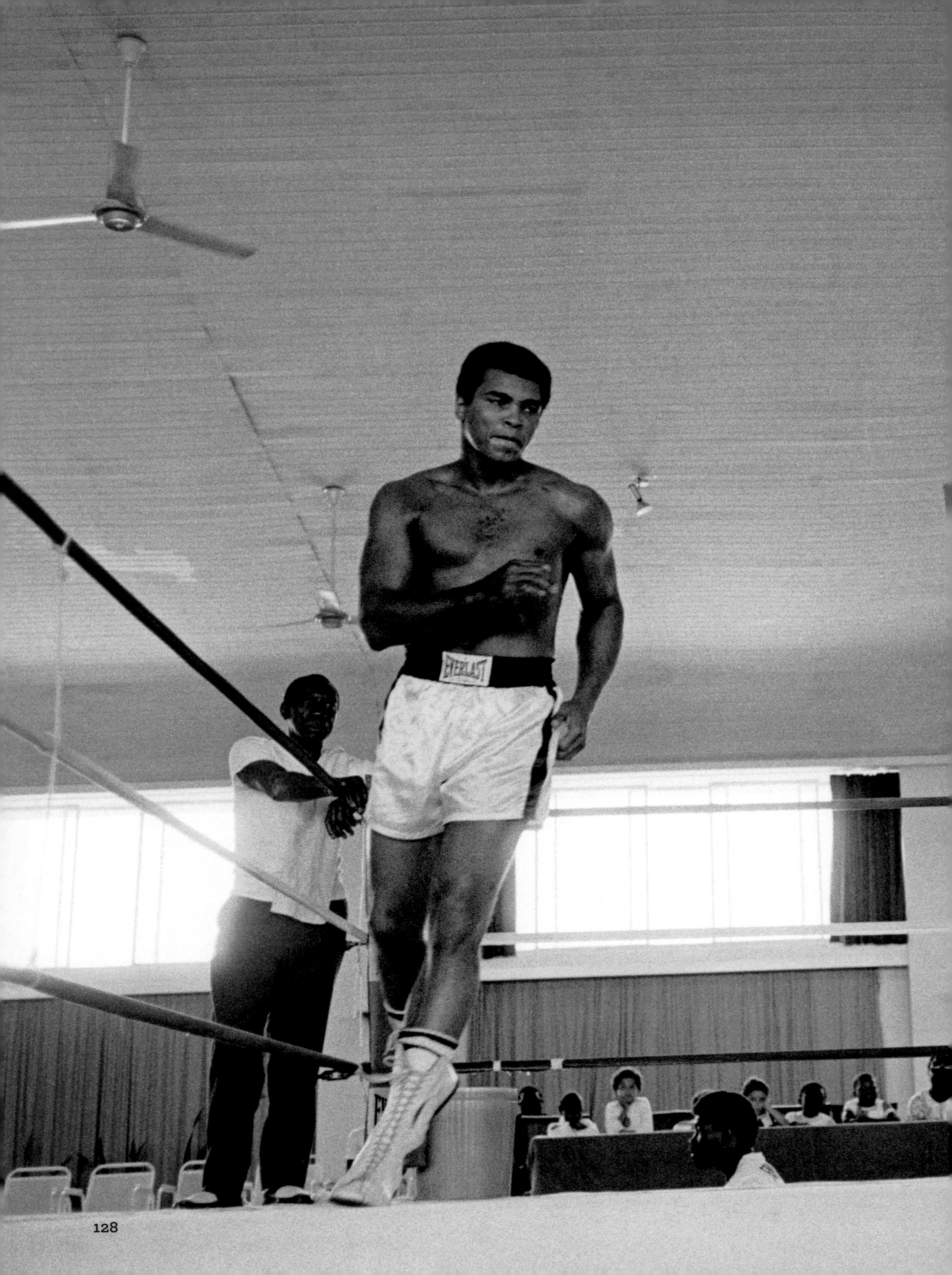
EVERLAST

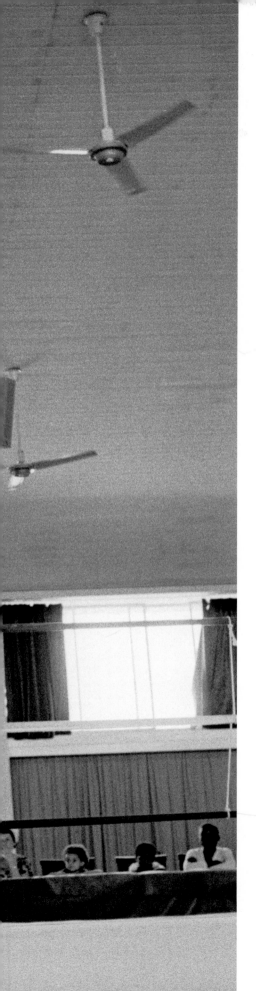

century." First world championship match between two unbeaten champions who were total opposites in terms of style, the match was also the first of the great combats that would define boxing in the 1970s. Hit in the face, Ali falls to the floor and rises on the count of 4 to continue the fight, which he eventually lost on points. This first defeat put an end to his dream to end his career unbeaten like Rocky Marciano. Ali would always hold a grudge against Frazier.

JUNE 28th 1971 The Supreme Court definitively clear Ali of all charges. The 8 judges unanimously acquit him.

JUNE 25th 1971 – OCTOBER 30th 1974 After his defeat, Ali fought 14 matches and 39 exhibition fights between the June 25 1971 and October 30 1974 to get back to the top of the category. The aim was to get back to the highest level of intense boxing and to rack up enough victories to be named challenger for World #1.

JANUARY 22nd 1973 Ali's career plans are brought to a halt; on January 22 in Kingston, Jamaica, Joe Frazier is destroyed in two rounds and hits the floor six times against George Foreman.

MARCH 31st 1973 San Diego against Ken Norton. The Californian boxer breaks his jaw in the 2nd round. Ali, handicapped by the pain, lasts until the final punch of the 12th round, but is proclaimed loser by two of the three judges.

SEPTEMBER 10th 1973 Ali takes his revenge against Norton in Los Angeles (and not in San Diego to deprive Norton of home-town supporters). Ali rightfully wins on points.

JANUARY 28th 1974 Then he gets revenge on points against Frazier in Madison Square Garden. Their rivalry continues even further when they come to blows on a television show.

All that remains for Ali to accomplish is the most difficult: take the title from George Foreman, the unmerciful heavy hitter unbeaten in 40 fights, 27 of those by KO.

SEPTEMBER 1974 Press conference in New York on his meeting with Foreman. Ali mocks Foreman, who he calls a mummy. He keeps repeating that he'll move and dance around him in the ring.

1974 Ali sees a witch doctor who tells him Foreman will be attacked by a woman with trembling hands.

JULY 21-22-23rd 1974 Arrival of James Brown, BB King, and the Spinners to announce the fight at the 20th May Stadium in Zaire.

NIGHT OF OCTOBER 29th TO 30th 1974 Nicknamed the Rumble in the Jungle, the fight takes place in Kinshasa, Zaire at the arena named the 20th May Stadium. Ten million dollars are put into play by Don King. The fight begins at 4am local time in order to be broadcast on US prime time.

Ali, whose best hit is the jab and whose best asset is his mobility, spends the majority of the fight against the ropes and surprises Foreman by sending more right hooks than left ones in the first rounds. Maintaining his guard up and taking all the pain of the violent hits from the champion while leaning on the ropes, Ali resists, countering with several combinations which tire and hurt Foreman who is forced to fight more than 5 rounds. His face swollen by Ali's punches, he falls in the 8th round after enduring an immeasurable series of hits.

Counted into KO, he arises a second too late. Ali thus reclaims his title ten years after his first fight against Liston.

It was Ali's greatest tactical victory, also named fight of the year, and Ali was again proclaimed boxer of the year. He also won the 1974 Hickok Belt, recognizing the best professional athlete of the year, as well as the trophy of Sportsperson of the year from *Sports Illustrated* magazine.

The date of the fight was chosen to just avoid monsoon season. One hour after the end of the fight, the locker rooms were flooded with water after the heavens opened.

1975 Ali converts to Sunni Islam.

1975 He is once again named boxer of the year, and reaches his peak with his third meeting against eternal rival Joe Frazier (in what was once again named fight of the year).

Ali begins the year against Chuck Wepner in Cleveland, in what was supposed to be an easy New Year's match against an unknown boxer destined to be beaten within 3 rounds. However, Wepner surprises the entire world by clinging on until the 15th round before being knocked out, and enjoyed the rare luxury of sending Ali to the ground.

Sylvester Stallone, not yet famous at the time, attended the match, which would give him the inspiration for the movie *Rocky*, released the next year.

MAY 16th 1975 Ali believes he can come out of a match with Ron Lyle, a boxer with the same caliber as Foreman, without a scratch. He attempts to use the same technique as in Africa, but the challenger doesn't fall for the trap and forces Ali into the center of the ring.

Nonetheless, Ali claims victory when the referee stops the fight in the 11th round.

OCTOBER 1st 1975 The battle against Frazier in Manilla dubbed "the Thrilla in Manilla" would eventually be his most intense duel.

1976 Ali fights Jean-Pierre Coopman, Jimmy Young and Richard Dunn. The fight against up-and-coming Young was his last real discernible success, and Dunn his last KO.

Muhammad Ali travels to Japan to fight against wrestler Antonio Inoki. According to the rules of the fight (fought behind closed doors), Inoki could not kick him in the face. Instead, his kicks caused serious injury to Ali's legs, causing reduced mobility. The fight was called a draw, and some commentators herald this as the unofficial beginning of Mixed Martial Arts.

1977 He manages to hold on to his title against Alfedo Evangelista and Earnie Shavers, though both fights particularly destroy him physically. He had been too worried about losing weight, and hadn't concentrated enough on his training.

JUNE 29th 1979 He goes into retirement, thinking that the World Champion's split titles would be reconciled by Leon Spinks.

This was not to be the case (in fact it would have to wait until Mike Tyson, who reunited the title in 1987). Ali accepts Don King's offer to fight Larry Holmes, his old sparring partner turned WBC champion.

OCTOBER 2nd 1980 Seeking to beat a new record and become the only boxer to win the World Heavyweight Champion title four times, Ali loses before the end bell for the first time in his career, when Angelo Dundee refuses to let him go into the 11th round. The fight against Holmes, organized as "The Last Hurrah" is viewed with scorn by many fans and experts, as they felt they were seeing a diminished version of Ali.

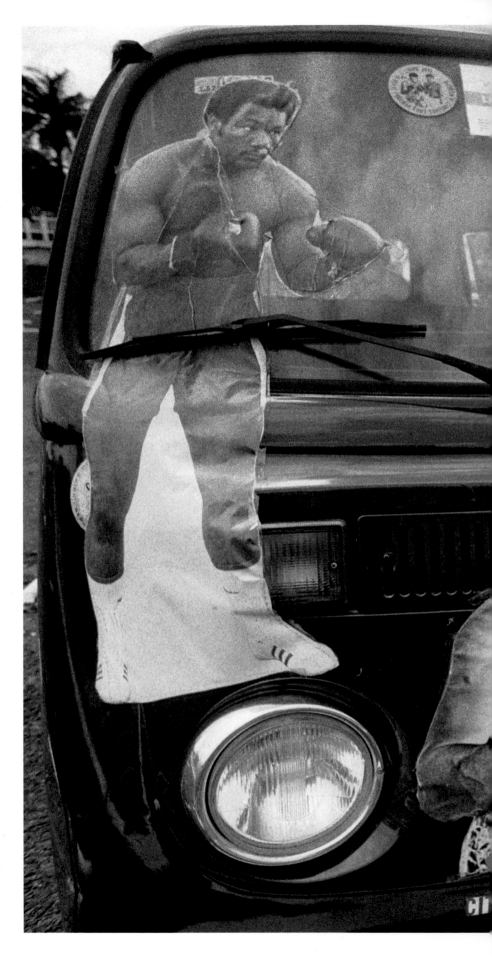

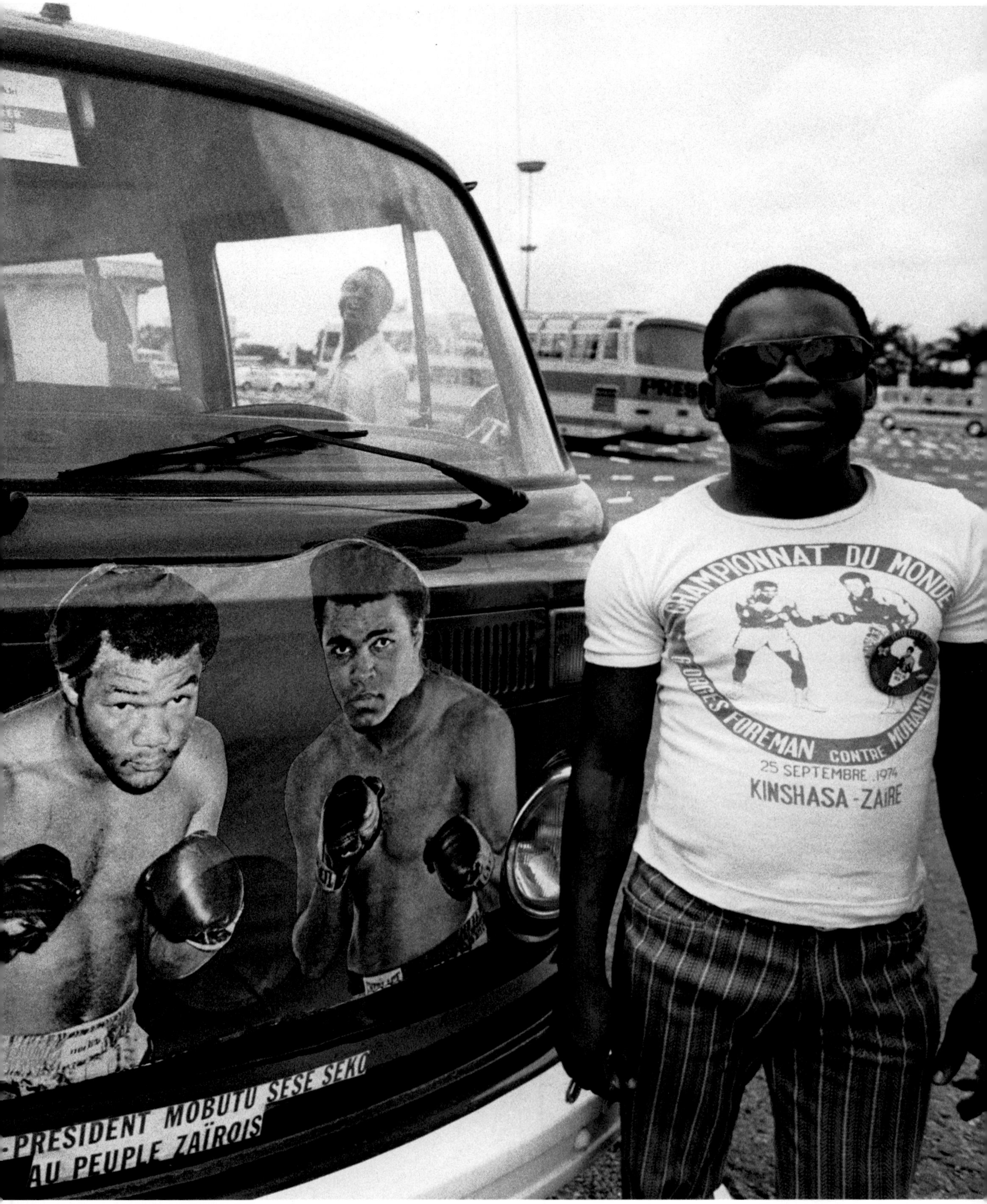
CHAMPIONNAT DU MONDE
FOREMAN CONTRE MOHAMED
25 SEPTEMBRE 1974
KINSHASA-ZAIRE
PRESIDENT MOBUTU SESE SEKO
AU PEUPLE ZAÏROIS

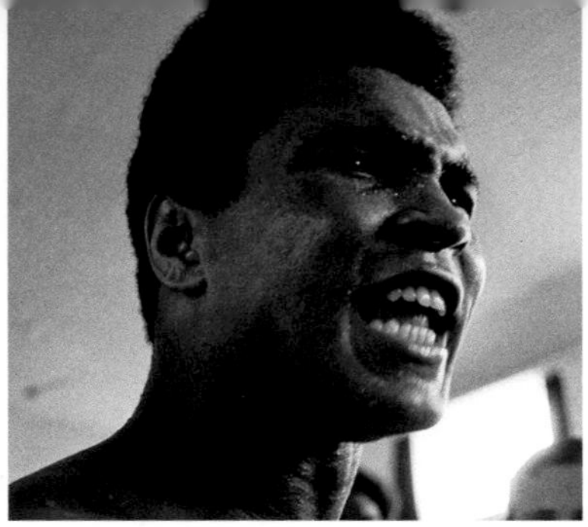

DECEMBER 11th 1981 Ali takes on a challenger well on his way to becoming world champion, Trevor Berbick, in what would be known as "The Drama in the Bahama." Ali is now truly considered a broken boxer.

1982 Ali is diagnosed with Parkinson's disease.

1985 He is asked to negotiate the release of his compatriots kidnapped in Libya.

1990 On the eve of the Gulf War, he travels to Baghdad to meet with Saddam Hussein and to plead for peace by persuading him not to pursue the conflict. He did not achieve this end-result, but did assure the release of 15 hostages taken by Iraq in Operation Desert Shield.

1996 He lights the Olympic Flame in Atlanta. During these same Olympic games, he is offered a gold medal to replace the one he won in 1960, but had thrown away in the Ohio River after a restaurant refused to serve him due to the color of his skin.

1999 Crowned 'Sportsperson of the Century' by Sports Illustrated and 'Sports Personality of the Century' by the BBC. His daughter Laila Ali becomes a boxer in her own right.

DECEMBER 17th 2005 First sportsperson to win the prestigious Otto-Hahn peace medal in Berlin from the United Nations "for his lifelong commitment to the American Civil Rights movement and the cultural and spiritual emancipation of Black people around the world."

JUNE 3rd 2016 Death in Scottsdale Arizona.

AWARDS
Amateur: 136 fights without defeat. Six-time winner of the Kentucky Golden Gloves in five categories. Double American Amateur Champion. Heavyweight Olympic Champion gold medalist 1960.
Professional: 61 fights, with 56 victories of which 37 by KO. 5 defeats.

Three-time Heavyweight World Champion from 1964 – 1978.

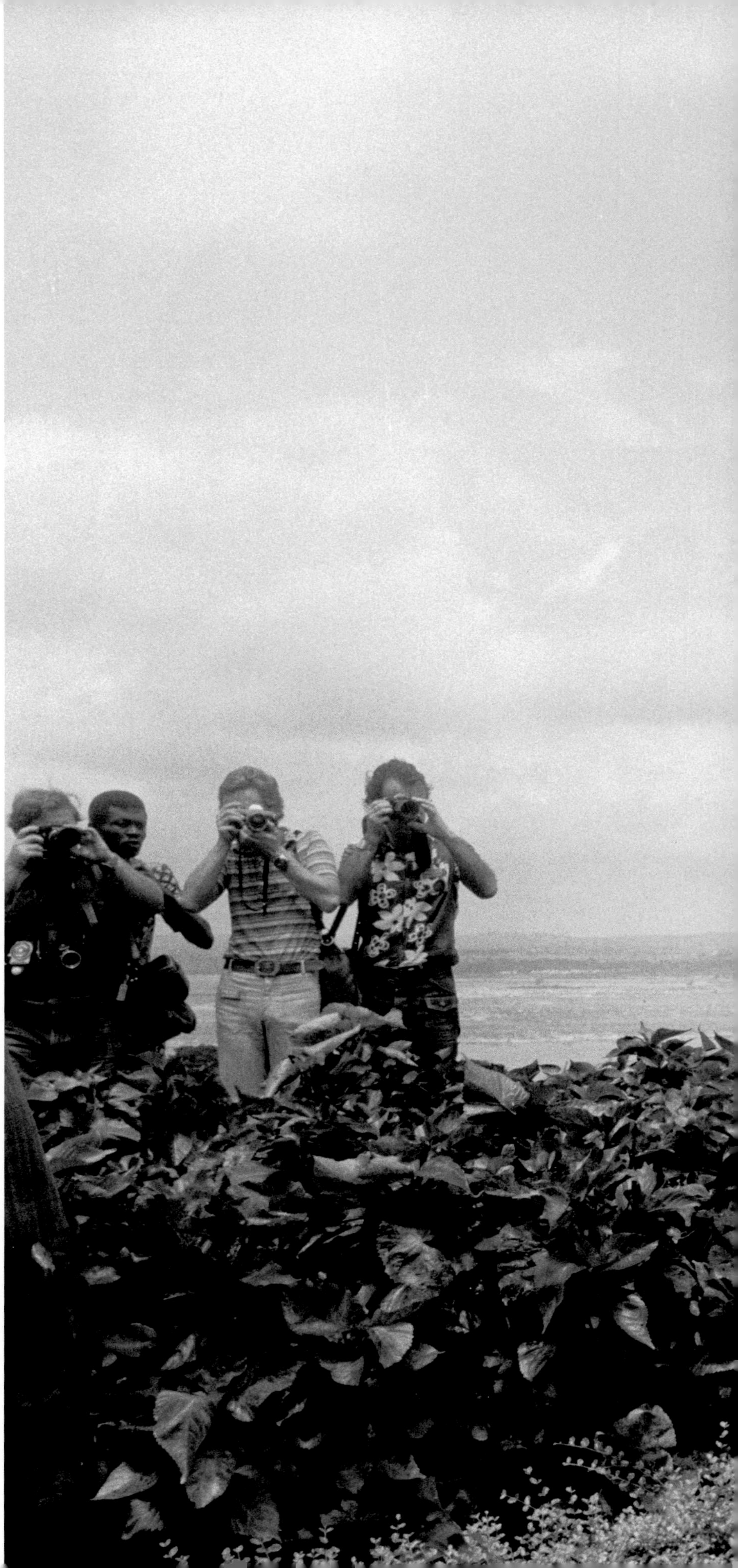

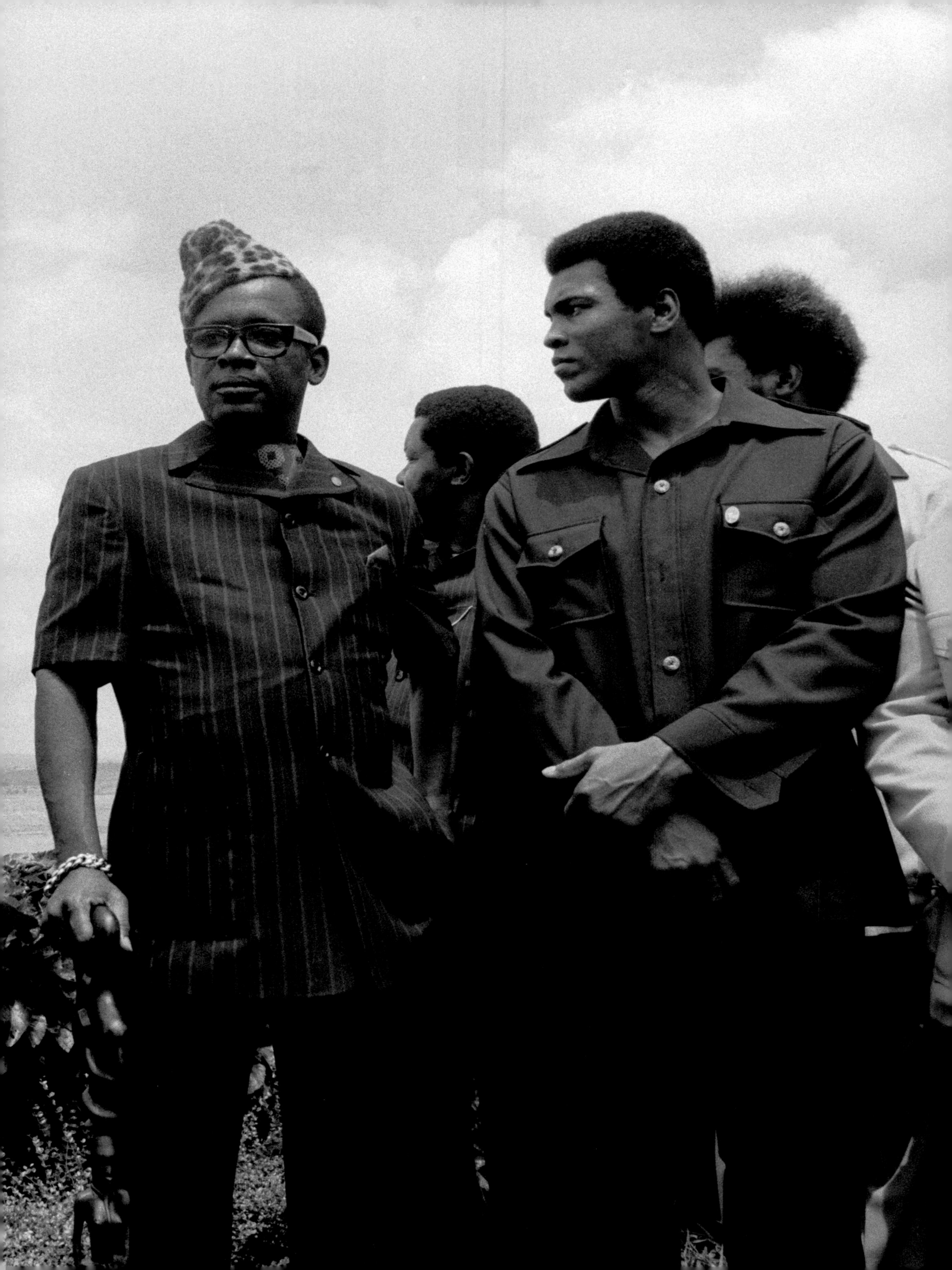

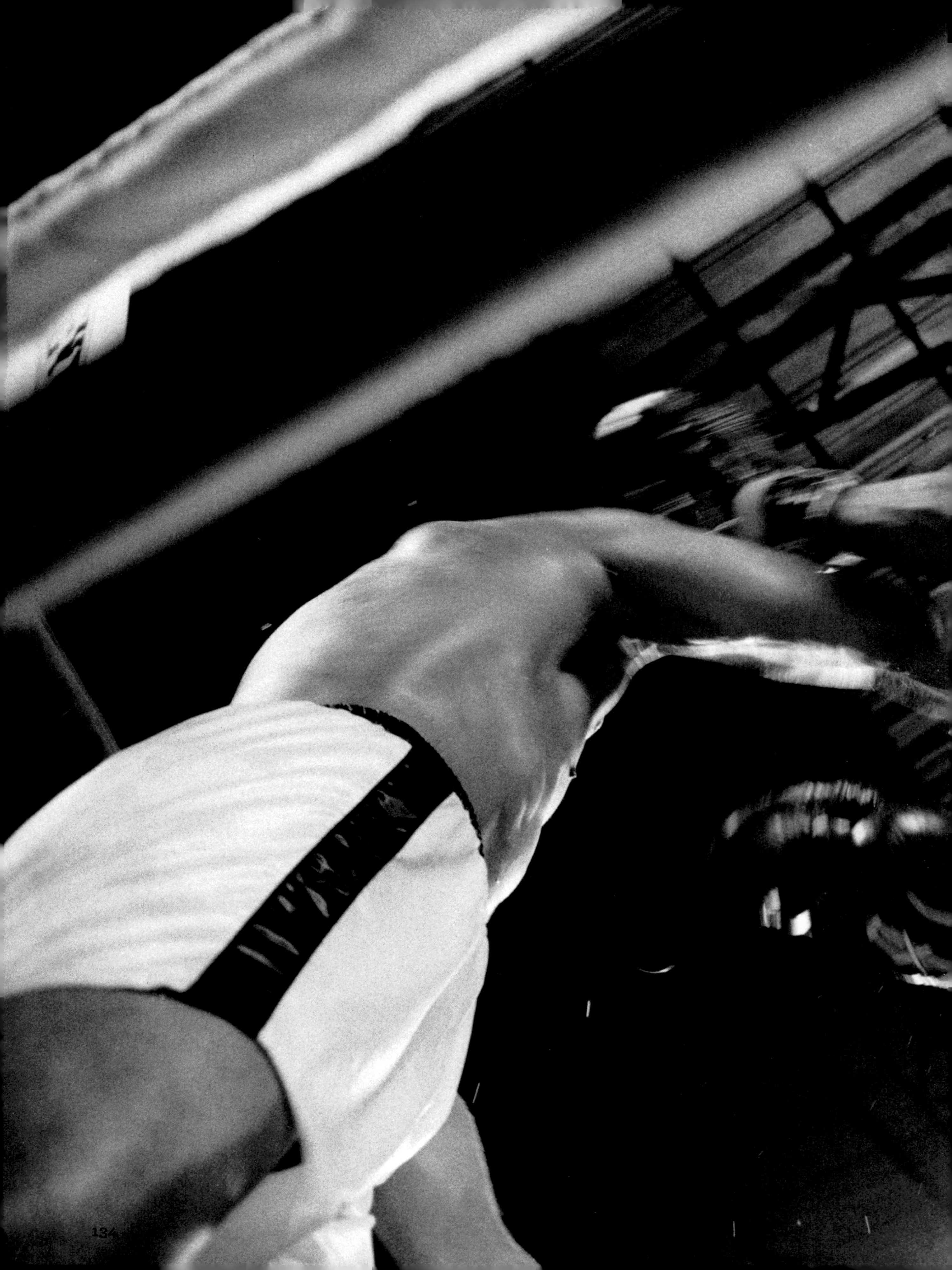

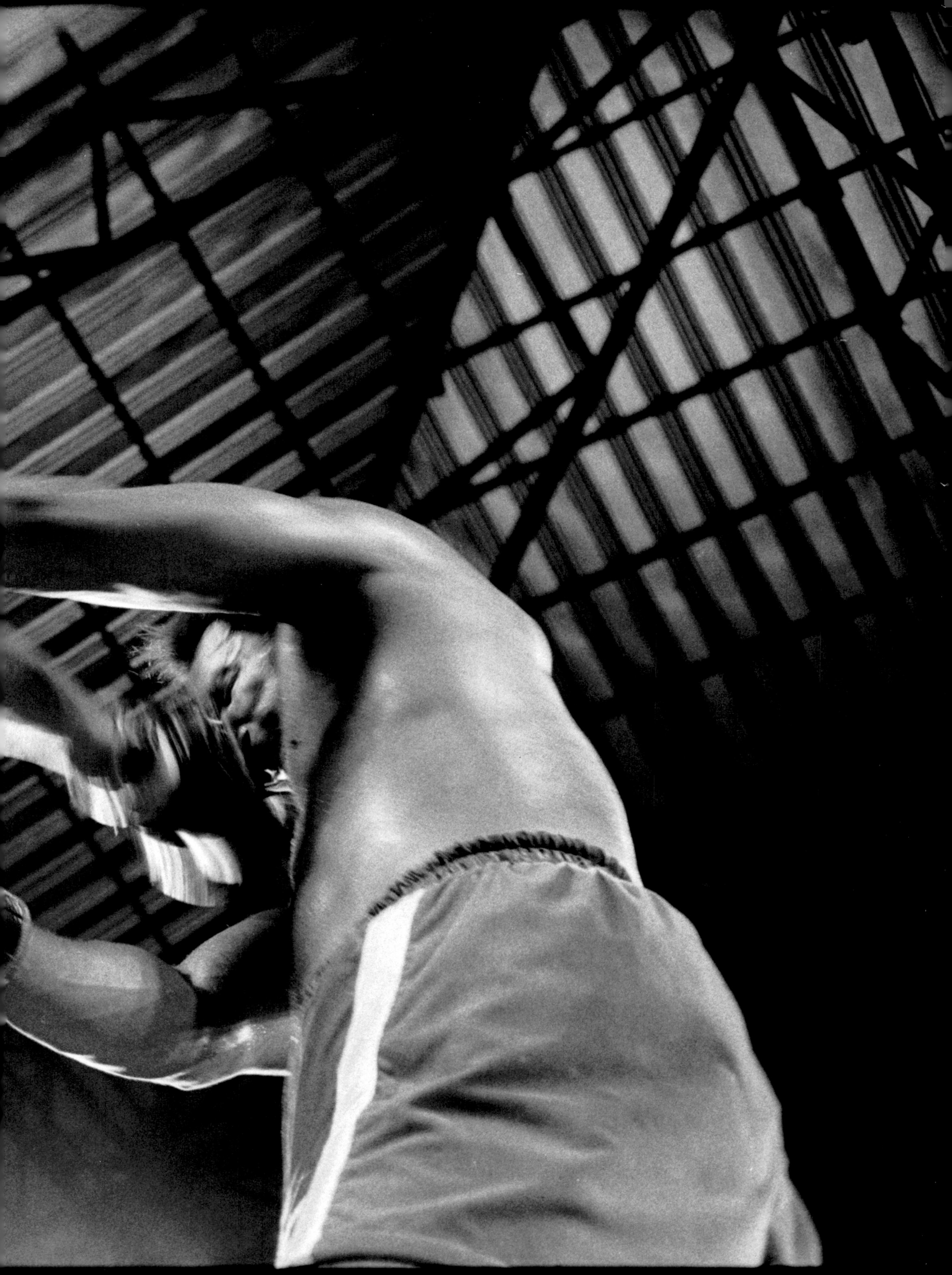

AUTHOR BIOS

ABBAS

Abbas is a world renowned photographer, originally from Iran. He dedicated a lot of his work to political and social coverage of developing southern nations, and from 1970 onwards, many of his works appeared in magazines across the world. After capturing the Iranian revolution, he self-exiled for 17 years before returning. One of his most controversial subjects has been religion, extensively documenting different faiths, from Islam to Buddhism, with accompanying essays. He has produced many books of his photographic works and has held exhibitions all over the globe. In 1981 he joined Magnum Photography Agency and was a governing member until he died in 2018.

JD MORVAN

Jean-David Morvan started out as a comic artist before realizing his masterful talent for storytelling. Born in France, he studied art at the Instiut St Luc in Brussels. In 2004, he became the writer of classic Franco-Belgian comic, *Spirou & Fantasio*. Over the years he has produced over 230 comics, winning multiple awards including the Youth Award in 2006 at Angouleme International Comics Festival, and Best Story in 2008 at Prix Saint-Michel.

RAFAEL ORTIZ

Rafael Ortiz is an Argentinian cartoonist whose work includes *Dan the Unharmable* and *God is Dead*. He collaborated with the screenwriter Jean-Davide Morvan on a biography of Mao Zedong. In 2018, Rafael worked with screenwriter Frédéric Richaud on *l'Envers des Nuages*, a fictitious account of the French Red Cross involved in African conflicts. In 2019, he began working with The Tribe, on graphic novels such as *The Division*.

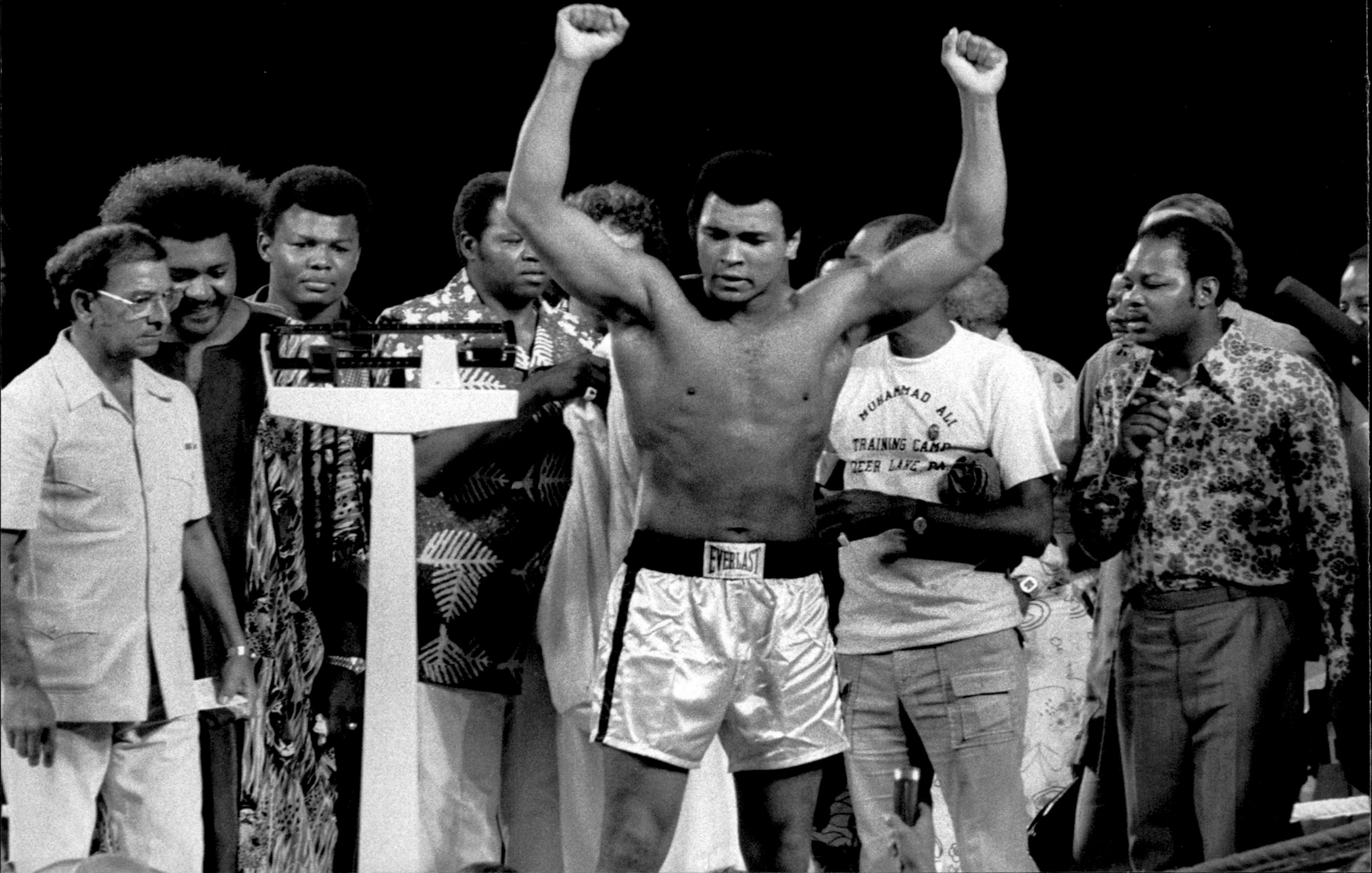

MUHAMMAD ALI
TRAINING CAMP
EVERLAST